Handology™

How to
Unlock the Hidden Secrets
of Your Life

By Gerry E. Biccum

Published by
Beyond Words Publishing, Inc.
Pumpkin Ridge Road
Route 3, Box 492-B
Hillsboro, OR 97123
Phone: 503-647-5109
Toll Free: 1-800-284-9673

Handology
Box 4, Clarkson P.O.
Missisauga, Ontario
Canada L5J 3X9

Manufactured in Canada and the United States of America

Library of Congress Catalog Card Number: 89-061267
ISBN: 0-941831-39-6

Special Thanks

To my two children, Adrian and April, for their patience and understanding on such a long project.

To John Wesley, a special friend, for his vision and inspiration, and to all the other people who made this book possible.

My most grateful appreciation to Maurice Simms for his astute hard work and editorial guidance, and to Syd Guishard for his spirit, ideas and support.

Dear Reader:

Welcome to the world of Handology! Like
many others you are probably just a bit
skeptical and uncertain that your hands
can truly reveal your life.

Perhaps you are worried that Handology is
difficult to understand.

Well, as you will learn in this book,
discovering yourself, identifying your
strengths and weaknesses, pinpointing your
natural abilities, is both fun and easy.

Every hand tells its own story. Therefore,
you hold in your hands the means of
achieving your own success.

HANDOLOGY -- efficiency through
                personal knowledge.

Gerry Biccum

Contents

Introduction

First, let me share with you how Handology started.

I still remember that fateful day when I came across a fascinating book called *The Science of Chirognomy*, by Dr. William G. Benham. The book was a gold mine of information, containing interviews with thousands of people from every walk of life. It explained a system of interpreting psychological character through a person's hands.

Unfortunately, the information which Dr. Benham had collected was complex and difficult to understand. But his results were so powerful and astounding that I felt compelled to share them with everyone. I decided to dedicate my time to researching the hand and to organizing this information so that everyone could enjoy its benefits.

My knowledge of computers helped me to organize the information, but that was only half the task — I still had to test and verify all the results. Ten years later, after I had interviewed thousands of people myself, Handology was born!

Why the Hand?
How can the lines in your palm, the shapes of your fingers, and all the other parts of your hand reflect character and destiny?

Everybody's hands can reveal hidden details about his or her life. Scientists have long known that the hand has more nerve endings than any other part of the body. In recent years, neurologists have proven that 60 percent of the gray matter of your brain is used to operate your thumb as a tool.

The most startling evidence was discovered while studying victims of paresis, a disease that causes the softening of the brain. When the brain softens, lines in the hand fade and disappear in the same proportion as the mind is destroyed.

These scientific findings prove beyond the shadow of a doubt that the operation of the hands occupies a large portion of the brain and reflects its physical makeup. Your hand is like a tape recorder recording your life as you live it!

What Is Handology?

Handology is a practical and scientific way to discover yourself, to identify your strengths and weaknesses, and to determine your natural aptitudes.

Because of a lack of knowledge about themselves, millions of people choose careers and endeavors for which they are not suited. Conversely, many people are unaware that they possess aptitudes that promise success and personal satisfaction.

Success doesn't happen by accident. It must be organized and planned using practical common sense. You hold in your hands the means of achieving your goals.

Prevent Failure Before It Occurs

The amount of information which can be extracted from the hand is amazing. This should not be a great surprise.

A doctor can look at your tongue and tell that you have liver problems. The liver and tongue are not connected through the alimentary canal, but the tongue reflects the liver. Heart disorders can be diagnosed through fingernails and skin color.

Similarly, using Handology one can look at your thumb, for instance, and see that you are lacking in willpower. The brain is directly connected to the thumb, and willpower is a mental quality.

You no longer need to be hampered, impeded or ruined because you are working in a job that is not right for you. Through the conscientious use of Handology you can be guided to your proper sphere in life.

Your hands are the key to obtaining the information you need. The time to prevent failure is before it occurs.

When Handology tells you the sphere of life for which you are best suited, and the studies which you can more readily master, it greatly reduces your likelihood of failure and contributes to your chances of success. Handology can prevent the marriage of people whose temperaments make it absolutely impossible for them to live together harmoniously; it can decrease the number of divorces and troubled lives.

The Hands of a Child
If we could go back in time to your birth and examine your hands, we would make a remarkable discovery. Your hands would look very similar to the hands of your parents! (Or parent, if one parent was genetically dominant.) However, as you grew and developed your personality, your hands changed to reflect this development. You may still find interesting similarities between your hands and those of your parents. The changes depend on your genetic makeup and the strength of your personality.

Your Two Hands
The Active hand (the right hand if right-handed, left hand if left-handed) reflects life as you live it. It will always reflect the ways in which you have developed. The Passive hand reflects life as it should have been.

The Passive hand reflects your genetic lifestyle. It is the life you inherited from your parents. This includes all your special talents and gifts. Interestingly, this genetic lifestyle never changes.

3

Your genetic lifestyle and your present lifestyle can be positive and negative. Handology allows you to compare these lifestyles by interpreting your hands. By comparing your genetic lifestyle with the lifestyle you are living, you can gain the edge needed to overcome obstacles and achieve success in life.

If your Passive hand reveals a negative lifestyle and your Active hand reveals a positive one, you are moving in a positive direction. If you find you are moving in a negative direction, you can correct your lifestyle to be more positive.

Handology vs. Palmistry

Many people have asked me, "What is the difference between Handology and palmistry?"

Handology is like an encyclopedia of the hand. Like an encyclopedia, you use it to look up information. Would you ever think of memorizing a 36-volume encyclopedia so that you could recall its contents? Of course not! The information stored is too lengthy and complex. Besides, you can always look things up when you need to. It's the same with Handology. I ask you: would you trust anyone who claimed to have memorized the enormously complex information that is required to understand the hand? That's what you are doing if you let a palmist read your hand.

They claim they can tell everyone about love, wealth and the future, but palmists can't begin to understand the complexities of the hand. The lines in your hand change to display only those things that have strongly influenced the mind. If, for example, you are not interested in money, nothing concerning money will show up in your hand. Every hand tells its own story.

It is important to make the distinction that palmistry reads the hand and Handology analyzes the hand. Unlike palmistry, Handology is based on years of proven, scientific research.

The Lines in Your Hand

There are two well-established facts which together explain how lines function. First, lines change to reflect a shift in mental attitude when a person undergoes a large mood or personality change. Second, lines respond to changes in health.

So how do lines in your hand project the future? Your life may be changed by many circumstances. These may include the influence of other people, an accident, a strong desire to change, or perhaps failing health. When these changes occur, lines appear, cross, disappear, strengthen and so on. The main lines, which are the original map of life, fade and disappear as you change your attitude and outlook. Lines just beginning to form show emotions and ideas just starting. By closely examining these lines, you can discover your mental attributes and your probable future.

Your Future Projection

For each lifestyle you live, you also project a new destiny. This projection is enhanced by examining your past and present lifestyle.

It must be understood that it takes one to three years before your Active hand records major changes. Therefore, your lifestyle must be consistent for at least one to three years for a clear projection to emerge. If your lifestyle is not consistent, your projection will not show any clear signs and the road ahead will be confused.

Handology has the power to play back your personality. The results depend largely on the strength of your emotions and your personality as a whole. Some people will have difficulty understanding themselves because of a multiple-personality makeup. However, understanding will always come eventually if you keep an open mind.

Scientists can project a missile's impact by calculating its velocity and angle of flight. If the missile changes course because of outside events, they must recalculate its impact. Handology works on the same principle, calculating where you are and the road you have taken. You have total control of your destination and the road you choose to take. In some cases, people lead confused lives, projecting several paths. It is up to you to look carefully at those paths and take a course of action which will place you on the path you desire.

Handology can only extract the information. It is your responsibility to understand and interpret this information to your advantage.

Part 1

Character styles

A profile of your character style can be assembled by identifying features of the hand — referred to as "descriptions" — and noting the Description code on the left side of the page. This Description code can then be looked up in Part 3.

Description "A" is texture of skin, Description "B" is consistency (firmness) of the hand, Description "C" is flexibility of the hand, and so on.

Most Description codes are cross-referenced in the back of the book for detailed analysis.

Example

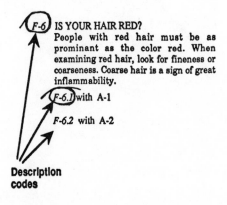

F-6 IS YOUR HAIR RED?
People with red hair must be as prominant as the color red. When examining red hair, look for fineness or coarseness. Coarse hair is a sign of great inflammability.

F-6.1 with A-1

F-6.2 with A-2

Description codes

In the previous example, I have circled Description code F-6.1 because the hair is red and A-1 was recorded previously. I recorded A-1 earlier because the skin is fine in texture. If I did not circle A-1 or A-2 previously, I would have circled only F-6.

"Mount" refers to the seven Mounts of the hand, found at the base of the fingers and along the side of the hand.

Mounts "A" to "D" are at the base of the fingers, beginning with "A" at the base of the index finger. The Mounts are referred to by the letters "A" to "G." See "Map of the Mounts" below.

Map of the Mounts

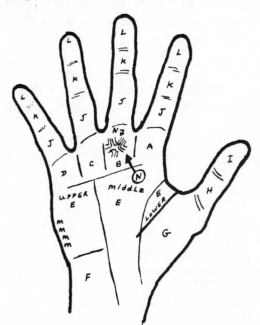

A - Mount
B - Mount
C - Mount
D - Mount
E - Lower "E" Mount
E - Middle "E" Mount
E - Upper "E" Mount
F - Mount
G - Mount
H - Thumb, 2nd phalange
I - Thumb, 1st phalange
J - 3rd finger phalange
K - 2nd finger phalange
L - 1st finger phalange
M - Percussion
N - Apex

When Reading Your Description Codes
Please remember the following statements when reading your selected Description codes.

Information from the Character style section is about traits of character that you:

    a) express now,
    b) have expressed in the past,
    c) are capable of expressing.

They are not necessarily the character traits you display all the time. Different emotional situations warrant different character expressions. The character traits you uncover are those you possess now.

It's So Easy to Use Handology
1. Use a pencil and paper to record your Description codes or circle the number in the book itself.

2. A magnifying glass with a built-in light source will help identify some features. Otherwise, use only daylight. Room temperature must be about 70 degrees Fahrenheit or 21 degrees Celsius.

3. Remember to use the right hand if right-handed, the left hand if left-handed. If ambidextrous, use the right hand.

4. It will not be necessary to go through the whole book because you only need to get information about the features you actually have in your hand. For example, if your fingers are not short, the section on short fingers can be ignored.

5. If you cannot identify a description easily, do not record it. Continue on. It's better to omit than to make a wrong selection.

6. Start with Description "A" (texture of the skin) in this section.

7. When you have selected your Description codes, look them up in Part 3.

8. Have fun!

9

A — TEXTURE

The texture of your skin holds the key to knowledge of your natural refinement.

Confine your examination to the back of your hand. The hair will either be coarse or fine, but coarse hair does not grow from finely textured skin. This will help you confirm your analysis of skin texture.

A-1   IS THE TEXTURE OF YOUR SKIN FINE?
Your skin is fine with small pores, soft and delicate. Touch your hand. Is it almost as soft and delicate as a baby's hand?

A-2   IS THE TEXTURE OF YOUR SKIN COARSE?
Touch your hand. Does your skin feel rough and coarse? Is it like leather compared with soft, flexible skin?

A-3   IS THE TEXTURE OF YOUR SKIN MEDIUM?
Touch your hand. Is it elastic? Your skin doesn't show delicate pores like a baby's hand, nor is it coarse. Your skin feels elastic, not soft; firm, not hard.

A-4   ARE THE FINGERTIP PADS LARGE AND SMOOTH?
Observe the inside part of the first phalanges of your fingers. On many hands there will be a pad of flesh which in some cases is quite prominent. The finger-print will be smooth.

B — CONSISTENCY

The consistency of your hands can tell you how well your energies are directed. You can determine consistency by pressing the center of your hand with your index finger on the back of the hand and your thumb on the palm. The roughness or softness of the skin should be ignored.

B-1 ARE YOUR HANDS FLABBY?

The flabby hand offers no resistance to pressure. If you squeeze your hand very firmly, the flesh and bones seem to squeeze together. Thumbs will be seemingly quite flat, looking as though they have been pressed until the substance has gone out of them. People with flat thumbs usually have flabby hands.

B-2 ARE YOUR HANDS SOFT?

The soft hand will not have the boneless, flabby feeling, yet will be soft. You will find more difficulty among women in distinguishing the flabby hand from the soft, for women's hands are naturally softer than men's. But by observing the lack of bony feeling in the hand under pressure, and following closely the description of the flabby hand, you will attain a clear idea of how to distinguish between the two.

B-3 ARE YOUR HANDS ELASTIC?

As you close your finger and thumb on it, the elastic hand has the feeling of life and resistance. It seems, when pressed with the tip of your thumb, as though the flesh rebounds like rubber. It lacks entirely the spongy quality of flabby or soft hands. You will find it best exemplified among active men and women, those who not only talk but also act.

B-4 ARE YOUR HANDS HARD?

Hard hands will not be encountered as often as soft or elastic hands because extreme types are much rarer than might be thought. The hard hand will give no sign of yielding under pressure; it will have no spring, no elasticity, but a hardness that resists any effort to dent it. The skin will be coarser in texture.

C — FLEXIBILITY

The flexibility of your hand shows the degree of flexibility of your mind. Flexibility is shown by how easily your hand bends backwards.

Start with your right hand pointing up. Exert pressure downward with your left hand. Bend it as far backwards as you can. Repeat with your other hand. Notice whether the whole hand is flexible or whether the bending occurs only at your knuckle joints.

C-1 **ARE YOUR HANDS STIFF AND DIFFICULT TO OPEN?**

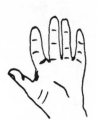

The hand which is stiff and difficult to open has fingers forming a curve inwards. A person with a stiff hand has difficulty closing the hand into a fist and then opening it.

Movements are slower than those of an average person and the fingers will not straighten themselves out.

C-2 **ARE YOUR HANDS MEDIUM OR NORMAL IN DEVELOPMENT?**
When pressed backwards, these hands open readily until the fingers straighten themselves naturally, so that the hands open with ease to their full extent.

C-3 **ARE YOUR HANDS FLEXIBLE IN THE EXTREME?**

Your fingers bend back without giving you pain, until a 90-degree angle is formed. Your fingers seem mobile, the bones like cartilage.

C-4 **IS THERE FLEXIBILITY WITH YOUR FIRST PHALANGES?**

Only the first phalanges of your fingers are flexible; the rest of your hand is normal.

C-5 **ARE BOTH HANDS FLEXIBLE?**
Shows whether you are improving in mentality or going in the opposite direction.

C-5.1 IS YOUR PASSIVE HAND STIFF AND YOUR ACTIVE HAND
FLEXIBLE?
Remember, the Passive hand is the left hand, if you are right-handed.

C-5.2 IS YOUR PASSIVE HAND FLEXIBLE AND YOUR ACTIVE HAND
STIFF?
Remember, the Passive hand is the left hand, if you are right-handed.

D — COLOR

*Your temperament and indications of health or disease are shown by the color of
your hands. The temperature of the room must be just right, say 70 degrees F., to
correctly judge color. Anything that accelerates or retards the flow of blood will
affect the color of your hand. When examining your hand for color, be guided
largely by the palm, not the back of your hand, and look at the lines and the nails
as well. A combination of these factors can accurately determine the normal color
of your hand.*

D-1 IS THE COLOR DEAD WHITE?
Learn to recognize the watery, pallid look of a dead-white hand, the
corpse-like whiteness that means a lack of heat, one which gives an
impression of a lack of blood supply. This is not a white hand which is
white only because of fineness. Any hand may have this pallid whiteness,
which indicates a lack of red corpuscles in the blood. You can also use
the nails as an indication of color. Nails give a clue to the predominant
quality — coldness — of the white hand.

D-2 IS THE COLOR PINK?
As whiteness shows deficiency of blood supply, pink shows a normal
amount of blood. Learn to recognize the color of the nail well, because all
hand colors can be judged from it.

D-3 IS THE COLOR RED?
Redness must be a clear, full red, not a pink or dark pink.

D-4 IS THE COLOR YELLOW?
Yellow can be caused by a vacation in a warm climate. Your hand may be
"bleached out." You can also use the nails to judge color.

13

D-5 IS THE COLOR BLUE OR PURPLE?
Two kinds of blueness must be distinguished, one which tinges the whole nail and the other which settles darkly at the base. Blueness or purpleness is usually caused by improper circulation of the blood. This is not necessarily a negative quality, however. It is useful to consider this blue color primarily from the health aspect; beyond showing physical weakness, poor circulation does not in any marked degree affect temperament.

E — NAILS

Your nails are like windows which allow you to look into your interior organization. Nails show quality, just like skin.

Your nails are composed of minute, hair-like fibers. The fibers are so tightly knit together that they adhere to each other and form a compact, horn-like substance. The part which lies under the nails is called the quick.

The nails on the right hand grow faster on right-handed people. Left-handed nails grow faster on lefties. Nails also grow faster in summer and faster during the day than at night. Nails protect delicate fingertip nerve fibers.

The horn of the nail should be even and smooth on the surface. The grain, which runs from top to base, should be smooth, not ridged or fluted. Nail texture is smooth if all the filaments forming the nail substance are the same size, while fluted nails occur when fibers of different sizes grow together. Normal nails will be pliable, not brittle, and will look alive and elastic.

E-1 CIRCLE E-1 FOR GENERAL DATA ON TEXTURE.

E-2 DO YOU HAVE COARSE NAILS AND FINE SKIN?
In some hands the skin texture is fine while the nails tend to coarseness. The coarse nail may be a short, heavy nail, belonging more often to large hands with coarse skin and hard or at least elastic consistency.

E-3 ARE YOUR NAILS FLUTED OR DO THEY HAVE WHITE SPOTS?
The fluting, or ridging, of the nail from the top to the base is an indication of nervous disorder. White spots appearing on the nails are the first warning signs of delicate nerves. As the disorder increases, the white flecks grow larger, then grow together and finally cover the whole nail, taking away transparency and clearness.

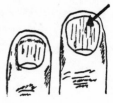

E-4   DO YOUR NAILS GROW UPON THEMSELVES?
The nail has been bitten down into the quick, the oil dried out, and the filaments, instead of binding themselves together in a homogeneous mass, are piling on top of each other in progression.

E-5   DO YOUR NAILS RIDGE, CROSSWISE?
Your nails have horizontal grooves.

E-6   IS YOUR NAIL NEWLY GROWN?
One nail died and another has grown to replace it.

E-7   IS YOUR NEW NAIL BADLY FLUTED?
If the new nail is badly fluted, a problem is indicated. It takes approximately six months to grow a new nail. A badly fluted nail has had its vitality interrupted.

E-8   ARE YOUR NAILS NARROW AND LONG?
A narrow nail will be either yellow, blue or pink, never red, and may be found with the blue color at the base, denoting poor circulation. None of these is indicative of special disease.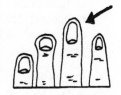

E-9   ARE YOUR NAILS BROAD?
The broad nail is sometimes red in color.

E-10 ARE YOUR NAILS SHORT?

E-11 ARE YOUR NAILS EXTREMELY SHORT AND FLAT?
This nail has the skin growing down on it.

E-12 ARE YOUR NAILS FLAT AND BLUNT, 1/4 INCH IN LENGTH?
Often less than a quarter of an inch long and sometimes broad, covering the entire visible end of the finger and giving the tip an exceedingly flat, blunt appearance, this nail appears almost clubbed. The skin seems to cling to the nail and grow down on it until it can stretch no farther and breaks. This usually results in a ragged appearance where the skin joins the nail. Strong examples of this type are common.

E-13 DO YOUR NAILS APPEAR OPEN AND
FRANK?

These are nails that are broad at the tip, curving
around the fingers, broadening at the base, pink in
color, and fine in texture. They are a broad, open-
looking nail type.

E-13.1 with A-1 or D-2

E-14 IS YOUR NAIL BLUE?

Small in size though regular in form, with the
end quite square and tapering towards the base,
or with the base the same width as the outer end,
this nail is often found on long fingers or large
hands, though it may be found on small hands. It
is quite distinctive in appearance and is easily

recognized. The nail is a small one, though it does not have the appearance
of a critical nail, nor is it like the narrow nail. A short nail, yet well-
proportioned.

E-15 IS YOUR NAIL TINGED WITH A FAINT BLUE?

A deep blue color is often found with this nail, which is most pronounced
at the base. Be careful to note the age of females with blue-colored nails.
There is some disturbance of circulation at age 12 to 14, at which time
childhood is giving way to womanhood. This ceases when menstruation
becomes regular. Blueness is also found at change-of-life.

E-16 ARE YOUR NAILS BULBOUS?

The end of your finger thickens on the underside
until it forms a distinct bulb or pad, which is sometimes
as round as a marble. Over this bulbous tip the nail is
curved, creating a complete clubbed, blunt end, the
top curved with the nail, the underside fleshy. This
formation makes the end of the finger a complete
knot; the appearance is most striking.

E-17 ARE YOUR NAILS LARGE?

Your nail shows a decided inclination to curve. This
nail can be found on any-shaped tip — it is the curve
alone that distinguishes it.

E-18 ARE YOUR NAILS CLUBBED?
Your nail has an exaggerated upward curve and curls
around the fingertip.

E-19 DO YOU HAVE SPOON NAILS?
Your nail is depressed and appears to be flat or spoonlike.

E-20 ARE THERE BEAU'S LINES ON YOUR NAILS?
You have depressed horizontal furrows across your nail.

E-21 DO YOU HAVE TERRY'S NAILS?
Most of the skin under the nail appears white, with the
normal pink area reduced to a band near the nail tip.

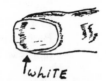

E-22 DO YOU HAVE LINDSAY'S NAILS?
The half near the nail tip appears pink or brown while
the half near the cuticle looks white. Also known as
half-and-half nails.

E-23 DO YOU HAVE YELLOW-NAIL SYNDROME?
Fingernail growth slows; the nails become thick and
very hard, and appear yellow or yellow-green.

E-24 DO YOUR NAILS SPLINTER OR HEMORRHAGE?
The nails have longitudinal red streaks that may signify
bleeding of the capillaries.

E-25 DO YOUR NAILS HAVE IRREGULAR PITTING
OR PITTING IN ROWS?
Your fingernails resemble hammered brass.

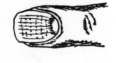

E-26 DO YOUR NAILS HAVE BROWN OR BLACK
DISCOLORATION?
There may be a single large patch or a collection of
small freckles. The thumb and big toes are the most
common sites. Such marks may spread from the nail to
surrounding finger tissue.

F — HAIR

The hair on your hand tells how hardy you are. Hair shows strength. Humans do not usually have hairy bodies unless they belong to a certain type and have certain qualities. Hair on the backs of the hands deserves attention, its fineness or coarseness indicating physical vitality.

F-1 IS THERE NO HAIR ON THE BACKS OF YOUR HANDS?
Most hands will have little hair, especially the hands of women. Hair will more often be encountered on men's hands because men are more robust than women, but it is not true that the absence of hair on a man's hand in any way indicates effeminacy.

F-2 IS YOUR HAIR BLOND OR LIGHT?
Blond hair belongs to the Swede and Norwegian, particularly when the hair is yellow or straw-colored.

F-3 IS YOUR HAIR BLACK?
Black hair belongs to the Latin and Oriental races. They have lots of vital energy and strength. The iron in them is abundant but is not needed to sustain and feed their vital fires.

F-4 IS YOUR HAIR WHITE?
White hair is caused by the level of iron falling far below normal so that not enough is absorbed by the hair sacs to give even a blond color. There are isolated cases where the hair has turned white from fright or from many headaches.

F-5 IS YOUR HAIR GRAY?
When gray hair is present, look at the skin on the back of the hand to see if it has the wrinkled, satiny-brown color of an old hand. If the skin is aged, merely conclude that this is the cause of the gray color. Also, look at the color of the ends of the hair. If they are black or red and the texture of your skin is youthful, then your hair is not really gray. The hand may be flat and flabby, much rayed and lined.

F-6   IS YOUR HAIR RED?
People with red hair must be as prominent as the color red. When examining red hair, look for fineness or coarseness. Coarse hair is a sign of great inflammability.

F-6.1 with A-1

F-6.2 with A-2

F-7   IS YOUR HAIR AUBURN OR BROWN?
What is called auburn hair and is much praised and admired is a combination of the warmth and passion of black hair with a shade of added fire from the red, a combination which tinges the hair with a golden glow.

G — WHOLE HAND

Your hand as a whole reveals your mind as either being intellectual or driven by simpler instincts.

The best method of proceeding with this examination is to lay your two hands wide open before you with the palms up and your fingers straightened out to their natural length. If your hand is a flexible one, do not allow it to bend back, showing its flexibility, but extend your fingers in a natural manner until they are held straight. This gives a full view of your palm. First, note if your fingers are long enough to balance the palm, if they are shorter than the palm, or if they seem to be too long. If you cannot tell at a glance which part predominates, your hand is balanced.

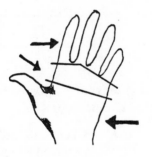

G-1   ARE YOUR FINGERS EXCESSIVELY LONG?
Close the fingers over the palm and note how far towards the wrist they reach. The 1st finger will be shortest; the 2nd, even though the longest finger, next; and the 3rd, by virtue of its position, will appear the longest of all. This is because they arrange themselves over the "G" Mount. It is generally believed that the fingers closing in this way should reach the wrist or be as long as the palm, but this is seldom the case because of the prominence of the Mounts. When the fingers extend between a little below

the center of the "G" Mount and the lines on the wrist, class the fingers as long.

G-1.1 with H-18 and a well-marked, long, pink-colored Head line
(see "Map of the Lines" in Part 2 for location of Head line).

G-2   IS THE MIDDLE OF YOUR HAND PROPORTIONATELY LARGER?

G-3   IS THE BASE OF YOUR HAND PROPORTIONATELY LARGER?

G-4   IS YOUR HAND BALANCED?

G-5   IS ONE PART SLIGHTLY SMALLER?
When a hand is not balanced, note which part is the smallest.

G-6   IS THE BASE SLIGHTLY SMALLER?

G-7   ARE YOUR FINGERS SLIGHTLY SMALLER?

G-8   IS THE MIDDLE PORTION SMALLER?

H — FINGERS IN GENERAL

Fingers tell a lot about character and the chances of success.

A series of tests for each finger must be done. Circle the Description codes that best describe you.

H-1   IS YOUR 1ST FINGER LONGER OR DOES IT SIT HIGH?
A normal 1st finger will reach the middle of the first phalange of the 2nd finger. Also, the 1st finger may appear long because of the way it sits on your hand. A finger longer than this is a high 1st finger.

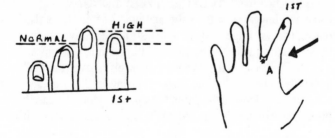

H-2   IS YOUR 2ND FINGER LONGER OR DOES IT SIT HIGH?

A normal 2nd finger will tower above the others. Only if it is half a phalange longer than normal is it a long 2nd finger. Also, the 2nd finger may appear long because of the way it sits on your hand. A finger longer than this is a high 2nd finger.

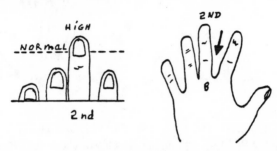

H-3   IS YOUR 3RD FINGER LONGER OR DOES IT SIT HIGH?

A normal 3rd finger will reach the middle of the first phalange of the 2nd finger. A finger longer than this should be classed as a long 3rd finger. Also, the 3rd finger may appear long because of the way it sits on your hand.

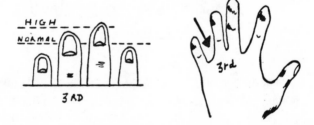

H-4   IS YOUR 4TH FINGER LONGER OR DOES IT SIT HIGH?

A normal 4th finger should reach the first knot on the 3rd finger. If longer than this, your finger should be classed as a long 4th finger. Usually, the 4th finger appears shorter than the other fingers. Also, the 4th finger may appear long because of the way it sits on your hand.

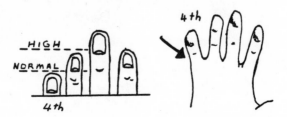

H-5   IS YOUR 1ST FINGER SHORTER OR DOES IT SIT LOW?

A normal 1st finger should reach the middle of the first phalange of the 2nd finger. If it does not, then it is classed as being short. Also, the 1st finger may appear short because of the way it sits on your hand.

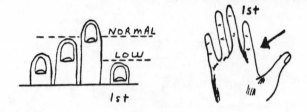

H-6   IS YOUR 2ND FINGER SHORTER OR DOES IT SIT LOW?

A normal 2nd finger should always tower above the others, but only by half a phalange. If not, then it is a short finger. Also, the 2nd finger may appear short because of the way it sits on your hand.

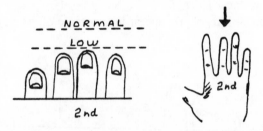

H-7   IS YOUR 3RD FINGER SHORTER OR DOES IT SIT LOW?

A normal 3rd finger should reach the middle of the first phalange of the 2nd finger. Also, the 3rd finger may appear short because of the way it sits on your hand.

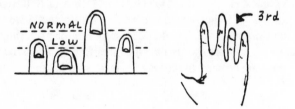

H-8 IS YOUR 4TH FINGER SHORTER OR DOES IT SIT LOW?
A normal 4th finger should reach the first phalange on the 3rd finger. Also, the 4th finger may appear short because of the way it sits on your hand.

H-9 ARE YOUR FINGER SETTINGS NORMAL?
It is best if your hands have normally placed fingers set evenly on the palm.

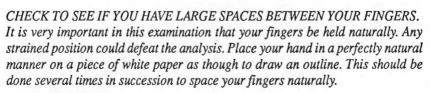

CHECK TO SEE IF YOU HAVE LARGE SPACES BETWEEN YOUR FINGERS. It is very important in this examination that your fingers be held naturally. Any strained position could defeat the analysis. Place your hand in a perfectly natural manner on a piece of white paper as though to draw an outline. This should be done several times in succession to space your fingers naturally.

Another method is to extend the arm and bend your hand back at the wrist, so as to look at the nails. This shows finger spaces quite accurately.

H-10 ARE YOUR THUMB AND 1ST FINGER WIDE?

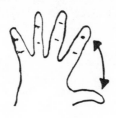

H-11   ARE YOUR 1ST AND 2ND FINGERS WIDE?

H-12   ARE YOUR 2ND AND 3RD FINGERS WIDE?

H-13   ARE YOUR 3RD AND 4TH FINGERS WIDE?

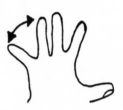

H-14   ARE YOUR FINGERS EQUALLY SEPARATED?

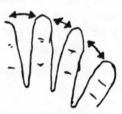

H-15   ARE YOUR FINGERS CLOSE TOGETHER AND YOU CANNOT
         SPREAD THEM WIDE?

H-16   THE THREE PHALANGES OF THE FINGERS
Your three phalanges will tell you whether mental quickness, business or common instinct rules you.

Fingers are made up of phalanges, and in this examination we measure the size of the phalange. From the tip to the first joint is the 1st phalange. Between the joints is the 2nd phalange, and the 3rd phalange is from the 2nd joint to the hand.

H-17   IS YOUR 1ST PHALANGE LONG?
Is the 1st phalange long on all four fingers?

H-18   IS YOUR 1ST PHALANGE THICK AND LONG?

H-19   IS YOUR 1ST PHALANGE SHORT?
Use the same principle as H-17.

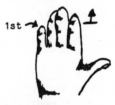

H-19.1 with D-2

H-20   IS YOUR 1ST PHALANGE EXCESSIVELY SQUARE?

H-21   IS YOUR 2ND PHALANGE LONG
OR THICK?

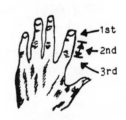

H-22   IS YOUR 2ND PHALANGE SHORT?

H-22 1 with D-2

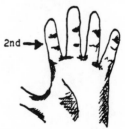

H-23 IS YOUR 3RD PHALANGE LONG OR
THICK?

> *H-23.1* with D-3
>
> *H-23.2* with A-2

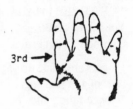

H-24 IS YOUR 3RD PHALANGE NARROW?

> *H-24.1* with B-1

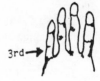

H-25 IS YOUR 3RD PHALANGE SHORT OR
WAIST-LIKE?

> *H-25.1* with D-2

H-26 ARE ALL OF YOUR 1ST PHALANGES SHORT, 2ND NORMAL,
3RD THICK?

H-27 ARE YOUR 1ST PHALANGES SHORT, 2ND NORMAL, 3RD
MODERATE?

H-28 WIDE CHINKS WITH G-1
Chinks are the lines at the wrist.

I — FINGERTIPS

Your fingertips show what kind of a machine you are, whether there is water in the boiler and fire to turn it into steam. They show whether the machine is acting in its intended fashion.

Fingertips can be spatulate, square, conic or pointed and all refer to appearance. You must consider only the shape of the tips of your fingers and not your whole hand.

I-1   ARE THE TIPS SPATULATE?
The spatulate is the broadest tip, named because of its resemblance to a druggist's spatula.

    I-1.1 with B-2

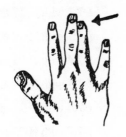

I-2   ARE SOME, OR ALL, SQUARE TIPS?
The square tip is distinctly square.

I-3   ARE THEY VERY SQUARE?

I-4   ARE THEY A LITTLE CONIC?

    I-4.1 with B-2

I-5   ARE THEY CONIC?
This is found mostly on women's hands, though it is possessed by many men. The tip forms a distinct cone at the end of the fingers and has many degrees of development.

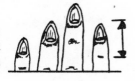

    I-5 1 with B-2

I-6   ARE SOME, OR ALL, POINTED?

Pointed tips are an exaggerated form of the conic. Their appearance is so striking that, once seen, the type is never mistaken for any other. They have a long, narrow, extremely pointed look. The finger narrows from the base to the tip.

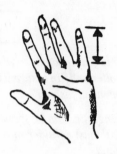

I-6.1 with B-1

I-7   FINGERTIPS AND THEIR 1ST PHALANGES

There is a variety of effects which the phalanges and fingertips have in conjunction with each other.

Look back to see if you have circled the items listed in the following "with" statements. If you have, record the corresponding Description codes.

I-7.1 with H-17 and I-5

I-7.2 with H-17 and I-2

I-7.3 with H-17 and I-1

I-7.4 with H-21 and I-5

I-7.5 with H-21 and I-2

I-7.6 with H-21 and I-1

I-7.7 with H-23 and I-5

I-7.8 with H-23 and I-2

I-7.9 with H-23 and I-1

J — KNOTTY FINGERS

Knotty joints tell you about your qualities of analysis, reasoning, investigation and thoughtfulness. They keep enthusiasm and spontaneity in check.

Your fingers will have either smooth or knotty joints. Knotty joints are noticeable at first glance. If you can't tell, do not class your fingers as knotty.

J-1 DO SOME OF YOUR JOINTS HAVE DEVELOPED KNOTS?

    J-1.1 with I-1 or I-2

    J-1.2 with I-5 or I-6

J-2 DO ALL OF YOUR 1ST JOINTS HAVE DEVELOPED KNOTS?

    J-2.1 with I-1 and B2

J-3 DO ALL OF YOUR 2ND JOINTS HAVE DEVELOPED KNOTS?

K — SMOOTH FINGERS

Smooth fingers indicate quickness of thought, inspiration, impulse and spontaneity. Many hands have fingers which are distinctly smooth in appearance. These may have any shape of tip. It is only the absence of developed joints which leads you to recognize them.

K-1 ARE YOUR FINGERS SMOOTH?

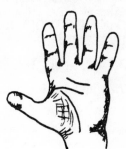

K-1.1 with B-4

K-1.2 with D-3

K-1.3 with I-1

K-1.4 with I-2

K-1.5 with I-5

K-1.6 with I-6

K-1.7 with J-3

L — LONG FINGERS

Long fingers reveal an irresistible tendency towards detail, towards observing little and trifling things, and a tinge of suspicion. If the shape of the fingers bears this tendency out it may indicate selfishness and hypocrisy.

When looking at your hand, fingers will appear to be long, in balance with the rest of the hand, or decidedly short. This examination requires closing the fingers over the palm and noting how far they reach towards the wrist. The 1st finger will be the shortest, the 2nd and 4th fingers will be even, and the 3rd finger, by virtue of its position, will appear to be the longest of all. This is due to the way the fingers arrange themselves over the Mount under the thumb. When the measurement taken extends anywhere between a little below the center of the thumb Mount and the Rascette at the wrist, class your fingers as long.

L-1   ARE YOUR FINGERS LONG?

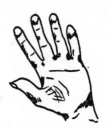

    L-1.1 with I-2

    L-1.2 with J-1

    L-1.3 with K-1

    L-1.4 A description of your professions

    L-1.5 A description of your faults

L-2   IS YOUR HAND LONG?
Long hands are those in which both the palm and the fingers are exceedingly long, though the fingers themselves may be only slightly over normal length in proportion to the palm.

L-3   ARE YOUR FINGERS LONG AND THIN?

    L-3.1 with J-3

    L-3.2 with E-11

L-4   ARE THE "C" AND "G" MOUNTS MORE DEFICIENT THAN THE OTHERS?
Check "Map of the Mounts" in the beginning of Part 1.

L-5   IS THE "F" MOUNT LARGER THAN THE OTHERS?
Check "Map of the Mounts" in the beginning of Part 1.

L-6   ARE YOUR FINGERS LONG AND THICK?

    L-6.1 with I-2

    L-6.2 with I-1

M — SHORT FINGERS

Short fingers can reveal how you will handle detail and quickness of thought and action.

The test for long fingers is also used for short fingers (see Description L). Short fingers will barely reach the center of the "G" Mount and will appear short in proportion to the rest of the hand. The palm may be long and the fingers short. In this case, they will be far short of the normal line.

M-1   ARE YOUR FINGERS SHORT?

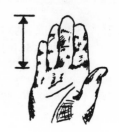

   M-1.1 with B-1

   M-1.2 with B-2

   M-1.3 with B-3

   M-1.4 with B-4

   M-1.5 with C-3

   M-1.6 with I-1

   M-1.7 with I-2

   M-1.8 with I-5 or I-6

   M-1.9 with J-1

   M-1.10 with J-2

   M-1.11 with J-3

   M-1.12 with H-17

   M-1.13 with H-22

   M-1.14 with H-25

M-2   A DEEP, WELL-CUT HEAD LINE, NO DEFECTS, WITH SHORT
   FINGERS.
   Check "Map of the Lines" in Part 2.

N — THUMB

The thumb is the fulcrum around which all the fingers must revolve. In proportion to its strength or weakness, it will maintain, enhance or detract from the strength of your other descriptions. The thumb alone can strongly contradict your other descriptions.

The thumb cannot be called a finger because it is infinitely more. It is really four fingers because it can oppose the four fingers at will. In this test, compare your thumb with the rest of the hand.

N-1   IS YOUR THUMB LARGE COMPARED WITH THE HAND?

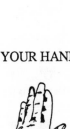

    N-1.1 with E — all nails

    N-1.2 with J — knotty fingers

    N-1.3 with K — smooth fingers

    N-1.4 with I-1 or I-2

    N-1.5 with I-5 or I-6

    N-1.6 with M — short fingers

    N-1.7 with women

    N-1.8 with L — long fingers

N-2   IS YOUR THUMB SMALL COMPARED WITH YOUR HAND?

    N-2.1 with E — all nails

    N-2.2 with J — knotty fingers

    N-2.3 with I-1 or I-2

    N-2.4 with I-5 or I-6

    N-2.5 with K — smooth fingers

    N-2.6 with L — long fingers

    N-2.7 with M — short fingers

    N-2.8 with women

N-3 THE THUMB AS A WHOLE CAN SHOW THE AMOUNT OF
MORAL FORCE YOU HAVE, WITHOUT WHICH NO BRILLIANCE
IS OF GREAT VALUE (CIRCLE N-3).

The thumb is composed of three phalanges, divided into mental and
abstract worlds and the thumb Mount.

The tip of the thumb should normally reach the
middle of the third phalange of the 1st finger. If
shorter, it could be because of a low setting or, if
higher, a high setting. Take care when examining
the phalanges because their long or short length
could cause an error in determining the proper
setting.

N-4 IS YOUR THUMB SET HIGH?
Hold the hand up with the palm towards you to
determine the setting.

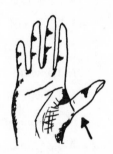

N-5 IS YOUR THUMB SET LOW?
If the set of the thumb is low it will open wide and
will not lie close along the side of the hand. This
low-set thumb will have a large space between
itself and the 1st finger. Illustration N-3 can be
used for comparison. Take care when noting the
length of the phalange of the thumb.

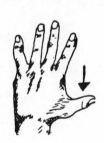

N-6 IS YOUR LOW-SET THUMB GENERALLY LONG?

N-7 IS YOUR LOW-SET THUMB GENERALLY SHORT?

N-8 IS YOUR THUMB MEDIUM-SET?
Neither too high nor too low, not tied closely
to the hand and not lying away from it, the medium-
set thumb seems to stand upright. Illustration N-3
can be used. Take care when noting the length of
the phalanges.

N-9 IS YOUR THUMB STRAIGHT? (DO NOT CIRCLE N-9 IF YOU
HAVE ALREADY CIRCLED N-8.)
A straight-set thumb is set close to the hand, placed
high, low or normally, and has, as its distinctive marks,
the closeness with which it lies by the side of the hand,
the straightness of its carriage, and its lack of flexibility
at the joint. (This is not a stiff thumb because the joint
is not always stiff, although the joint is not flexible or
supple. The marked peculiarity of this thumb is its
carriage, as a whole, and its disposition to lie close to
the side of the hand.)

N-9.1 with E-10 or E-11 or E-12

N-10 YOUR THUMB SHAPE AS A WHOLE WILL SHOW UPON WHICH
PLANE THE THUMB QUALITIES OPERATE (CIRCLE N-10).
In this examination, begin at the bottom and go upwards in the scale,
starting with heavy, elementary development.

N-11 IS YOUR THUMB HEAVY AND
ELEMENTARY?
This thumb is shaped rather like a banana. The
two joints do not show where they separate.

N-12 IS YOUR THUMB FLAT?
Some thumbs are seemingly quite flat, looking as though they have been pressed until the substance has gone out of them. It is this flatness that is their distinguishing mark.

N-12.1 with M — short fingers

N-13 IS YOUR THUMB BROAD?
When viewed from the nail side, it has a broad look in both phalanges and has a strong, healthy appearance.

N-14 IS IT A ONE-THICKNESS THUMB?
This thumb appears to be one thickness throughout its entire length. It is delicate and shapely. The nail is smooth in texture (no ridges on nail) and pink in color.

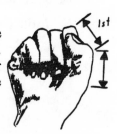

N-15 THE PHALANGES (CIRCLE N-15).
These two phalanges are for will and reason. Examine the phalanges as to length, shape of tips and form. The rule is that the first phalange should be shorter than the second. The first phalange is for will; the second is for reason or logic.

N-16 THE FIRST PHALANGE SHOWS WILL, DECISION AND ABILITY TO COMMAND OTHERS (CIRCLE N-16).

N-17 IS THE 1ST PHALANGE LONG?
In a normally shaped hand, the ratio between the first and second phalange is two to three. In other words, if you measure a thumb from its base to the tip, the first phalange must extend over two-fifths of the total length and the second phalange should extend over three-fifths. Use Illustration N-15 to measure your phalanges.

N-18   IS YOUR 1ST THUMB PHALANGE
VERY SHORT?

N-19   THE 2ND PHALANGE (CIRCLE N-19).
Shows perception, judgment and reasoning faculties.

N-20   IS YOUR 2ND THUMB PHALANGE LONG?
Use Illustration N-15 to measure your phalanges.

N-21   IS THE 2ND PHALANGE LONG, THE 1ST SHORT?

N-22   ARE BOTH THUMB PHALANGES THE SAME LENGTH?
Use Illustration N-15 to measure your phalanges.

N-23   IS YOUR 3RD THUMB PHALANGE LARGE?
The 3rd thumb phalange is actually the "G" Mount.

N-24   THE THUMB TIP WILL INCREASE OR DIMINISH STRENGTH.
The tip of the thumb follows the same formation as the tips of the fingers.
Several other shapes of the first phalange, which are often seen and yet
which cannot be classed as belonging strictly to any of the four basic
shapes (paddle-shaped and clubbed thumb, Illustration N-34), must be
considered.

N-25   IS YOUR THUMB TIP CONIC?

N-25.1 with N-17

N-25.2 with N-18

N-26   CIRCLE IF YOU HAVE NOT SELECTED I-5 OR I-6.

N-27   IS YOUR THUMB TIP SQUARE?

N-28 CIRCLE IF YOU HAVE NOT SELECTED I-2.

 N-28.1 with N-17

N-29 IS YOUR THUMB TIP SPATULATE?

N-30 CIRCLE, IF YOU HAVE SELECTED N-29 BUT NOT I-1.

 N-30.1 with N-18

N-31 IS YOUR 1ST PHALANGE NORMAL?

 N-31.1 with N-17

N-32 IS YOUR 1ST PHALANGE WEAK OR STRONG?

N-33 IS YOUR THUMB TIP PADDLE-SHAPED?
Many thumbs have a broad 1st phalange, as viewed from the nail side, but are not thick all the way through. This is not the flat thumb, for it is not thin enough, and is not as thick as the clubbed thumb. It is its extreme breadth, often called paddle-shaped, that is its distinguishing feature, and this breadth belongs to a long phalange; thus it has both length and breadth but not thickness. It is always a strong phalange and must be analyzed as such, even if its length is somewhat deficient.

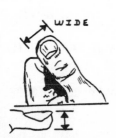

N-34 IS YOUR THUMB CLUBBED?
Occasionally, a thumb may have a 1st phalange that is thick and rounded, or broad and thick, with a nail that is short and very coarse in texture. This is not the consumptive formation of nail and tip but is found on the hands of healthy people. The clubbed thumb requires careful study.

 N-34.1 with B4 + H-21 + M-1

 N-34.2 with M-1

N-34.3 with big "G" Mount + B-4 + C-1 + M-1 + H-21 + E-10 and deep red lines in the palm of the hand

N-35 IS YOUR THUMB JOINT LARGE?

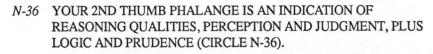

N-35.1 with N-17

N-35.2 with N-25

N-35.3 with any of N-25 to N-29

N-35.4 with N-21

N-36 YOUR 2ND THUMB PHALANGE IS AN INDICATION OF REASONING QUALITIES, PERCEPTION AND JUDGMENT, PLUS LOGIC AND PRUDENCE (CIRCLE N-36).

N-36.1 with N-9

N-37 IS YOUR 2ND THUMB PHALANGE LONG?
When examining the 2nd phalange, consider its length. Look at the thumb held up naturally and compare it to the rest of the hand. Next, bend the thumb as shown in the illustration. Accustom yourself to noting whether this phalange is in proportion to the hand and whether it is longer or shorter than the 1st phalange. It should normally be a little longer.

N-37.1 with N-25

N-37.2 with N-27

N-37.3 with N-29

N-38 IS YOUR 2ND THUMB PHALANGE SHORT?

N-38.1 with M-1 — short fingers

N-39 IS YOUR 2ND PHALANGE SHORT AND THICK?

N-39.1 with N-25

N-39.2 with N-27

N-39.3 with N-29

N-40 IS YOUR 2ND THUMB PHALANGE EXCEEDINGLY SHORT?

   N-40.1 with N-17

   N-40.2 with N-25 or N-27

N-41 IS YOUR 2ND THUMB PHALANGE FLAT AND
FLABBY?
If the thumb tip is flat, assume the 2nd phalange to be
flabby, even if slender and round.

   N-41.1 with N-11

   N-41.2 with A-1

N-42 CIRCLE IF YOU USUALLY HAVE A NEGATIVE ATTITUDE
TOWARDS LIFE.

N-43 CIRCLE IF YOU USUALLY HAVE A POSITIVE ATTITUDE
TOWARDS LIFE.

N-44 IS YOUR 2ND THUMB PHALANGE WAIST-LIKE?

N-45 SHAPES OF THE THUMB PHALANGES SHOW
GOOD MUSCULAR STRENGTH AND ROBUSTNESS IN YOUR
REASONING FACULTIES (CIRCLE N-45).

N-46 IS YOUR THUMB PHALANGE MERELY BROAD?

   N-46.1 with N-44

   N-46.2 with N-27

   N-46.3 with N-25

N-47 IS YOUR THUMB SUPPLE?
The supple thumb can bend back at the joint, as
does the low-set thumb.

   N-47.1 with N-27 + a good Head line

   N-47.2 with N-29

   N-47.3 with N-25

N-48   IS YOUR THUMB STIFF?
This thumb is stiff in the joint and does not bend back as does the supple thumb. It tries to carry itself erect and close to the hand. The joint must be used as a guide in determining the stiff thumb.

N-48.1 with A-2

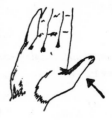

P — FINGER STANCE

Every finger leaning towards another gives up some of its strength to the finger towards which it leans. This shows if your character is balanced or not.

Note whether any finger stands more erect than the others, with one or more fingers inclined towards it. A leaning finger and a bent finger are not the same.

NOTE: Circle only the Description code that describes the finger with the largest Mount at its base.

P-1   IS YOUR 1ST FINGER ERECT OR STRAIGHT?

P-2   DOES YOUR 1ST FINGER LEAN TO THE 2ND FINGER?

P-3   IS YOUR 2ND FINGER ERECT OR STRAIGHT?

P-4   DOES YOUR 2ND FINGER LEAN TO THE 1ST FINGER?

P-5   DOES YOUR 2ND FINGER LEAN TO THE 3RD FINGER?

P-6   IS YOUR 3RD FINGER ERECT OR STRAIGHT?

P-7   DOES YOUR 3RD FINGER LEAN TO THE 2ND FINGER?

P-8   DOES YOUR 3RD FINGER LEAN TO THE 4TH FINGER?

P-9   IS YOUR 4TH FINGER ERECT OR STRAIGHT?

P-10   DOES YOUR 4TH FINGER LEAN TO THE 3RD FINGER?

Q — THE APEX

Every apex leaning towards another gives up some of its strength to the finger towards which it leans. This shows if your character is balanced or not.

A Triangle is formed at the base of each finger. The center of the Triangle is the center of the apex and Mount. The center will show whether the apex is leaning or not. Note where the center of the apex is as you answer the following questions. You will need a magnifying glass to view the apex.

NOTE: Circle only the Description code that describes the apex on the largest Mount.

Q-1   IS THE APEX UNDER YOUR 1ST FINGER CENTERED ON THE "A" MOUNT?

Q-2   DOES THE APEX UNDER YOUR 1ST FINGER LEAN OUTWARDS?

Q-3   DOES THE APEX UNDER YOUR 1ST FINGER LEAN TOWARDS THE APEX UNDER YOUR 2ND FINGER?

Q-4   DOES THE APEX UNDER YOUR 1ST FINGER POINT UPWARDS?

Q-5   DOES THE APEX UNDER YOUR 1ST FINGER POINT DOWNWARDS?

Q-6   IS THE APEX UNDER YOUR 1ST FINGER NEAR THE HEART LINE?

Q-7   IS THE APEX UNDER YOUR 1ST FINGER NEAR THE HEAD LINE?

Q-8   IS THE THE APEX UNDER YOUR 2ND FINGER CENTERED ON THE "B" MOUNT?

Q-9   DOES THE APEX UNDER YOUR 2ND FINGER LEAN TOWARDS THE APEX UNDER YOUR 1ST FINGER?

Q-10   DOES THE APEX UNDER YOUR 2ND FINGER LEAN TOWARDS THE APEX UNDER YOUR 3RD FINGER?

Q-11   DOES THE APEX UNDER YOUR 2ND FINGER POINT UPWARDS?

Q-12   DOES THE APEX UNDER YOUR 2ND FINGER POINT DOWNWARDS?

Q-13   IS THE APEX UNDER YOUR 3RD FINGER CENTERED ON THE "C" MOUNT?

Q-14   DOES THE APEX UNDER YOUR 3RD FINGER LEAN TOWARDS THE APEX UNDER YOUR 2ND FINGER?

Q-15   DOES THE APEX UNDER YOUR 3RD FINGER LEAN TOWARDS THE APEX UNDER YOUR 4TH FINGER?

Q-16   DOES THE APEX UNDER YOUR 3RD FINGER POINT UPWARDS?

Q-17   DOES THE APEX UNDER YOUR 3RD FINGER POINT DOWNWARDS?

Q-18   IS THE APEX UNDER YOUR 4TH FINGER CENTERED ON THE "D" MOUNT?

Q-19   DOES THE APEX UNDER YOUR 4TH FINGER LEAN TOWARDS THE APEX UNDER YOUR 3RD FINGER?

Q-20   DOES THE APEX UNDER YOUR 4TH FINGER LEAN OUTWARDS?

Q-21   DOES THE APEX UNDER YOUR 4TH FINGER POINT UPWARDS?

Q-22   DOES THE APEX UNDER YOUR 4TH FINGER POINT DOWNWARDS?

Q-23   IS THE 4TH APEX CENTERED, AND DO THE 1ST, 2ND AND 3RD APEXES LEAN TOWARDS THE 4TH?

R — THE 7 MOUNTS

Study of the Mounts helps considerably in determining your strongest character points. Check the following diagrams and compare them with your hands. Is any one Mount bigger than the others?

It is necessary to become familiar with exact positions and boundaries. The apexes are located on the "A", "B", "C" and "D" Mounts at the base of the 1st, 2nd, 3rd and 4th fingers. Physiologically, these Mounts are the balls or pads of flesh which bulge from the palm at different points in the hands. In some cases there are holes or depressions. Mounts which are very prominent (in excess) are considered strong Mounts. Flat Mounts are ordinary, and depressions show weakness.

R-1   IS YOUR "A" MOUNT LARGE?

R-2   IS YOUR "B" MOUNT LARGE?

R-3   IS YOUR "C" MOUNT LARGE?

R-4   IS YOUR "D" MOUNT LARGE?

R-5   IS YOUR "E" MOUNT LARGE?

R-6   IS YOUR "F" MOUNT LARGE?

R-7   IS YOUR "G" MOUNT LARGE?

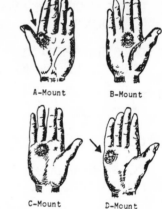

A-Mount   B-Mount

C-Mount   D-Mount

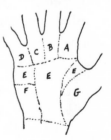

upper-E Mount   puffy lower-E Mount   F-Mount   G-Mount

Are there any smooth Mounts (no bulges)?

R-8   IS YOUR "A" MOUNT SMOOTH OR ORDINARY?

R-9   IS YOUR "B" MOUNT SMOOTH OR ORDINARY?

R-10 IS YOUR "C" MOUNT SMOOTH OR ORDINARY?

R-11   IS YOUR "D" MOUNT SMOOTH OR ORDINARY?

R-12   IS YOUR "E" MOUNT SMOOTH OR ORDINARY?

R-13   IS YOUR "F" MOUNT SMOOTH OR ORDINARY?

R-14   IS YOUR "G" MOUNT SMOOTH OR ORDINARY?

Are there any Mounts showing depressions?

R-15   IS YOUR "A" MOUNT DEPRESSED?

R-16   IS YOUR "B" MOUNT DEPRESSED?

R-17   IS YOUR "C" MOUNT DEPRESSED?

R-18   IS YOUR "D" MOUNT DEPRESSED?

R-19   IS YOUR "E" MOUNT DEPRESSED?

R-20   IS YOUR "F" MOUNT DEPRESSED?

R-21   IS YOUR "G" MOUNT DEPRESSED?

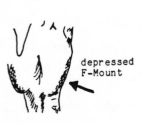

depressed
and
deficient

upper E-Mount

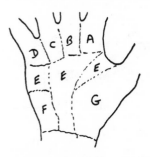

depressed
F-Mount

Locate any of following marks on a big Mount and circle the Description code for that Mount.

R-22   ARE THERE 1 TO 3 VERTICAL LINES ON A BIG "A" MOUNT?

R-23   ARE THERE 1 TO 3 VERTICAL LINES ON A BIG "B" MOUNT?

R-24   ARE THERE 1 TO 3 VERTICAL LINES ON A BIG "C" MOUNT?

R-25   ARE THERE 1 TO 3 VERTICAL LINES ON A BIG "D" MOUNT?

R-26   ARE THERE 1 TO 3 VERTICAL LINES ON A BIG "E" MOUNT?

R-27   ARE THERE 1 TO 3 VERTICAL LINES ON A BIG "F" MOUNT?

R-28   ARE THERE 1 TO 3 VERTICAL LINES ON A BIG "G" MOUNT?

R-29   IS THERE A TRIDENT ON A BIG "A" MOUNT?

R-30   IS THERE A TRIDENT ON A BIG "B" MOUNT?

R-31   IS THERE A TRIDENT ON A BIG "C" MOUNT?

R-32   IS THERE A TRIDENT ON A BIG "D" MOUNT?

R-33   IS THERE A TRIDENT ON A BIG "E" MOUNT?

R-34   IS THERE A TRIDENT ON A BIG "F" MOUNT?

R-35   IS THERE A TRIDENT ON A BIG "G" MOUNT?

R-36   IS THERE A PERFECT STAR ON A BIG "A" MOUNT?

R-37   IS THERE A PERFECT STAR ON A BIG "B" MOUNT?

R-38   IS THERE A PERFECT STAR ON A BIG "C" MOUNT?

R-39   IS THERE A PERFECT STAR ON A BIG "D" MOUNT?

R-40   IS THERE A PERFECT STAR ON A BIG "E" MOUNT?

R-41   IS THERE A PERFECT STAR ON A BIG "F" MOUNT?

R-42   IS THERE A PERFECT STAR ON A BIG "G" MOUNT?

R-43   IS THERE A TRIANGLE ON A BIG "A" MOUNT?

R-44   IS THERE A TRIANGLE ON A BIG "B" MOUNT?

R-45   IS THERE A TRIANGLE ON A BIG "C" MOUNT?

R-46   IS THERE A TRIANGLE ON A BIG "D" MOUNT?

R-47   IS THERE A TRIANGLE ON A BIG "E" MOUNT?

R-48   IS THERE A TRIANGLE ON A BIG "F" MOUNT?

R-49   IS THERE A TRIANGLE ON A BIG "G" MOUNT?

R-50   IS THERE A CIRCLE ON A BIG "A" MOUNT?

R-51   IS THERE A CIRCLE ON A BIG "B" MOUNT?

R-52   IS THERE A CIRCLE ON A BIG "C" MOUNT?

R-53   IS THERE A CIRCLE ON A BIG "D" MOUNT?

R-54   IS THERE A CIRCLE ON A BIG "E" MOUNT?

R-55   IS THERE A CIRCLE ON A BIG "F" MOUNT?

R-56   IS THERE A CIRCLE ON A BIG "G" MOUNT?

R-57   IS THERE A SQUARE ON A BIG "A" MOUNT?

R-58   IS THERE A SQUARE ON A BIG "B" MOUNT?

R-59   IS THERE A SQUARE ON A BIG "C" MOUNT?

R-60   IS THERE A SQUARE ON A BIG "D" MOUNT?

R-61   IS THERE A SQUARE ON A BIG "E" MOUNT?

R-62   IS THERE A SQUARE ON A BIG "F" MOUNT?

R-63   IS THERE A SQUARE ON A BIG "G" MOUNT?

R-64   IS THERE A CROSS ON A BIG "A" MOUNT?

R-65   IS THERE A CROSS ON A BIG "B" MOUNT?

R-66   IS THERE A CROSS ON A BIG "C" MOUNT?

R-67   IS THERE A CROSS ON A BIG "D" MOUNT?

R-68   IS THERE A CROSS ON A BIG "E" MOUNT?

R-69   IS THERE A CROSS ON A BIG "F" MOUNT?

R-70   IS THERE A CROSS ON A BIG "G" MOUNT?

R-71   IS THERE A GRILLE ON A BIG "A" MOUNT?

R-72   IS THERE A GRILLE ON A BIG "B" MOUNT?

R-73   IS THERE A GRILLE ON A BIG "C" MOUNT?

R-74   IS THERE A GRILLE ON A BIG "D" MOUNT?

R-75   IS THERE A GRILLE ON A BIG "E" MOUNT?

R-76   IS THERE A GRILLE ON A BIG "F" MOUNT?

R-77   IS THERE A GRILLE ON A BIG "G" MOUNT?

R-78   IS THERE A CROSSBAR ON A BIG "A" MOUNT?

R-79   IS THERE A CROSSBAR ON A BIG "B" MOUNT?

R-80   IS THERE A CROSSBAR ON A BIG "C" MOUNT?

R-81   IS THERE A CROSSBAR ON A BIG "D" MOUNT?

R-82   IS THERE A CROSSBAR ON A BIG "E" MOUNT?

R-83   IS THERE A CROSSBAR ON A BIG "F" MOUNT?

R-84   IS THERE A CROSSBAR ON A BIG "G" MOUNT?

R-85   IS THERE AN ISLAND ON A BIG "A" MOUNT?

R-86   IS THERE AN ISLAND ON A BIG "B" MOUNT?

R-87   IS THERE AN ISLAND ON A BIG "C" MOUNT?

R-88   IS THERE AN ISLAND ON A BIG "D" MOUNT?

R-89   IS THERE AN ISLAND ON A BIG "E" MOUNT?

R-90   IS THERE AN ISLAND ON A BIG "F" MOUNT?

R-91   IS THERE AN ISLAND ON A BIG "G" MOUNT?

R-92   ARE THERE DOTS, SPOTS OR BLOTCHES ON A
       BIG "A" MOUNT?

R-93   ARE THERE DOTS, SPOTS OR BLOTCHES ON A
       BIG "B" MOUNT?

R-94   ARE THERE DOTS, SPOTS OR BLOTCHES ON A BIG
       "C" MOUNT?

R-95   ARE THERE DOTS, SPOTS OR BLOTCHES ON A BIG
       "D" MOUNT?

R-96   ARE THERE DOTS, SPOTS OR BLOTCHES ON A BIG
       "E" MOUNT?

R-97   ARE THERE DOTS, SPOTS OR BLOTCHES ON A BIG
       "F" MOUNT?

R-98   ARE THERE DOTS, SPOTS OR BLOTCHES ON A BIG
       "G" MOUNT?

R-99   IS THERE AN IMPERFECT STAR ON A BIG
       "A" MOUNT?

R-100 IS THERE AN IMPERFECT STAR ON A BIG
       "B" MOUNT?

R-101 IS THERE AN IMPERFECT STAR ON A BIG
       "C" MOUNT?

R-102 IS THERE AN IMPERFECT STAR ON A BIG "D" MOUNT?

R-103 IS THERE AN IMPERFECT STAR ON A BIG "E" MOUNT?

R-104 IS THERE AN IMPERFECT STAR ON A BIG "F" MOUNT?

R-105 IS THERE AN IMPERFECT STAR ON A BIG "G" MOUNT?

R-106 ARE THERE MORE THAN 3 VERTICAL LINES ON A BIG "A" MOUNT?

R-107 ARE THERE MORE THAN 3 VERTICAL LINES ON A BIG "B" MOUNT?

R-108 ARE THERE MORE THAN 3 VERTICAL LINES ON A BIG "C" MOUNT?

R-109 ARE THERE MORE THAN 3 VERTICAL LINES ON A BIG "D" MOUNT?

R-110 ARE THERE MORE THAN 3 VERTICAL LINES ON A BIG "E" MOUNT?

R-111 ARE THERE MORE THAN 3 VERTICAL LINES ON A BIG "F" MOUNT?

R-112 ARE THERE MORE THAN 3 VERTICAL LINES ON A BIG "G" MOUNT?

Part 2

Handology Interprets Past, Present and Future Projections

The Surface of Your Hand
Handology looks at the surface features of the palm and takes note of lines and other marks. For the location of all lines and their direction, use "Map of the Lines" in this section.

But first, a little reading before you begin will make it easier for you to use this section and to produce accurate results.

Future Profile
This is the section where past and present lifestyles can be projected into the future. If you are unhappy with this projection, remember that it can be changed by a change in lifestyle.

Follow the "Current"
You may at first have difficulty in accepting the idea of a life current flowing through the body. Nevertheless, the faithful and careful application of the theory of life currents is very helpful when making an analysis. You will find that, whether you believe the theory or not, you will be able to correctly analyze the lines in the hand and to produce amazing insights. Thus it matters little whether you believe the theory to be true or false.

To understand how to analyze lines, imagine that an electrical life current is in operation along the lines. It begins through the 1st finger, reaches the Heart line and sets in motion the circulation, then passes to the Head line and awakens the mind.

When circulation and mind begin to operate, the current passes on to the Life line. It then travels over the Career, Fate and Health lines and finds its outlet through the 2nd, 3rd and 4th fingers.

It is not until the current reaches a line that it begins to operate. So, because the Career line receives the current from the end of the Life line, it is analyzed from the bottom of the hand upwards. The Fate line and Health line are analyzed in the same direction.

The beginnings of these lines cover early years of life, the middle portions cover the middle years of life, and the ends of the lines cover the later years. Some lines are analyzed in these three separate parts, not as complete lines. The parts are referred to as the "beginning," the "course" and the "termination." Please remember this when matching your hands to the pictures.

Marks on a Line
The marks on a line can either hinder the current or help it along. If a mark is present with other, similar marks on other lines, and at the same age, this is a physical indication. If other main lines show no marks or similar characteristics at that age, it is an emotional indication, not a physical one.

Lines indicate, first, the physical effect; second, mental characteristics and qualities of affection (love, hate and so on); third, the times when this mental attitude has exerted an influence powerful enough to draw lines in different directions.

All of these are not shown in every hand. The first and second always are, but the third is shown only at times.

THE DESCRIPTION CODE IN PART 2

The Description code used in Part 2 is the same code used in Part 1. Letters of the alphabet represent lines, and numbers represent marks:

Description **T** is the Heart line.
Description **U** is the Head line.
Description **V** is the Life line, etc.

For example, in Description code **T-10.6** the letter **T** represents the Heart line, **10** represents a break, **.6** represents the 6th type of break.

The numbers and their significance are as follows:

1 — meaning of line
2 — line is ABSENT
3 — the STARTING POINT
4 — LENGTH
5 — COURSE
6 — TERMINATION
7 — CHARACTER
8 — COLOR
9 — SPLIT
10 — BREAK
11 — TRIDENTS
12 — DOTS
13 — ISLANDS
14 — CIRCLES
15 — STARS
16 — CROSSES
17 — SISTER LINES

THE YEAR INDICATOR

Age is calculated by means of a "Year Indicator" system which works by drawing an imaginary mark at the midway point of a line, this midway point representing midlife — age 36.

HANDOLOGY

Each half of the line is then divided into equal spaces. The spaces must be in proportion — the larger the hand, the larger must be the spaces, as shown in the diagrams.

The Heart, Head, Life, Career, Fate and Health lines are analyzed as shown below.

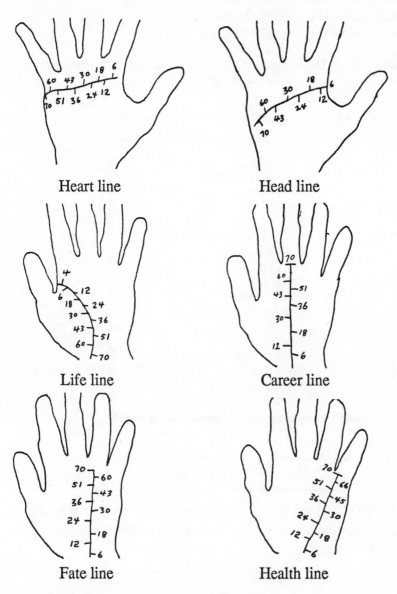

Heart line

Head line

Life line

Career line

Fate line

Health line

The Affection lines can be numerous; they run parallel to the Heart line. The length of each Affection line determines the length of that affection. You can have strong affection for material things as well as people. This area needs more research but is helpful when used in conjunction with the rest of the hand.

The Affection and Influence lines are analyzed as shown below.

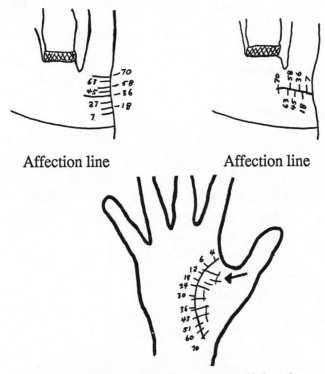

Affection line   Affection line

Influence lines are the parallel and
vertical lines on the "G" Mount

HOW TO USE THE PICTURES

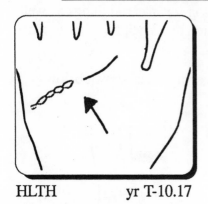

The arrow indicates where you should look to find the year using the Year Indicator.

"yr" indicates the need to determine the year by using the Year Indicator.

"HLTH" indicates significance of mark.

HLTH   yr T-10.17   Description code: T-10.17

Line chained after break.

IMPORTANT NOTE: Some pictures, such as the above, contain the words "Health," "Accident," etc. in abbreviation. If you wish to remain unaware of knowledge pertaining to one of these subject areas, do not record the corresponding Description codes. Abbreviations are: FEML — females, MALE — males, MNTL — mental, ACC — accident, HLTH — health, DTH — death.

It's So Easy to Use Handology
Handology is designed as an easy 1-2-3 operation. As soon as you understand its content, all you have to do is:

1. Match the line or mark in your hand to the pictures.
2. Remember the Description codes under the pictures.
3. Look up the Description codes in Part 3.

It's that simple.

This method is good at parties and family gatherings, but to develop a complete and accurate analysis, use the worksheet and the Year Indicator to record all the Description codes you have selected.

What you will need

Magnifying glass ...... Preferably with a light-source attached. It makes some visual analysis easier.

A pencil .... Keep a couple of sharp pencils handy.

Lined paper .... Used to create your own worksheets before you begin.

You Are Now Ready to Begin

1. Create a worksheet as shown to record the Description codes as you go through Part 2.

2. Turn to page 60.

3. Match the hand to the pictures.

   Remember, it is not necessary to check every picture and every section. Simply record what is in your hand. For instance, if there are no breaks on the line, the section on breaks can be ignored. This also applies to the lines themselves. If you don't have a Fate line, for instance, skip that section.

   If there is a "yr" in the picture, calculate the age using the Year Indicator and write the number in the appropriate age box on the same line on the worksheet.

4. When the worksheet is completed, turn to Part 3 and look up the interpretation of each Description code, column by column. For example, look up all the codes on the left of the worksheet, then all the codes under the year 4-6, then 6-12 and so on.

   The Description codes concern events that:
   a) have occurred in the past,
   b) may occur if you continue on the same course,
   c) may be changed if you so desire it.

Remember, not all future events will occur. Therefore, anything in Part 3 which refers to the future can only be interpreted as an insight. For example, if your age is 30 at the time of the analysis, statements about a later age are future projections, not facts.

Also keep in mind that lines change weekly, monthly and yearly and that future analysis could produce different projections if your life-style has changed substantially.

The Golden Rule
No single feature in the hand should be taken in isolation as an adequate indication of character. Each facet of personality revealed by examination must be assessed in the light of each and every other indication. Only if this is done properly can accuracy be ensured.

WORKSHEET EXAMPLE

Check which hand   Age: 30

☑ Active   ☐ Passive

Title	Description Code	4 6	6 12	12 18	18 24	24 30	30 36	36 43	43 51	51 60	60 70	70 Up
Heart L.	T-1.1											
					Tic -17							
						T14 .1						
	T-16.2											
Head L.	U-1.1											
	U-3.1											
	U-4.10											
							U13 .6					

Year Indicator

MAP OF THE LINES

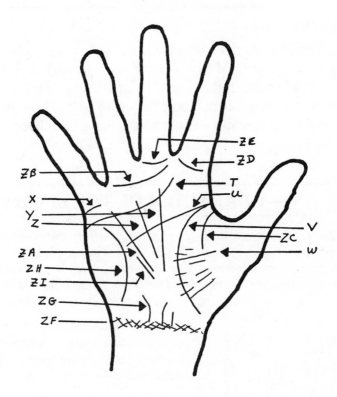

T — Heart	ZB — Neurosis
U — Head	ZC — Warrior
V — Life	ZD — Mystical
W — Influence	ZE — Balance
X — Affection	ZF — 1st Rascette
Y — Career	ZG — Travel
Z — Fate	ZH — Intuition
ZA — Health	ZI — Lascivia

Start Here to Analyze Your Hands

Begin with the "Active" Hand

Analyze the active hand first — the right hand if right-handed, left hand if left-handed, right hand if ambidextrous. The active hand reflects life as it has been lived; the opposite hand — the passive hand — reveals how life was intended to have been lived.

S — CHARACTER OF THE LINES

This refers to the clearness, depth and evenness of the lines, and to whether they are spoiled by defects such as broadness, shallowness or poor coloration. The first general principle governing lines is that the more even a line is, the less it is crossed, broken, has islands, or is chained, and the nearer it is to being pink in color, the better is the line and the more vigorous is the operation of its attributes.

S-1.1

Character of the lines.

When examining lines, note the character of the lines themselves — their clearness, depth, evenness, and whether they are perfect or defective.

S-1.2

Multiplicity of lines.

In some hands there are hundreds of lines crossing the palm in every direction. This multitude is made up of Chance lines, Worry lines and lines showing various emotions. Every line which is not a main line or minor line is such a line. Decide whether your hand has a multiplicity or non-multiplicity of lines.

S-1.3

Lines clearly cut and deep.

Heart   S-1.4

Small hands, large lines — hand is small and the lines very large and deep.

S-1.5

Broad, shallow, poorly colored lines — lines are broad and shallow, rather than deep and clear.

S-1.6

Large hands with tiny, narrow lines. Compare the size of the hand with the size of the lines, noting whether the lines are proportionately too small.

T — THE HEART LINE

The Heart line reveals not only the muscular, vital strength and action of the heart itself but, as a result of these conditions, the strength and character of the affections.

T-1.1

Heart line.

The Heart line rises from a point under or near the index finger and traces its way across the hand under the Mounts, ending on the left side. It is not proper to say this line has any normal starting or stopping place. When a single line is seen occupying a position which is, relatively, where the Head line ought to be, it should be classified as a Head line and the Heart line should be considered to be absent.

Its disposition·

T-2.1

Line is absent.

T-3 STARTING POINT

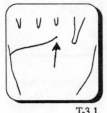

T-3.1

Rising from the index finger Mount.

T-3.2

Rising between 1st and 2nd finger.

T-3.3

Rising from the Mount under 2nd finger.

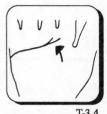

T-3.4

Starting from two different sources.

T-3.4

Rising from three different sources.

T-3.5

Starts near Head line.

T-3.6

Line starts from Head line.

yr T-3.7

Line starts anywhere along Head line.

T-3.8

Line starts under index finger.

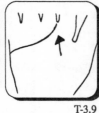

T-3.9

Starts high between 1st and 2nd fingers.

T-3.10

Heart line joined to Head and Life lines.

DTH   T-3.11

Cuts through Head and Life lines.

 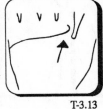  

| T-3.12 | T-3.13 | T-3.14 | T-3.15 |

Starts high on the Mount and crosses entire hand.

Curves around Mount.

Line starts with two lines under 1st finger.

Line starts with three lines under 1st finger.

T-4 ITS LENGTH

yr T-4.1   T-4.2

Line is short.

Line crosses entire hand.

T-5 ITS COURSE

  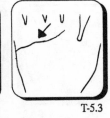 

| yr T-5.1 | T-5.2 | T-5.3 | T-5.4 |

Line curves up towards the fingers.

Rises to the 2nd finger.

Rises to the 3rd finger.

Rises to the 4th finger.

yr T-5.5

yr T-5.6

yr T-5.7

Line dips down in its course.

Line merges into the Head line.

Line, after deflection, regains its course.

yr T-5.8

T-5.9

T-5.10

Line deflects and cuts the Head line.

Line curves down close to the Head line.

Line lies high above the Head line.

T-6 ITS TERMINATION

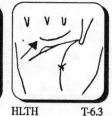

T-6.1

HLTH   T-6.2

HLTH   T-6.3

T-6.4

Line terminates under 2nd finger.

Line terminates under 2nd finger with any defect. Other lines at age 25.

Line terminates under 3rd finger with any defect. Other lines at age 50.

Line terminates under 3rd finger.

64

T-6.5

Line terminates
under 4th finger.

T-6.6

Not a Heart line.

T-6.7

Not a Heart line.

T-6.8

Line ends on upper
"E" Mount.

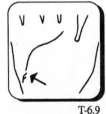

T-6.9

Line ends on the
"F" Mount.

HLTH   yr T-6.10

Line ends in the
center of the hand.
Any defects on other
lines at age 30.

HLTH   yr T-6.11

Line ends in the
center and no other
defects at age 30.

HLTH   yr T-6.12

Line ends on the
"G" Mount. Any
defect on other lines
at age 30.

yr T-6.13

Line ends on
"G" Mount with no
defect at age 30 on
other lines.

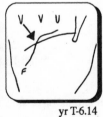

yr T-6.14

Line cuts Head line,
ends on "F" Mount.

T-7 ITS CHARACTER

PLEASE NOTE

Apply G-2,3,4,5 at different age periods if change shows following pictures.

yr T-7.2

Part of the line is deep-cut and smooth.

yr T-7.3

Part of the line is small and thin, other lines larger.

yr T-7.4

Part of the line is broad and shallow, other lines well marked.

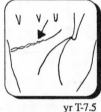

yr T-7.5

Part of the line is chained, other lines well marked.

yr T-7.6

Part of the line becomes thin and fine near the end.

yr T-7.7

Part of the line is broken up by lines running into it.

T-8 ITS COLOR

When beginning the examination of this line, it is useful to press the line from source to end with the finger and note the ease with which the blood flows under this pressure. This indicates the strength of the blood stream and helps to distinguish the color of the line. In some lines the blood flows freely while in others the whiteness under pressure indicates a weak blood supply. People from non-white races may be difficult to analyze, in which case press the nails to determine color.

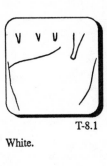

T-8.1

White.

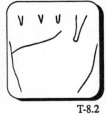

T-8.2

Pink.

T-8.3

Red.

T-8.4

Yellow.

T-8.5

Blue or Purple.

T-9 THE SPLIT

A MESSAGE ABOUT SPLITS.

T-9.1

Splits.

A MESSAGE ABOUT SPLITS THAT DEFLECT.

T-9.2

Splits deflect to Mounts.

yr T-9.3

Split rising to index finger.

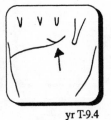

yr T-9.4

Split rising to 2nd finger.

yr T-9.5

Split rises under 3rd finger.

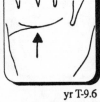

yr T-9.6

Split rises under 4th finger.

yr T-9.7

Fine or few lines fall from Heart line.

T-9.8

Short lines fall along its course.

yr T-9.9

Split line merges into
Head line.

HLTH   yr T-9.10

Crossbars cut line
with any crossbar on
other lines, same age.

yr T-9.11

Crossbar cuts Heart
line only.

T-9.12

Very fine lines
joining and leaving
Heart line.

T-9.13

Very fine lines point
towards fingers.

T-9.14

Very fine lines point
towards wrist.

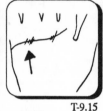

T-9.15

Very fine lines cross
Heart line.

yr T-9.16

Very short split lines.

T-9.17

A large split line
from 1st finger.

T-9.18

A large split line
from 2nd finger.

T-9.19

Split line from Heart
line cuts broken
Career line.

yr T-9.20

Split line falls
towards Head line.

yr T-9.21

Split line falls
towards Head line,
has a crossbar.

T-9.22

Split line falls
towards Head line,
has an island.

68

T-10 THE BREAK

HLTH   yr T-10.1

Line breaks and curls
up under 1st finger.
With any other
similar line.

yr T-10.2

Line breaks and curls
up on Heart line only.

yr T-10.3

Line breaks and curls
up under 2nd finger.
With any other
similar line.

yr T-10.4

Line breaks and curls
up under 2nd finger.
Heart line only.

yr T-10.5

Breaks and curls up
under 3rd finger.
With any other
similar line.

yr T-10.6

Breaks and curls up
under 3rd finger.
Heart line only.

yr T-10.7

Breaks under 3rd
finger with a line
that splits to the
3rd finger.

HLTH   yr T-10.8

Breaks and curls up
under 4th finger.
With any other
similar line.

yr T-10.9

Breaks under 4th
finger with a line
that splits to the
4th finger.

HLTH   T-10.10

Many breaks in the
line. With any other
similar line.

T-10.11

Many breaks, Heart
line only.

yr T-10.12

Broken lines, short
or long lines point
to the Head line.

yr T-10.13

Broken line merges
with Head or other
lines.

yr T-10.14

Broken line cuts
Head line.

yr T-10.15

Broken line with star
on Head line.

yr T-10.16

Line droops, cuts
Head line followed
by an island.

HLTH   yr T-10.17

Line chained after
break.

yr T-10.18

Island or islands after
break.

DTH   yr T-10.19

Well-marked star
between break.

DTH   yr T-10.20

Break is cut by a
crossbar.

DTH   yr T-10.21

Break has crossbars
on both ends.

HLTH   yr T-10.22

Sister line joins
crossbars.

HLTH   yr T-10.23

Broken line repaired
by a square.

yr T-10.24

A well-marked dot
before break.

T-10.25

Small breaks at the
beginning of the line.

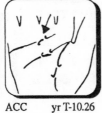

ACC   yr T-10.26

Hook breaks with
any other hook break
on other lines, same
year.

yr T-10.27

Hook break.

yr T-10.28

Chance lines and
sister repair marks.

yr T-10.29

Other repair signs.

yr T-10.30

Square repair signs.

yr T-10.31

Break in the line.

yr T-10.32

Break under
2nd finger.

yr T-10.33

Break under
3rd finger.

yr T-10.34

Break under
4th finger.

yr T-10.35

A square on the line.

71

T-11 THE TRIDENT

T-11.1

Line ends in a tassel.

T-11.2

Heart and other lines
that end in a tassel.

T-12 THE DOT

HLTH   yr T-12.1

Dots on the line with
any dot on any other
line.

yr T-12.2

Any dot on the line.

yr T-12.3

Small dot on the line.

yr T-12.4

A square repair sign.

T-13 THE ISLAND

HLTH   yr T-13.1

Island with an island
on any other line,
same year.

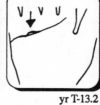

yr T-13.2

Island on the line.

yr T-13.3

Island terminated by
a split line.

T-14 THE CIRCLE

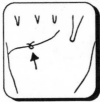

HLTH   yr T-14.1

A circle under the
3rd finger or on the
line itself.

T-15 THE STAR

HLTH   yr T-15.1

A small star or badly
formed star with any
other line, same year.

yr T-15.2

A small star or badly
formed star. Heart
line only.

DTH   yr T-15.3

Large well-formed
star with any other
line, same year.

ACC   yr T-15.4

A well-formed large
star on Heart line
only.

HLTH   yr T-15.5

After star, line is
chained. With any
other line, same year.

yr T-15.6

After star, line is
chained. Heart line
only.

HLTH   yr T-15.7

After star, an island.
With any other line,
same year.

yr T-15.8

After star, an island.
Heart line only.

73

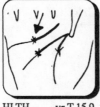

HLTH   yr T-15.9   yr T-15.10

After star, line is thin.
With any other line,
same year.

After star, line is thin.
Heart line only.

T-16 THE CROSS

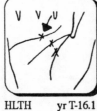

HLTH   yr T-16.1   yr T-16.2

Cross on line,
with any other
line, same year.

Cross on Heart
line only.

T-17 SISTER LINES

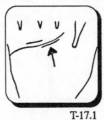

T-17.1

A line runs parallel
to Heart line.

U — THE HEAD LINE

This is an important line which indicates clearly your degree of mental prowess, your power of mental concentration and your ability to exert self-control. The importance of this line will be recognized when we consider what a tremendous part mental attitude plays in the shaping of our destiny.

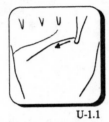

U-1.1

Head line.

The Head line traces its way across the hand below the Heart line.

Its disposition.

U-3 STARTING POINT

U-3.1

Line slightly attached to Life line.

U-3.2

Line rises farther along Life line.

U-3.3

Pointed angle formed by Head and Life lines.

U-3.4

Line rises well along its course.

U-3.5

Head and Life lines form an obtuse angle.

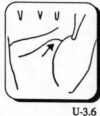

U-3.6

Obtuse angle with Heart, Head and Life lines only.

U-3.7

Line is separated from the Life line.

U-3.8

Line starts from lower "E" Mount, crossing the Life line.

U-3.9

Line starts from the Mount under the 1st finger.

U-3.10

Line starts from under the Mount, 1st finger.

U-3.11

Line starts from Life line with a branch line to the 1st finger.

U-3.12

Separated line droops to the "F" Mount.

U-3.13

Separated, split Head line.

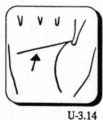

U-3.14

Starts from Life line and goes well across the palm with few defects.

U-3.15

Head and Life lines closely connected for some time.

U-3.16

Line starts inside the Life line. *Passive hand only.*

U-3.17

Line starts inside Life
line. *Passive and
active hands.*

U-4 ITS LENGTH

U-4.1

Line is short.

U-4.2

Line short, narrow
and thin, all other
lines deep and
well cut.

yr U-4.3

Life and Head lines
same length.

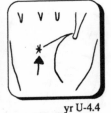

yr U-4.4

Short line ends with
a star.

HLTH   yr U-4.5

Short Head and Life
lines, ending in a star.

HLTH   yr U-4.6

Head and Life lines
short. Both end in
a cross.

yr U-4.7

Straight line across
the hand with no
Heart line.

U-4.8

Long and straight
but thinner than
other lines.

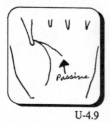

U-4.9

Short in passive, long in active.

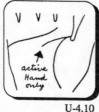

U-4.10

Long in passive, short in active.

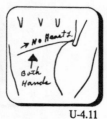

U-4.11

With no Heart line. Long in both active and passive hands.

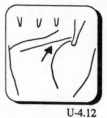

U-4.12

Separated straight Head line.

U-5 ITS COURSE

U-5.1

A straight line.

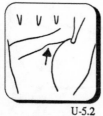

U-5.2

Line curves under 2nd finger.

U-5.3

Line curves under 3rd finger.

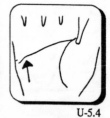

U-5.4

Line curves under 4th finger.

U-5.5

Line is wavy from start to end.

U-5.6

Line deflects in a curve towards the Heart line.

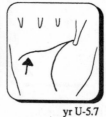

yr U-5.7

Line deflects in a curve near the end.

U-5.8

A slight curve towards the Heart line.

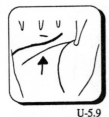

U-5.9

Line deflects to
Heart line but the
Heart line is deeper
and stronger.

U-5.10

Line deflects to
Heart line but the
Head line is deeper
and stronger.

yr U-5.11

Line deflects
downwards.

U-5.12

The whole line
deflects downwards.

U-5.13

Head and Heart lines
are close together.

U-5.14

Head and Heart lines
are widely separated.

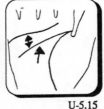

U-5.15

Lines are widely
separated, Head line
has a very slight
slope along its length.

U-5.16

Heart, Head and
Life lines are
widely separated.

U-6 ITS TERMINATION

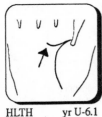

HLTH   yr U-6.1

Line turns up towards
2nd finger.

HLTH   yr U-6.2

Line runs up to
the base of the
2nd finger.

HLTH   yr U-6.3

Line under the base
of 2nd finger ends in
a star, cross or dot.

yr U-6.4

Line ends in a tassel.

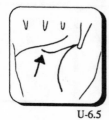

U-6.5

yr U-6.6   HLTH   yr U-6.7

Line turns up towards 3rd finger.

Line touches the Heart line.

Line ends on the base of the 3rd finger.

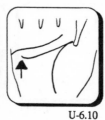

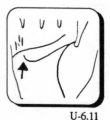

HLTH   yr U-6.8   HLTH   yr U-6.9   U-6.10   U-6.11

Star where Head and Heart lines cross.

A star is followed by an island.

Line turns up towards 4th finger.

Line turns up with vertical lines under the 4th finger.

HLTH   yr U-6.12   HLTH   yr U-6.13   U-6.14   U-6.15

Line ends under the 4th finger.

Line ends under the 4th finger with a star.

Line ends on upper Warrior Mount.

Line slopes downwards.

U-6.16

Line ends on the
"F" Mount.

MNTL   U-6.17

Line droops, ends in
a star.

MNTL   U-6.18

Line droops, ends in
a chain.

MNTL   U-6.19

Line droops, ends in
a cross.

MNTL   U-6.20

Line droops, ends in
an island.

MNTL   U-6.21

Line droops, ends in
a dot.

U-6.22

Line droops, end
is broken and
intermittent

U-6.23

Line droops from
its beginning.

U-6.24

Line straight, then
droops down.

U-6.25

Line slightly forked
at the end.

U-6.26

Line forks largely at
the end.

U-6.27

Line forks,
then droops and
forks again.

81

HANDOLOGY

  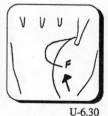 

MNTL   U-6.28   U-6.29   U-6.30   MNTL   yr U-6.31

Second line forks, ends in a star, cross or dot.

Line divides widely into three branches.

Line curves and ends on the "F" Mount.

Line ends at the 2nd finger on both hands.

yr U-6.32   U-6.33   U-6.34

Line ends in the middle of the palm.

Line ends in upper "F" Mount.

Sloping line forks.

U-7 ITS CHARACTER

 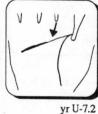  

U-7.1   yr U-7.2   yr U-7.3   yr U-7.4

Deep and well cut, thin during deflection, chained afterwards

Thin line, then deep and well cut

Deep and well cut, then a thin line.

Line is normal, then becomes chained.

U-7.5

Deep and well-
cut Head line.
No defects.

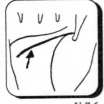

U-7.6

Long, deep and well-
cut Head line.

U-7.7

Line thin and narrow,
traces delicately
across the hand.

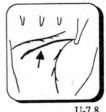

U-7.8

Line deeper
and clearer than
other lines.

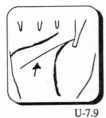

U-7.9

Line is thin, other
lines are larger.

HLTH   yr U-7.10

Thin at start, chained
during deflection,
ends in a star.

U-7.11

Line cuts more
deeply than the
other lines.

U-7.12

Line is broad
and shallow.

yr U-7.13

Line broad and
shallow, then turns
deep and well cut.

MNTL   U-7.14

A chained line.

yr U-7.15

Line chained,
then turns deep
and well cut.

yr U-7.16

Line chained, turns
thin, then deep and
well cut.

yr U-7.17

Line is thick, then
thin, then thick.

U-8 ITS COLOR

Press the line from source to end with the finger and note the ease with which the
blood flows under this pressure. People from non-white races may be difficult to
analyze for color; in this case, press the nails.

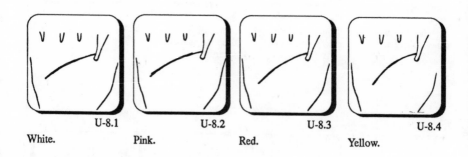

U-8.1

White.

U-8.2

Pink.

U-8.3

Red.

U-8.4

Yellow.

U-8.5

Blue.

84

U-9 THE SPLIT

U-9.1

Rising splits are
small and frequent.

U-9.2

Rising splits are large
and long.

U-9.3

Splits drop below
the line.

U-9.4

A single split rises
under the 1st finger.

U-9.5

Split line rises to the
2nd finger.

U-9.6

Any rising split line
ends in a star.

U-9.7

Split runs to
3rd finger.

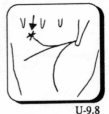

U-9.8

Split line ends in
a star under the
3rd finger.

U-9.9

Split lines end in a
dot, cross or island.

U-9.10

Any split that
touches the
Heart line.

yr U-9.11

Split merges into the
Heart line.

yr U-9.12

Merged split line cuts
Career or Fate lines.

U-9.13

Merged line cuts
Career and Fate lines.

HLTH   yr U-9.14

Deep crossbars.

U-9.15

Fine crossbars.

U-9.16

Split line branches
from under 1st finger.

U-9.17

Split line
branches from
under 2nd finger.

U-9.18

Split line branches
from under 3rd
finger.

U-9.19

Split line droops
downwards.

MNTL   U-9.20

A dual Head line.

yr U-9.21

Small and frequent
cuts on the line.

HLTH   yr U-9.22

Cuts are deeper than
the line itself.

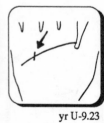

yr U-9.23

A cut on a thin line.

U-9.24

Branch line turns up
under 4th finger.

U-9.25

Split line rises
between 1st and
2nd fingers.

U-9.26

Split line rises
between 2nd and
3rd fingers.

U-9.27

Split line rises
between 3rd and
4th fingers.

U-10 THE BREAK

yr U-10.1

Breaks in the line.

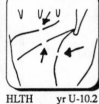

HLTH   yr U-10.2

Breaks with any
other breaks on other
lines, same year.

MNTL   U-10.3

Line continually
broken and
ladder-like.

U-10.4

Many breaks in
the line.

yr U-10.5

A square on the line.

U-11 THE TRIDENT

U-11.1

Tassel or trident
ending the line.

U-12 THE DOT

MNTL   yr U-12.1

Large and deep dots
on the line.

HLTH   yr U-12.2

Small, white or
pink dots.

yr U-12.3

Dot followed by a
thin line.

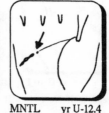

MNTL   yr U-12.4

Dot followed by a
chained line.

HLTH   yr U-12.5

Dot followed by a
chain, then a deep-
cut line.

HLTH   yr U-12.6

Dot followed by
an island.

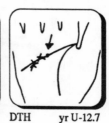

DTH   yr U-12.7

A star or a cross after
a dot.

DTH   yr U-12.8

An island follows the
dot, ending in a star.

88

MNTL   yr U-12.9

Dot, island, star,
then line continues
normally.

yr U-12.10

Dot on a thin Head
line. All other lines
are deeper.

yr U-12.11

Red spots on the line.

yr U-12.12

Dark spots on
the line.

U-13 THE ISLAND

yr U-13.1

Fine islands on
the line.

HLTH   yr U-13.2

Deep-cut and
red island.

HLTH   yr U-13.3

After island, a dot.

HLTH   yr U-13.3

After island, a cross.

MNTL   yr U-13.3

After island, a star.

MNTL   yr U-13.3

After island, a
severe break.

yr U-13.4

Deep-cut line
preceding island.

U-13.5

Island under the
1st finger.

89

yr U-13.6

Line terminates in
an island.

U-13.7

Line is made up of
small islands.

U-13.8

Line is made up
of small islands
and lines.

U-13.9

Line is chained.

U-14 THE CIRCLE

U-15 THE STAR

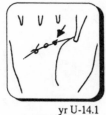

yr U-14.1

A circle on the line.

yr U-14.2

A circle under the
3rd finger.

HLTH   yr U-15.1

Stars on the line.

yr U-15.2

Stars on a thin and/or
narrow line.

U-16 THE CROSS

U-17 SISTER LINES

HLTH   yr U-16.1

Cross on the line.

yr U-16.2

Cross on a thin or
narrow line.

U-17.1

Sister line to
Head line.

90

V — LIFE LINE

The Life line indicates health during the various periods of life, physical strength in general, and whether life has been lived during each period with nervous force or with muscular robustness. It records many events in life and forms a basis to fall back on when seeking confirmation or explanations of indications found elsewhere on the hand.

V-1.1

Life line.

The Life line rises at the side of the hand under the 1st (index) finger, circles the lower "E" and "G" Mounts and, in most cases, ends at the base of the hand. As a guide, remember that the Life line should enclose the "G" Mount, not run on top of it.

V-2.1

Line is absent.

The inside line is the Life line.

The outside line is the Life line.

V-3 STARTING POINT

V-4 ITS LENGTH

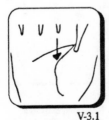

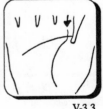

V-3.1

V-3.2

V-3.3

V-4.1

Line rises at the side of the hand under the 1st finger.

Line starts under the 1st finger.

Line starts under 1st finger and crosses Head line

A short line.

V-5 ITS COURSE

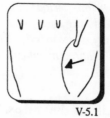

V-5.1

Line runs close to the Thumb.

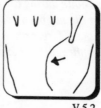

V-5.2

Line sweeps wide into the palm.

V-6 ITS TERMINATION

V-6.0

Passive hand does not show the defect termination of the active.

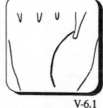

V-6.1

Line is deep and strong, ends strongly.

yr V-6.2

Short, thin line.

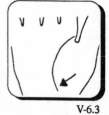

V-6.3

Ends clearly without any defects.

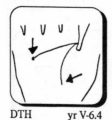

DTH   yr V-6.4

Head line ends in a dot, Life line ends same year.

DTH   yr V-6.4

Head line ends in a star, Life line ends same year.

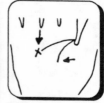

DTH   yr V-6.4

Head line ends in a cross, Life line ends same year.

DTH   yr V-6.5

Heart line ends in a crossbar, Life line ends same year.

DTH   yr V-6.5

Heart line ends in a
dot, Life line ends
same year.

DTH   yr V-6.5

Heart line ends in a
star, Life line ends
same year.

DTH   yr V-6.5

Heart line ends in a
cross, Life line ends
same year.

DTH   yr V-6.6

Dot on a wavy
Health line, Life
line ends same year
as dot.

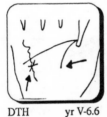

DTH   yr V-6.6

Cross on a wavy
Health line, Life
line ends same year
as cross.

DTH   yr V-6.6

Crossbar on a wavy
Health line, Life
line ends same year
as crossbar.

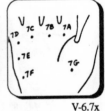

V-6.7x

Line ends with a
dot on any Mount.
Record corres-
ponding Reference
numbers.

yr V-6.8

Line deep and
strong, begins to
fade and disappears.

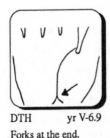

DTH   yr V-6.9

Forks at the end.

yr V-6.10

Short forks at
the end.

yr V-6.11

Forks are
close together.

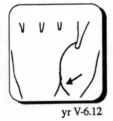

yr V-6.12

Forks diverge widely.

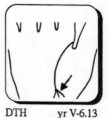

DTH   yr V-6.13

Line ends in
three prongs.

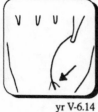

yr V-6.14

The middle prong is
stronger and deeper.

DTH   yr V-6.15

Line ends in a tassel.

HLTH   yr V-6.16

Line deflects to
1st finger.

HLTH   yr V-6.-17

Line deflects to
2nd finger.

HLTH   yr V-6.18

Line deflects to
3rd finger.

HLTH   yr V-6.19

Line deflects to
4th finger.

HLTH   yr V-6.20

Line deflects to upper
"E" Mount.

HLTH   yr V-6.21

Line deflects to
"F" Mount.

HLTH   yr V-6.22

Line deflects to
"G" Mount.

DTH   yr V-6.23

Line ends in a cross.

DTH   yr V-6.24

Line ends in
a crossbar.

DTH   yr V-6.25

Line ends in a dot.

HLTH   yr V-6.26

Line ends in a star.

DTH   yr V-6.27

A fine line leaving
the line ends in a star.

yr V-6.28

Line stops with a few
lines at the end.

V-7 ITS CHARACTER

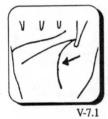

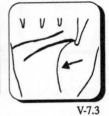

V-7.1

Deep and well cut,
few other lines.

V-7.2

Deep and long, few
other lines.

V-7.3

A narrow and
thin line.

V-7.4

Line deep, all other
lines are thin.

V-7.5

A thin line.

V-7.6

Line thin, all other
lines deep and
well cut.

V-7.7

Broad and
shallow line.

V-7.8

Lines run like
a ladder.

95

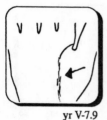

yr V-7.9

Fine lines
close together.

HLTH   V-7.10

Line is chained.

V-7.11

First years chained or
poorly marked.

yr V-7.12

Chained, then deep
and well cut.

yr V-7.13

Chained, followed by
a thin line.

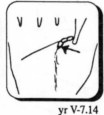

yr V-7.14

Chained, followed by
a poorly marked line.

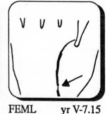

FEML   yr V-7.15

Lines is deep,
becoming thin, then
deep at approx. age
of 42 to 46.

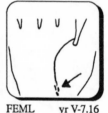

FEML   yr V-7.16

Line is broad and
shallow at age 42
to 46.

FEML   yr V-7.17

Line becomes
broad and shallow
at the end.

FEML   yr V-7.18

Broad and shallow
at the end with a
break on Head line,
same year.

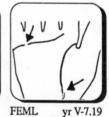

FEML   yr V-7.19

Broad and shallow
at the end with a
break on Heart line,
same year.

FEML   yr V-7.19

Broad and shallow at
the end with a dot on
Heart line, same year.

V-8 COLOR

With this examination, press the line from source to end with the finger and note how the blood flows under pressure. This will help to distinguish the color of the line. People from non-white races may be difficult to analyze for color, in which case press the nails to determine color.

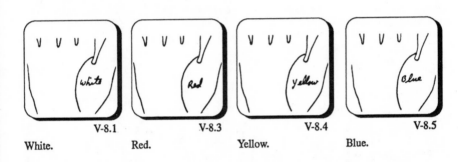

| V-8.1 | V-8.3 | V-8.4 | V-8.5 |

White.   Red.   Yellow.   Blue.

V-9 THE SPLIT

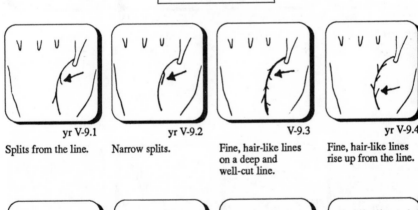

yr V-9.1   yr V-9.2   V-9.3   yr V-9.4

Splits from the line.   Narrow splits.   Fine, hair-like lines on a deep and well-cut line.   Fine, hair-like lines rise up from the line.

 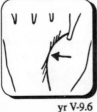 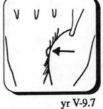 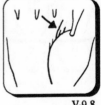

yr V-9.5   yr V-9.6   yr V-9.7   V-9.8

Fine, hair-like lines fall downwards.   Point where rising lines end and falling lines begin.   Rising lines end at island, then falling lines begin.   Rising lines and a single line to the index finger.

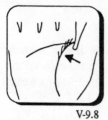   

V-9.8	yr V-9.9	yr V-9.10	yr V-9.11
Rising lines at the beginning of the line.	Line rises to the 2nd finger.	Line rises to the 3rd finger.	Line rises to the 4th finger.

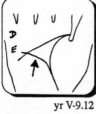   

yr V-9.12	yr V-9.12	yr V-9.13	yr V-9.14
Line rises to upper "E" Mount.	Line rises to upper "E" Mount.	Line goes to the "F" Mount.	Fine bars do not cut the line.

  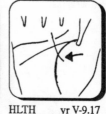 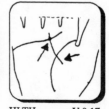

HLTH yr V-9.15	HLTH yr V-9.16	HLTH yr V-9.17	HLTH yr V-9.17
Crossbar cuts line in two.	Crossbar cuts line and ends in a grille under 2nd finger.	Bar to Heart line. Heart line breaks at the junction.	Bar to Heart line, dot at the junction.

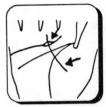

HLTH   yr V-9.17

Bar to Heart line,
island at the junction.

HLTH   yr V-9.18

A bar to a wavy
Health line.

HLTH   yr V-9.19

Crossbar ends in a
grille on the upper
"E" Mount.

HLTH   yr V-9.20

Bar to Heart line,
break at the junction
under 3rd finger.

HLTH   yr V-9.20

Bar to Heart Line,
dot at the junction
under 3rd finger.

HLTH   yr V-9.20

Bar to Heart line,
island at the junction
under 3rd finger.

HLTH   yr V-9.21

Bar runs to
"F" Mount.

HLTH   yr V-9.22

Confirms 9.21.
A bar with an
island runs to
the 2nd finger.

HLTH   yr V-9.23

A bar points to
a grille on the
"F" Mount.

HLTH   yr V-9.23

A bar points to
a cross on the
"F" Mount.

HLTH   yr V-9.24

Confirms 9.23. A star
on Health line at
Head line junction.

HLTH   yr V-9.24

Confirms 9.23. A
star on Health line
at Head line junction.

yr V-9.25

Line is deep and well cut after crossbar.

yr V-9.26

Crossbar cuts line, runs to Head line with break. Life line has island and becomes broad and shallow.

yr V-9.26

Crossbar cuts line, runs to Head line with a dot. Life line has island and becomes broad and shallow.

yr V-9.26

Crossbar cuts line, runs to Head line. Life line has island and becomes broad and shallow.

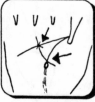

yr V-9.26

Crossbar cuts line, runs to Head line with a star. Life line has island and becomes broad and shallow

yr V-9.26

Crossbar cuts line, runs to Head line with a cross. Life line has island and becomes broad and shallow.

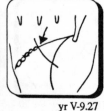

yr V-9.27

After crossbar, Head line becomes chained.

yr V-9.28

Crossbar begins on Influence line.

HLTH   yr V-9.29

Crossbar creates narrow quadrangle, a 4-sided figure.

HLTH   yr V-9.30

Crossbar runs to a ladder-like Health line.

HLTH   yr V-9.31

Crossbar runs to an island on the Health line.

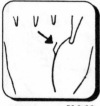

yr V-9.32

A single branch line rises to the 1st finger.

yr V-9.33

Branch line
sweeps up close
to the Life line.

yr V-9.34

Branch line
ends alongside
Career line.

yr V-9.35

Branch line sweeps
to "F" Mount.

yr V-9.36

Bar cuts Life and
Career lines.

yr V-9.37

Crossbar cuts Life
and Head lines and
ends between Heart
and Head lines.

yr V-9.38

Crossbar cuts Life,
Head and Heart lines.

yr V-9.39

Crossbar ends at the
Head line under the
2nd finger.

V-9.40

Any crossbar that
has an island along
its length.

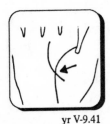

yr V-9.41

Crossbar ends under
the 2nd finger.

DTH   V-9.42

Crossbar has a star
on it.

DTH   V-9.42

Crossbar has a cross
on it.

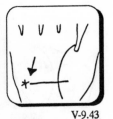

V-9.43

Crossbar ends
in a star on the
"F" Mount.

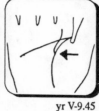

yr V-9.44

yr V-9.45

yr V-9.46

V-9.47

Crossbar stops under the 1st finger.

Branch line stops under the 1st finger.

Branch line stops under 1st finger with a grille.

Branch line crosses Career line.

V-9.47

yr V-9.48

yr V-9.49

V-9.50

Branch line stops at the Career line.

Split line stops at the Head line.

Split line stops at the Heart line under the 2nd finger.

Split line falls from the Life line.

yr V-9.51

yr V-9.52

yr V-9.53

yr V-9.54

Line to upper "E" Mount.

Line to upper "E" Mount with an island on the Life line

Line to upper "E" Mount with a spot after the line

Line stops at the Head line.

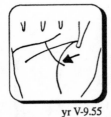

yr V-9.55

Line stops at the
Heart line.

yr V-9.56

Line stops at the
Career line.

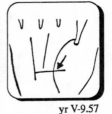

yr V-9.57

Line stops at the
Fate line.

yr V-9.58

Line stops at the
Health line.

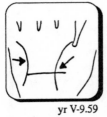

yr V-9.59

Line stops at the
Intuition line.

yr V-9.60

Line cuts Life line.

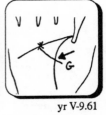

yr V-9.61

Line from "G" Mount
to Head line ends
with a star.

yr V-9.61

Line from "G" Mount
to Head line ends
with a dot.

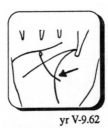

yr V-9.62

Island on the
line stops at the
Heart line.

V-10 THE BREAK

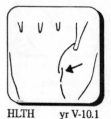

HLTH   yr V-10.1

Break on the line.

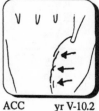

ACC   yr V-10.2

Small breaks
repaired.

yr V-10.3

Wide breaks.

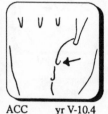

ACC   yr V-10.4

The ends turn back
after breaks.

HLTH   V-10.5

A series of
small breaks.

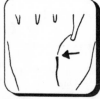

HLTH   yr V-10.6

Line becomes thin
after each break.

yr V-10.7

Starts thin after
each break, then
grows deeper.

ACC   yr V-10.8

Island after a break.

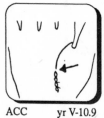

ACC   yr V-10.9

Chained line after
a break.

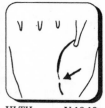

HLTH   yr V-10.10

Line thin before
break at age 50.

V-12 THE DOT

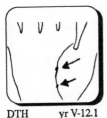

DTH   yr V-12.1

Dots on the line.

HLTH   yr V-12.2

Dot precedes island, chain or other defect.

HLTH   yr V-12.3

Dot precedes any defect with a line running to a split on the Head line.

HLTH   yr V-12.3

Dot precedes any defect with a line running to a dot on the Head line.

HLTH   yr V-12.3

Dot precedes any defect with a line running to an island on the Head line.

HLTH   yr V-12.3

Dot precedes any defect with a line running to a cross on the Head line.

HLTH   yr V-12.3

Dot precedes any defect with a line running to a star on the Head line.

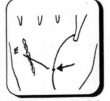

HLTH   yr V-12.4

Dot with a line to upper "E" Mount. Health line is islanded.

HLTH   yr V-12.5

Dot, line to 1st finger and grille on the "F" Mount.

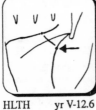

HLTH   yr V-12.6

Dot with a line to 2nd finger and a dot on the Heart line.

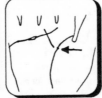

HLTH   yr V-12.6

Dot with a line to the 2nd finger and an island on the Heart line.

HLTH   yr V-12.6

Dot with a line to the 2nd finger and a cross on the Heart line.

HLTH   yr V-12.7

Dot, line to wavy
Health line with a
bar on it.

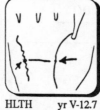

HLTH   yr V-12.7

Dot, line to wavy
Health line with a
dot on it.

HLTH   yr V-12.7

Dot, line to wavy
Health line with
a cross on it.

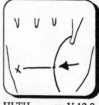

HLTH   yr V-12.8

Dot, line to the
"F" Mount with
a cross on it.

HLTH   yr V-12.8

Dot, line to the
"F" Mount with
a grille on it.

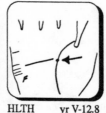

HLTH   yr V-12.8

Dot, line to the "F"
Mount with crossbars
on the percussion.

HLTH   yr V-12.8

Dot, line to the
"F" Mount with an
imperfect star on it.

HLTH   yr V-12.9

Dot, line to 2nd
finger with a dot on
it. Line to "F" Mount
with a cross on it.

HLTH   yr V-12.9

Dot, line to 2nd
finger with a dot
on it. Line to "F"
Mount, crossbars on
percussion.

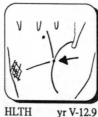

HLTH   yr V-12.9

Dot, line to 2nd
finger with a dot on
it. Line to "F" Mount
with a grille on it.

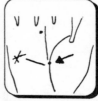

HLTH   yr V-12.9

Dot, line to 2nd
finger with a dot on
it. Line to "F" Mount
with an imperfect star
on it.

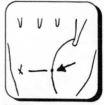

HLTH   yr V-12.10

Dot, line to
"F" Mount with
a cross on it and
yellow hands.

HLTH   yr V-12.10

Dot, line to "F"
Mount with a grille
on it and yellow
hands.

HLTH   yr V-12.10

Dot, line to "F"
Mount with crossbars
in the hand opposite
thumb.

HLTH   yr V-12.11

Dot, line to 2nd
finger with a dot
on it.

HLTH   yr V-12.11

Dot, line to 2nd
finger with a cross
on it.

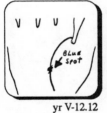

yr V-12.12

Blue spot on the line.

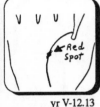

yr V-12.13

Red spot on the line.

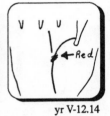

yr V-12.14

Red spot with a line
from the 2nd finger.

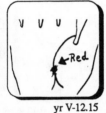

yr V-12.15

Red spot followed
by a split line.

V-13 THE ISLAND

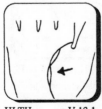

HLTH   yr V-13.1

Large islands on
the line.

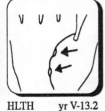

HLTH   yr V-13.2

Small islands on
the line.

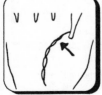

HLTH   yr V-13.3

A series of islands
on the line.

HLTH   yr V-13.4

A series of islands
starts small and
grows larger.

HANDOLOGY

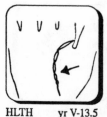

HLTH   yr V-13.5

A series of islands starts big and grows smaller.

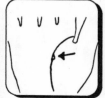

HLTH   yr V-13.6

Islands appear larger than mere dots.

yr V-13.7

An island with many lines in the hand.

HLTH   yr V-13.8

Island with fine crossbars on the Head line.

HLTH   yr V-13.9

Island with deep crossbars on the Head line.

HLTH   yr V-13.9

Crossbars are deeper than the Head line, island on the Life line.

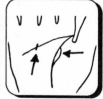

HLTH   yr V-13.9

Crossbar on a thin Head line, island on the Life line.

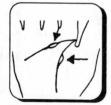

HLTH   yr V-13.10

Islands on Head and Life lines.

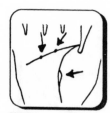

HLTH   yr V-13.11

Island on line with dots on the Head line.

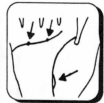

HLTH   yr V-13.12

Island on line with dots on the Heart line.

HLTH   yr V-13.13

Island on line with an island on the Heart line and a red hand.

HLTH   yr V-13.13

Island on line with an island on the Heart line and a blue or purple hand.

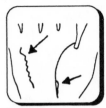

HLTH   yr V-13.14

Island on the
line with a wavy
Health line.

HLTH   yr V-13.15

Island on the line
with a ladder-like
Health line.

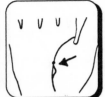

HLTH   yr V-13.16

A dot before
the island.

HLTH   yr V-13.17

Islanded line running
to 2nd finger and
a line running to
"F" Mount.

HLTH   yr V-13.18

Islands on Life and
Head lines connected
by a line with a grille
under 2nd finger.

HLTH   yr V-13.18

Island on line, dot on
Head line, connected
by a line with a grille
under 2nd finger.

HLTH   yr V-13.19

Island connected to
a dot under 1st
finger with a red
or purple hand.

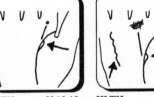

HLTH   yr V-13.20

Island connected
to a grille under
2nd finger with a
wavy Health line.

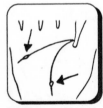

FEML   yr V-13.21

Island with an island
on the Head line.

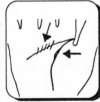

HLTH   yr V-13.21

Island with fine
crossbars on the
Head line.

HLTH   yr V-13.21

Island with small and
frequent cuts on the
Head line.

FEML   yr V-13.22

Island at ages 42
to 56.

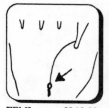

FEML   yr V-13.23

Island followed by a deep line.

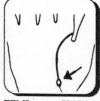

FEML   yr V-13.24

Island followed by a thin line, ages 42 to 56.

FEML   yr V-13.24

Island followed by a chained line, ages 42 to 56.

FEML   yr V-13.24

Island followed by a broad and shallow line, ages 42 to 56.

FEML   yr V-13.25

Island at ages 42 to 56 with a grille on "F" Mount.

FEML   yr V-13.26

Island and a line to a grille on "F" Mount.

FEML   yr V-13.27

Island and a line to a grille on "F" Mount with a star on the Health line.

FEML   yr V-13.27

Island and a line to a grille on "F" Mount with an island on the Health line.

V-15 THE STAR

V-16 THE CROSS

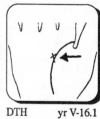

DTH   yr V-15.1

Star on the line.

yr V-15.2

Star at the start of the line.

DTH   yr V-16.1

Cross on the line.

V-16.2

Cross at the start of the line.

V-17 SISTER LINES

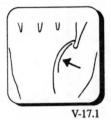

V-17.1

A Sister line to the
Life line.

W — THE INFLUENCE LINE

The Influence line indicates people who have strongly influenced your life either for good or ill, generally representing members of your own family or the closest of friends. If the latter, they are those who have grown into your life and have become a part of it. These lines exist because the influences have made strong impressions on the mind and these mental impressions have shown themselves in the hand.

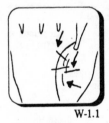

W-1.1

Influence line.

The Influence line is on the "G" Mount inside the Life line. Some lines run parallel to the Life line while others run across the "G" Mount.

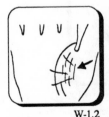

W-1.2

Many lines on
the Mount.

W-1.3

Few lines on
the Mount.

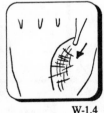

W-1.4

A grille on
the Mount.

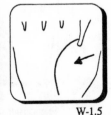

W-1.5

No grille on
the Mount.

111

W-3 STARTING POINT

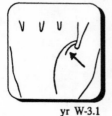

yr W-3.1

yr W-3.2

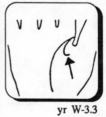

yr W-3.3

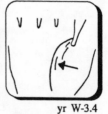

yr W-3.4

Line starts with
Life line.

Line starts from the
Life line.

Line turns towards
the Mount.

A new line seems to
appear.

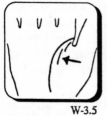

W-3.5

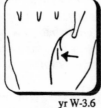

yr W-3.6

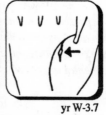

yr W-3.7

yr W-3.8

Line rises early,
supported by
another line

Line in between split
and Life line.

Island on the line.

Line starts and ends
on the line.

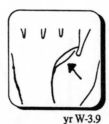

yr W-3.9

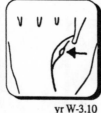

yr W-3.10

yr W-3.10

Starts inside the Life
line and then
connects.

Island on the line
after beginning inside
the Life line.

Line is connected to
Life line at both ends
with an island.

112

W-4 ITS LENGTH

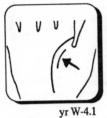

yr W-4.1

The length of any
Influence line.

yr W-4.2

Length of 3rd line.

W-5 ITS COURSE

W-5.1

Starts far away and
grows thicker as it
comes closer.

W-6 ITS TERMINATION

W-6.1

Line ends in a star.

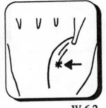

W-6.2

Another line ends in
a star.

W-7 ITS CHARACTER

W-7.1

Lines are deep,
strong and
well colored.

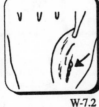

W-7.2

Lines are thin, shal-
low, chained, uneven
or broken in any way.

yr W-7.3

Line begins deep,
then fades away.

yr W-7.4

Line is strong,
grows thin, then
strong again.

113

 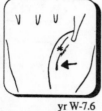 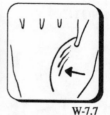 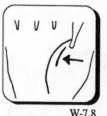

yr W-7.5   yr W-7.6   W-7.7   W-7.8

Line draws away, then grows thin.

Line begins early, ends in a star. Another line grows stronger beside it.

Repeated lines start thin, then grow stronger.

A strong line with a thin and narrow Life line.

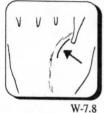  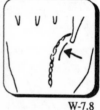 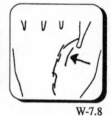

W-7.8   W-7.8   W-7.8   W-7.8

A strong line with a broad and shallow Life line.

A strong line with a ladder-like Life line.

A strong line with an island or islands on the Life line.

A strong line with any breaks on the line.

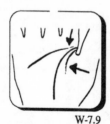 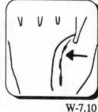 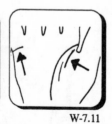

W-7.9   W-7.10   W-7.11

Line starts strong and grows thin, Head line weak at the beginning.

Line alternates from deep-cut to thin.

1st line is deep and well cut with a thin Affection line.

114

W-9 THE SPLIT

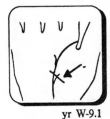

yr W-9.1

Split lines are cut by Worry line.

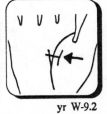

yr W-9.2

Worry line starts from Influence line.

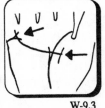

W-9.3

Line cuts branch line and cuts forked Affection line.

W-9.4

Worry line from star cuts branch line on Life line.

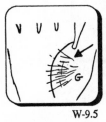

W-9.5

Horizontal lines on the "G" Mount.

W-9.5

Horizontal lines are deep and red on the "G" Mount.

W-9.6

Horizontal lines are thin and weak on the "G" Mount.

W-9.7

Horizontal lines cut the Life line continually.

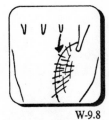

W-9.8

Deep horizontal lines cut the Life line continually.

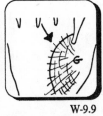

W-9.9

Horizontal lines cross the entire "G" Mount and Life line from top to bottom.

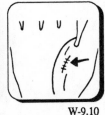

W-9.10

Horizontal lines cut an Influence line repeatedly.

W-9.11

Line is cut by a strong crossbar, then an island, and ends in a star.

115

   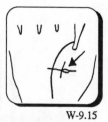

yr W-9.12	W-9.13	W-9.14	W-9.15
Any line is cut by numerous small lines.	A crossbar has an island on it.	Crossbar with an island cuts Influence line only.	Crossbar with an island cuts Life and Influence lines.

W-9.16	W-9.17	W-9.18
Split lines rise but do not touch the Life line.	Split lines fall from the line.	Split line rises to the Mount under the 1st finger.

W-10 THE BREAK

 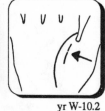

W-10.1	yr W-10.2
Breaks on the line.	One break on the line.

W-12 THE DOT

yr W-12.1

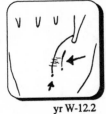

yr W-12.2

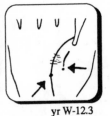

yr W-12.3

Line deep at the start, grows thinner, ends in a dot after worry line on Life line.

Line deep at the start, grows thinner, ends in a dot. Life line ends in a dot.

Line deep at the start, grows thinner, ends in a dot. Life line also has a dot.

W-13 THE ISLAND

yr W-13.1

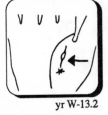

yr W-13.2

yr W-13.2

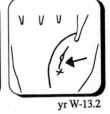

yr W-13.2

Island on the line.

Island on the line, ends in a star.

Island on the line, ends in a dot.

Island on the line, ends in a cross.

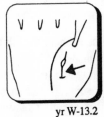

yr W-13.2

yr W-13.3

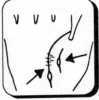

yr W-13.4

Island on the line, ends in a bar.

Island on the line with small lines cutting Life line.

Island on the line with small lines cutting Life line. Island on the Life line.

117

W-15 THE STAR

yr W-15.1

Line deep at start, grows thin, ends in a star after worry lines on Life line.

DTH   yr W-15.2

Line deep at start, grows thin, ends in a star. Life line ends in a dot.

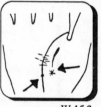

yr W-15.3

Line deep at start, grows thin, ends in a star. Dot on the Life line.

yr W-15.4

Line ends in a star, connected by a line to a dot on the Head line.

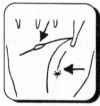

yr W-15.5

Line ends in a star, connected by a line to an island on the Head line.

X — THE AFFECTION LINE

The lines of Affection or Marriage, as they are commonly called, have been used as indications of marriage or unions of the sexes. To use the word "marriage" is misleading. The Affection line means you are more open to emotional or material affection at the age indicated; its length indicates how long the affection lasts.

X-1.1

Affection line.

The Affection line is under the 4th finger and runs from the outside towards the palm. In some hands there are none of these lines and in others many are seen. To use these lines as marriage lines is misleading and wrong.

 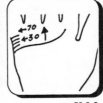 

X-2.1	X-2.2	X-2.3
Line is absent.	A year indication determining year of affection.	A year indication determining length of affection in years.

X-2.4	yr X-2.5	X-2.6
Many lines exist.	Record the year of the strongest Affection line.	A note about the meaning of these lines.

X-3 STARTING POINT

X-4 ITS LENGTH

X-3.1

Line begins with a
fork.

yr X-4.1	X-4.2
Record longest and deepest line.	Two lines are the same length.

X-6 ITS TERMINATION

yr X-6.1

Line ends in a star.

yr X-6.2

Line forks at end.

yr X-6.3

Fork is not wide
at end.

X-6.4

Line curves towards
Heart line.

X-6.5

Line curves and
touches Heart line.

X-6.6

Line curves up
towards 4th finger.

X-7 ITS CHARACTER

X-7.1

Numerous lines,
upper one deep at the
start, lower one deep
at termination

X-7.2

Top line is thin and
long, bottom line
short and thick.

X-7.3

Line is thin in
proportion to other
lines in the palm.

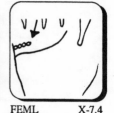

FEML   X-7.4

FEMALES ONLY:
Line is chained.

FEML   X-7.5

FEMALES ONLY:
Line is shallow.

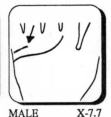

MALE   X-7.6

MALES ONLY:
Line is chained.

MALE   X-7.7

MALES ONLY:
Line is shallow.

X-7.8

Line is deep and
well cut.

X-7.9

Line is deep and
well cut to the end.

yr X-7.10

Line starts deep and
gradually grows thin.

yr X-7.11

Starts thin and
gradually grows
thinner.

X-9 THE SPLIT

X-9.1

A split line to the 3rd
finger ends in a star.

X-9.2

Branch lines fall
from the line.

X-9.3

Branch lines rise up
from the line.

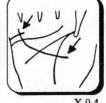

X-9.4

Worry line from
inside the Life
line cuts the
Affection line

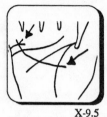 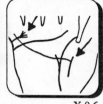 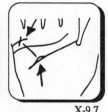 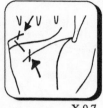

X-9.5	X-9.6	X-9.7	X-9.7
Line from Influence line cuts a forked Affection line.	Line from Influence line cuts a split line on Life line and a tassel on Affection line.	Cut by a crossbar, Chance line to island on the Head line.	Cut by a crossbar, Chance line to a crossbar on the Head line.

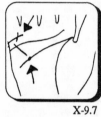   

X-9.7	X-9.7	yr X-9.8	yr X-9.9
Cut by a crossbar, Chance line to a dot on the Head line.	Cut by a crossbar, Chance line to a cross on the Head line.	Cut by a crossbar, line touches the Heart line.	Crossbar cuts the line.

X-10 THE BREAK

yr X-10.1	yr X-10.2	X-10.3
Line is broken.	A square mark around the break.	Line terminates in a hook.

X-11 TRIDENT AND TASSEL

yr X-11.1   yr X11.2

Line ends in   Line ends in a tassel.
a trident.

X-12 THE DOT

yr X-12.1 yr X-12.2 X-12.2 X-12.2

Dot on the line. Dot on the line, line Dot on the line, line Dot on the line, line
     ends in a fork. ends in a trident. ends in a tassel.

yr X-12.3

After dot, line
grows thin.

123

X-13 THE ISLAND	X-16 THE CROSS

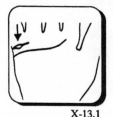  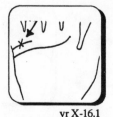

X-13.1   X-13.2   yr X-16.1

Island on the line.   Line is composed of   Cross on the line.
                      islands.

Y — THE CAREER LINE

The Career line indicates the course of your life from a standpoint of material success and shows whether you must make your way, will have a difficult time, or whether things will come easily to you. It could also locate your most productive periods. All indications refer to financial affairs.

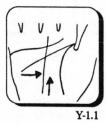

Y-1.1

Career line.

The Career line rises from the base of the hand and runs upwards to the fingers. It is analyzed from the bottom upwards. The course of the Career line is always towards the 2nd finger, sometimes reaching it, sometimes falling short. It always runs through the center of the hand and, with one exception, may terminate on any one of the Mounts.

Y-2.1

Line is absent

Y-3 STARTING POINT

Y-3.1

Line starts inside the Life line.

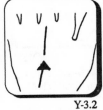

Y-3.2

Line starts from the center of the hand.

Y-3.3

Line starts from the "F" Mount.

Y-3.4

Line starts high up on the palm.

yr Y-3.5

Line starts high, Life line starts with a broad and shallow line.

yr Y-3.5

Line starts high, Life line runs like a ladder.

yr Y-3.5

Line starts high, Life line chained or poorly marked at the beginning.

yr Y-3.6

Line and Life line grow thicker.

yr Y-3.7

Line starts high, Head line starts thin and grows thicker.

yr Y-3.7

Line starts high, Head line starts normally, then grows chainlike

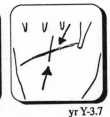

yr Y-3.7

Line starts high, Head line broad and shallow at the start.

yr Y-3.7

Line starts high, Head line chained at the start.

yr Y-3.8	yr Y-3.8	yr Y-3.9	yr Y-3.10
Line starts high, Heart line broad and shallow at end, Head line broad and shallow at start. A thin Life line.	Line starts high, chained Heart line at the end and chained Head line at the start. Thin Life line.	Low in passive hand, high in active hand.	Line starts high, Influence line ends in a star.

 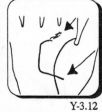 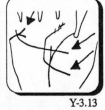 

Y-3.11	Y-3.12	Y-3.13	Y-3.14
Line starts inside Life line and ends under 1st finger.	Line starts inside Life line, becomes defective under 1st finger.	Line starts inside Life line, defective under 1st finger, branch line cuts split and Affection line.	Line starts on "F" Mount and ends under 1st finger.

Y-3.15

A defective line starts on the "F" Mount and ends under 1st finger.

126

Y-5 ITS COURSE

yr Y-5.1

A wavy line.

Y-5.2

A defective, uneven wavy line.

yr Y-5.3

Line is wavy between Heart and Head lines only.

Y-6 ITS TERMINATION

yr Y-6.1

Line stops at the Head line.

Y-6.2

Line ends under 1st finger.

Y-6.3

Line deflects to 3rd finger.

Y-6.4

Line deflects to 4th finger.

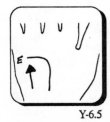

Y-6.5

Line deflects to the upper "E" Mount.

Y-6.6

Line runs deep to 2nd finger.

Y-6.7

Line ends in a wavy line under 2nd finger.

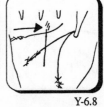

Y-6.8

Line breaks under 2nd finger; Life, Head and Heart lines defective at the end.

Y-6.9

Line ends in an
island, Life line ends
in three prongs.

Y-6.9

Line ends in an
island, Life line ends
in a tassel.

Y-6.9

Line ends in an
island, hairlike lines
fall from Life line.

Y-6.10

Crossbars cut line
under 2nd finger.

Y-6.11

Faint crossbars do
not cut line under
2nd finger.

Y-6.12

A cross on the line
under 2nd finger.

Y-7 ITS CHARACTER

Y-7.1

Line shallow, other
lines deeper.

Y-7.2

Line is deep and
well cut, other lines
not so clear.

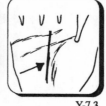

Y-7.3

Line is deep and
extends to 2nd
finger, other lines
not so clear.

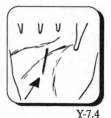

Y-7.4

Short, deep line,
other lines not
so clear.

128

Y-7.5	**Y-7.6**	**Y-7.7**	**Y-7.8**
Deepness of line starts low.	A thin line, other lines deeper.	A broad and shallow line.	A broad and shallow line, other lines deeper and well cut.

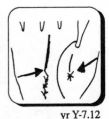

Y-7.9	**yr Y-7.10**	**yr Y-7.11**	**yr Y-7.12**
A chained line.	Line chained part-way.	Line is defective, then grows deep and well cut.	Line is defective at the start, Influence line ends in a star.

yr Y-7.13	**yr Y-7.14**	**yr Y-7.15**	**Y-7.16**
Line defective at the start, Influence Line ends in a star, Worry line to island on Head line.	Line is uneven: thin, then thick, then thin again.	Line defective after the Head line.	Line is made up of broken lines and is very defective.

129

Y-9 THE SPLIT

Y-9.1

Faint crossbars on
the line.

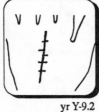

yr Y-9.2

Crossbars cut
the line.

yr Y-9.3

Fine lines rising.

yr Y-9.4

Fine lines falling.

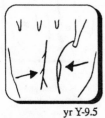

yr Y-9.5

Falling lines and
large island on the
Life line.

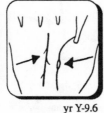

yr Y-9.6

Falling lines and
small islands on the
Life line.

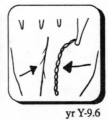

yr Y-9.6

Falling lines and the
Life line is chained.

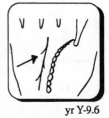

yr Y-9.6

Falling lines;
islands are small,
then grow larger
on the Life line.

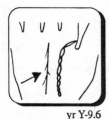

yr Y-9.6

Falling lines;
islands are large,
then grow smaller
on the Life line.

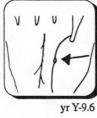

yr Y-9.6

Falling lines, islands
appear larger than
mere dots on the
Life line.

yr Y-9.7

Falling lines
between Head and
Heart lines, an island
on the Head line.

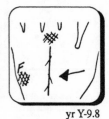

yr Y-9.8

Falling lines, Grille
on "F" Mount and
under 2nd finger.

Y-9.9

Rising lines and
horizontal lines
on "G" Mount.

Y-9.9

Rising lines and
horizontal lines
continually cut
the Life line.

Y-9.10

Worry and Chance
lines from all angles
cross or join the
Career line.

yr Y-9.11

Any line cutting
the Career line.

yr Y-9.12

Chance line from star
under 1st finger cuts
the Career line.

Y-9.13

Line from grille
under 4th finger cuts
the Career line.

yr Y-9.14

A defective line after
a split line from the
Influence line cuts
the Career line.

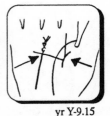

yr Y-9.15

A Chance line runs
to 1st finger.

yr Y-9.16

Line defective, cut by
a defective Life line.

yr Y-9.17

Line defective after
being cut by a
defective Life line.

Y-9.18

Many lines run
towards the line but
do not touch it.

Y-9.19

Some lines merge
into the line.

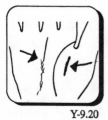

Y-9.20

Line thin or defective with a strong Influence line.

yr Y-9.21

Line chained, then is strong after merged Chance or Worry lines.

yr Y-9.22

Line is strong after a line from the "F" Mount merges into it.

yr Y-9.23

Line is strong after a merged Chance line from inside Life line.

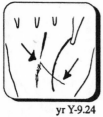

yr Y-9.24

Line is thin after merging with a Chance line from inside Life line.

yr Y-9.25

Chance lines run alongside the Career line.

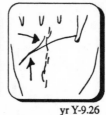

yr Y-9.26

Line is broken, split line from Head line runs alongside it.

yr Y-9.27

Line defective, a Chance line from upper "E" Mount runs alongside it.

yr Y-9.28

Crossbars cut line between the Head and Heart lines.

yr Y-9.29

Line below the Heart line is cut by crossbars.

yr Y-9.30

Crossbars are not strong enough to cut the line.

yr Y-9.31

Line between the Head and Heart lines is cut by a split line.

yr Y-9.32

Line cut by split lines from the Heart line.

yr Y-9.33

Lines from a defective Life line cut the Career line.

yr Y-9.34

A line from Influence line ends in a star. A line cuts Life and Career lines.

yr Y-9.35

Line from Influence line ends in a star. A line crosses a split Life line and a Career line.

Y-9.36

A split line runs to 1st finger.

Y-9.37

A split line runs to 3rd finger.

Y-9.38

A split line runs to 1st and 3rd fingers.

Y-9.39

A split line runs to 4th finger.

Y-9.40

A split line merges into the Head line.

yr Y-9.41

Line does not reach Head line; split line merges into Head line.

yr Y-9.42

With a merged split line, the Career line stops at any age period.

Y-9.43

With a merged split line, the Career line runs deep to 2nd finger.

133

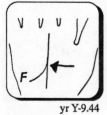

yr Y-9.44

Split line runs to the
"F" Mount.

yr Y-9.45

Chance line from
"F" Mount crosses
the Career line.

yr Y-9.46

Chance line from
"F" Mount runs
to a break in the
Career line.

yr Y-9.47

Split line rises
from line.

yr Y-9.48

Split line from line
merges into Fate line.

Y-10 THE BREAK

yr Y-10.1

Breaks in the line.

yr Y-10.2

Breaks in active but
not passive hand.

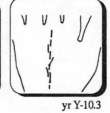

yr Y-10.3

Many breaks in
the line.

yr Y-10.4

Many breaks
in active but not
passive hand

yr Y-10.5

Any repaired breaks.

yr Y-10.6

Repaired breaks
in active but not
passive hand.

yr Y-10.7

Break repaired by a
square between Head
and Heart lines.

yr Y-10.8

Broken line
continues to
1st finger.

yr Y-10.9

Broken line
continues to
2nd finger.

yr Y-10.10

Broken line
continues to
3rd finger.

yr Y-10.11

Broken line
continues to
4th finger.

Y-13 THE ISLAND

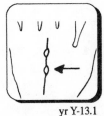

yr Y-13.1

Island on the line.

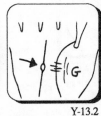

Y-13.2

Worry lines from
"G" Mount to
island on the line.

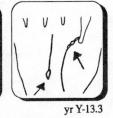

yr Y-13.3

Island at the start,
Life line chained
or poorly marked
at its beginning.

yr Y-13.4

Island at the start,
Head line chained
or poorly marked
at its beginning.

135

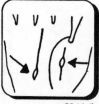

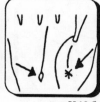

yr Y-13.5

Island at the start,
Influence line has
an island.

yr Y-13.5

Island at the start,
Influence line ends
in a star.

yr Y-13.5

Island at the start,
Influence line ends
in a dot.

yr Y-13.5

Island at the start,
Influence line ends
in a cross.

yr Y-13.5

Island at the start,
Influence line ends
in a crossbar.

yr Y-13.6

Worry lines to island
from a star at the end
of an Influence line.

yr Y-13.7

Worry lines from
inside Life line.
Lines travel to island
at start of Career line.

yr Y-13.8

A Chance line has a
star under the 1st
finger, cuts an island
on the Career line.

yr Y-13.9

Island between Head
and Heart lines.

Y-15 THE STAR

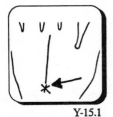

Y-15.1

Star at the base.

Y-15.2

Star at the base, passive hand only.

Y-15.3

Star at the base, both passive and active hands.

Y-15.4

Star on the Life line side of the Career line.

Y-15.5

Star on the Fate line side of the Career line.

Y-15.6

Line terminates in a star.

Y-16 THE CROSS

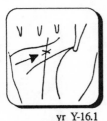

yr Y-16.1

Cross between Head and Heart lines.

yr Y-16.2

Cross on the line.

Y-16.3

Cross near the end of the line.

Y-16.4

Cross near the Career line on Life line side of line.

137

Y-16.5

Cross near the Career
line on the Fate line
side of the line.

Z — THE FATE LINE

*The Fate line indicates a capability or possibility of accomplishing a great deal, and
the field in which the capability will best operate. The Fate line must be estimated
continually in the light of how a person develops over a period of time.*

Z-1.1

Fate line.

The Fate line is a vertically rising line; if long,
from the base of the hand; if short, from the
center of the hand to the 3rd finger, sometimes
not reaching it. In its course through the hand,
the Fate line must run in the general direction
of the 3rd finger. You will not find a great
number of really fine Fate lines. Most hands
have no Fate line at all, though you will see a
good many of some value.

Z-2.1

Line is absent.

Split line from Life
line is not a Fate line.

Split line from Career
line is not a Fate line.

138

Z-3 STARTING POINT

Z-3.1

Line starts from the "F" Mount and rises to 3rd finger, with long fingers.

Z-3.2

Line rises sharply from the left side of the hand.

Z-3.3

Line starts from inside Life line.

Z-3.4

Line starts from the "F" Mount.

Z-3.5

Line rises near the wrist.

Z-4 ITS LENGTH

Z-4.1

Line is long from wrist to 3rd finger.

Z-4.2

Line starts low, runs a short distance.

Z-4.3

Line covers the space of Heart and Head lines only.

Z-4.4

Line starts between the Head and Heart lines only.

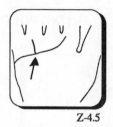

Z-4.5

Line starts from the
Heart line only.

Z-5 ITS COURSE

Z-5.1

A wavy line.

Z-5.2

A wavy line ends
strongly under
3rd finger.

Z-5.3

A wavy line ends
in a star.

Z-6 ITS TERMINATION

Z-6.1

Line ends near
a square.

Z-6.2

Line ends with a
dot near a square.

Z-6.2

Line ends with an
island near a square.

Z-6.2

Line ends with a star
near a square.

Z-6.2

Z-6.3

yr Z-6.4

yr Z-6.5

Line ends with a
cross near a square.

Line ends with
vertical lines under
the 3rd finger.

Line ends in a fork
from the Heart line.

Line ends in three
lines from the
Heart line.

Z-7 ITS CHARACTER

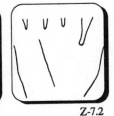

Z-7.1

Z-7.2

Deep, well-cut line.

A thin line.

Z-7.2

Z-7.2

Z-7.2

Z-7.3

A thin line, Head line
becomes thin after
being deep and
well cut.

A thin line, Head line
is thin and narrow.

A thin line, Head line
is thin, other lines are
deeper and well cut.

Line is broad
and shallow.

141

Z-7.4

A chained line.

Z-7.5

Line alternates between thick and thin.

Z-7.6

Line alternates between thick and thin and ends thickly under 3rd finger.

Z-7.7

A deep line grows thin, then fades away.

Z-9 THE SPLIT

yr Z-9.1

Crossbars cut the line.

yr Z-9.2

Crossbars do not cut the line.

Z-9.3

Small, fine crossbars.

yr Z-9.4

Line ends with a deep crossbar.

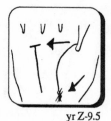

yr Z-9.5

Line ends in a deep crossbar, Life line ends abnormally.

yr Z-9.6

Line ends in a deep crossbar, Head line ends abnormally.

Z-9.7

Line ends in a deep crossbar, split line from Head line draws to it.

Z-9.8

Line ends in a fork.

142

Z-9.9

Z-9.10

Z-9.11

Z-9.12

Split lines run to 2nd and 4th fingers.

Fine split lines rise from line.

Fine split lines fall from line.

A split line runs to 1st finger.

Z-9.13

Z-9.14

Z-9.14

Z-9.14

A split line from the line ends in a star under 1st finger.

A split line from the line ends in vertical lines under 1st finger.

A split line from the line ends in a trident under 1st finger.

A split line from the line ends in a triangle under 1st finger.

Z-9.14

Z-9.14

Z-9.15

Z-9.16

A split line from the line ends in a circle under 1st finger.

A split line from the line ends in a square under 1st finger.

A split line runs to 2nd finger.

A split line from the line ends in a star under 2nd finger.

Z-9.17

Line ends in a
crossbar, a split line
runs to 2nd finger.

Z-9.18

Split line ends
under 1st finger
with Sister lines.

Z-9.19

Split line ends
under 2nd finger
with Sister lines.

Z-9.20

Split line ends
under 4th finger
with Sister lines.

Z-9.21

Split line reaches 2nd
finger. Vertical lines
under 2nd finger.

Z-9.22

Split line does not
reach 2nd finger.
Vertical lines
under 2nd finger.

Z-9.23

Split line does not
reach 4th finger.
Vertical lines
under 4th finger.

Z-9.24

Split line runs to
the 4th finger.

Z-9.25

Fate line and split
line to the 4th finger
both end in a star.

Z-9.26

Split line to upper
"E" Mount.

Z-9.27

Split line to upper
"E" Mount with
a Sister line.

Z-9.28

Split line to
"F" Mount.

Z-9.29

Split line to
"G" Mount.

Z-9.30

Split line to "G"
Mount, Fate line
ends in a square.

Z-9.30

Split line to "G"
Mount, Fate line
ends in a bar.

Z-9.30

Split line to "G"
Mount, Fate line ends
in a bar. Life line
ends in any mark.

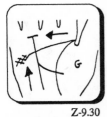

Z-9.30

Split line to "G"
Mount, Fate line ends
in a bar. Head line
ends in any mark.

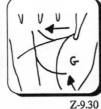

Z-9.30

Split line to "G"
Mount, split line
from Head line goes
to 3rd finger.

Z-9.30

Split line to "G"
Mount, Fate line
ends in a dot.

Z-9.30

Split line to "G"
Mount, Fate line
ends in a star.

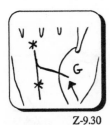

Z-9.30

Split line to "G"
Mount, Fate line
has a double star.

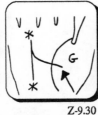

Z-9.30

Split line to "G"
Mount, Fate line
starts and ends
in a star.

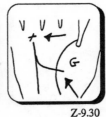

Z-9.30

Split line to "G"
Mount, Fate line
ends in a cross.

Z-9.31

Split line merges into
the Head line.

145

Z-9.32

Split line merges
into a deep and well-
cut Head line with
no defects.

Z-9.33

Split line meets with
Head line and forms
a triangle.

Z-9.34

Split line merges into
the Heart line.

Z-9.35

Influence line from
inside the Life line
runs alongside the
Fate line.

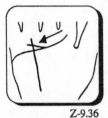

Z-9.36

Split line from
Heart line cuts the
Fate line.

yr Z-9.37

Line from Fate line
to Career line.

yr Z-9.38

Falling split line
on the thumb side
of the line

yr Z-9.39

Falling split line
on the percussion
side of the line.

Z-9.40

Many lines under
the 3rd finger

yr Z-9.41

A Chance or Sister
line, the Heart line
cuts the Fate line

yr Z-9.42

A Chance line from
under the 4th finger
cuts the Fate line

yr Z-9.43

A Chance line with
an island from the
4th finger cuts the
Fate line

yr Z-9.44

A Chance line from
upper "E" Mount
cuts the Fate line.

Z-10 THE BREAK

HLTH   yr Z-10.1

Fate and Heart
lines have breaks,
same year.

HLTH   yr Z-10.1

Fate and Head
lines have breaks,
same year.

HLTH   yr Z-10.1

Fate and Life
lines have breaks,
same year.

yr Z-10.2

Fate line breaks.

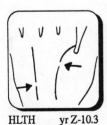

HLTH   yr Z-10.3

Break in line, Life
line shows break
same year.

HLTH   yr Z-10.4

Break in line, Head
line shows any mark
same year.

yr Z-10.5

Breaks in line,
one repaired by
Sister lines.

yr Z-10.6

Break has a Sister
repair sign.

147

yr Z-10.6   yr Z-10.6

Break has a square   Break has a crossbar
repair sign.   repair sign.

Z-11 THE TRIDENT AND TASSEL

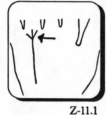
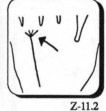

Z-11.1   Z-11.2

Line ends in   Line ends in a tassel.
a trident.

Z-12 THE DOT

yr Z-12.1   yr Z-12.2   yr Z-12.3   yr Z-12.4

A dot or dots on   The dot is large   The dot is small.   The line ends in
the line.   and deep.   a dot.

148

Z-13 THE ISLAND

yr Z-13.1

yr Z-13.2

Z-13.3

Line has an island.

Line has an island, Head and Life lines are widely separated.

Line ends in an island.

Z-15 THE STAR

  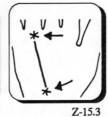 

Z-15.1

yr Z-15.2

Z-15.3

yr Z-15.4

Line ends in a star.

Line has a double star.

Line begins with a star and ends with a star.

A star on the line.

Z-16 THE CROSS

  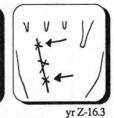

Z-16.1

Z-16.2

yr Z-16.3

Line ends in a cross.

Cross on thumb side of Fate line.

Many crosses on the line.

149

Z-17 SISTER LINES

Z-17.1   Z-17.2

Line ends with   Fate and Career lines
parallel Sister lines.   are Sister lines.

ZA — THE HEALTH LINE

The Health line has been variously called the line of liver and the Hepatica line. It is exceedingly useful as a guide to success, as no factor better enables one to cope with the affairs of the world than a clear brain, and nothing more surely keeps the brain from clogging than a good digestion and an active liver.

ZA-1.1

Health line.

The Health line should start on the "F" Mount and run upwards on the percussion to the 4th finger. The line is not found in all hands. I do not regard the absence of this line necessarily as a detriment, for the health of many of those who have no line was found to be uniformly good. While the line should rise from the "F" Mount, in practice it rarely does.

Disposition.   Disposition.   Disposition.   Not a Health line.

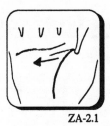

ZA-2.1

Line is absent.

ZA-4 ITS LENGTH

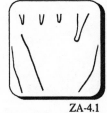  

ZA-4.1 ZA-4.1 ZA-4.1

Line is long from the base of the hand to the 4th finger.

Long and deep Health line.

Line is long and deep, Life line is defective in some way.

ZA-5 ITS COURSE

HLTH   ZA-5.1

A wavy line.

ZA-6 ITS TERMINATION

ZA-6.1

Affection line cuts
Health line.

ZA-6.2

Line ends in a
crossbar.

ZA-6.3

Line ends in a
bar, grille under
4th finger.

ZA-6.4

Line ends in a bar,
grille under 4th
finger, dot under
3rd finger.

ZA-6.5

Line ends in a fork.

ZA-7 ITS CHARACTER

ZA-7.1

Line is deep and
well cut.

ZA-7.2

Line is deep and
well cut, any
character defect
on the Life line.

ZA-7.3

Line is thin,
Heart line is well
cut and smooth.

ZA-7.3

Health and Head
lines are thin.

152

ZA-7.3

Health and Life lines
are thin.

HLTH   ZA-7.4

Broad and
shallow line.

HLTH   ZA-7.5

A chained line.

HLTH   yr ZA-7.6

Line starts
deep, grows
thin, then deep.

HLTH   yr ZA-7.7

Line starts deep, then
becomes chained.

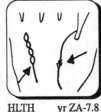

HLTH   yr ZA-7.8

Line becomes
chained. Life line
becomes defective,
same year.

HLTH   yr ZA-7.9

Line is uneven.

HLTH   yr ZA-7.10

Line becomes
chained, Head line
is short and ends in
a star, same year.

HLTH   yr ZA-7.10

Line becomes
chained, Head
and Life lines short
and end in a star,
same year.

HLTH   yr ZA-7.10

Line becomes
chained. Head line
becomes chained,
deflects and ends
in a star, same year.

HLTH   yr ZA-7.10

Line becomes
chained, a crossbar
on a thin Head line,
same year.

HLTH   yr ZA-7.10

Line becomes
chained, a dot on
a thin Head line,
same year.

153

HLTH   yr ZA-7.10

DTH   yr ZA-7.10

MNTL   yr ZA-7.10

ZA-7.11

Line becomes
chained. A cross
on a thin Head line,
same year.

Line becomes
chained. Head line
ends in a star, has an
island followed by a
dot, same year.

Line becomes
chained. Head line
has cross followed
by an island and a
dot, same year.

Line is made up of
numerous small lines.

ZA-9 THE SPLIT

HLTH   yr ZA-9.1

HLTH   yr ZA-9.2

HLTH   yr ZA-9.3

HLTH   yr ZA-9.4

Fine, fretting
crossbars cut the line

Deep crossbars cut
the line

Continuous cross-
bars cut the line from
start to finish

Crossbars on the line,
Head line shows
crossbars, same year

ZA-9.5

ZA-9.6

HLTH   yr ZA-9.7

HLTH   ZA-9.8

Rising split lines.

Falling split lines.

Split line to
2nd finger.

Split line to 1st
finger, a star under
1st finger.

ZA-9.9	ZA-9.10	ZA-9.11	ZA-9.12
Split line to 2nd finger.	Split line to 3rd finger.	Split line merges into the line from the "F" Mount.	Split line merges into Head line.

yr ZA-9.13	ZA-9.14
Split line merges into Fate line.	Split line to upper or middle "E" Mount.

ZA-10 THE BREAK

HLTH ZA-10.1	HLTH ZA-10.2	HLTH ZA-10.3	HLTH ZA-10.4
A poor line with a deep and well cut Head line, no defects.	Poor Health and Head lines, other lines deep and well cut.	Poor Health and Heart lines, other lines deep and well cut.	Poor Health and Heart lines, a deep, well-cut Head line.

155

HLTH   ZA-10.5

A ladderlike line.

HLTH   yr ZA-10.6

A ladderlike
line with a dot
on the line.

HLTH   yr ZA-10.7

Line is absent
between Head
and Heart lines.

HLTH   yr ZA-10.7

Line is defective
between Head
and Heart lines.

DTH   yr ZA-10.8

Line ends in a
crossbar, absent or
defective between
Head and Heart lines.

DTH   yr ZA-10.8

Line ends in a cross,
absent or defective
between Head and
Heart lines.

DTH   yr ZA-10.8

Line ends in a dot,
absent or defective
between Head and
Heart lines.

DTH   yr ZA-10.8

Line ends in an
island, absent or
defective between
Head and Heart lines.

DTH   yr ZA-10.8

Line ends with any
mark, absent or
defective between
Head and Heart lines.

HLTH   ZA-10.9

A broken line.

HLTH   ZA-10.10

Line is continually
broken.

HLTH   yr ZA-10.11

A square repair sign
over breaks.

yr ZA-10.12

Sister line repair, any
breaks.

ZA-11 THE TRIDENT

ZA-11.1   ZA-11.1

Line ends in a tassel.   Line ends in a trident.

ZA-12 THE DOT

HLTH yr ZA-12.1	HLTH yr ZA-12.2	HLTH yr ZA-12.3	HLTH yr ZA-12.4
A dot or dots on the line.	A dot on the line, a grille under 1st finger.	A dot on the line, a grille under 2nd finger.	Dot on the line, Chance line from 2nd finger to Life line and from "F" Mount to Life line

157

HLTH   yr ZA-12.5

Dots on Heart and
Health lines.

HLTH   yr ZA-12.5

Dot on line, island
on Heart line.

HLTH   yr ZA-12.5

Dot on line, break
on Heart line.

HLTH   yr ZA-12.6

Dot on line, grille
under 3rd finger,
defects on Heart line.

HLTH   yr ZA-12.7

Line ends abnormally
with a dot on the line.

HLTH   yr ZA-12.8

Grille on the upper
"E" Mount with a
dot on the line.

HLTH   yr ZA-12.9

Crossbars on the
percussion with
a dot on the line.

HLTH   yr ZA-12.9

Grille on the "F"
Mount with a dot
on the line.

HLTH   yr ZA-12.10

Grille on the "F"
Mount with a dot
on the line.

ZA-13 THE ISLAND

HLTH   yr ZA-13.1
Island on the line.

HLTH   ZA-13.2
Line is made up
of islands.

HLTH   ZA-13.3
Line is made up of
islands, grille on
upper "E" Mount.

ZA-15 THE STAR

ZA-15.1

Line ends in a star.

ZA-15.2

Line ends in a star,
Career and Fate lines
present and well cut.

FEML   yr ZA-15.3

Star on crossing
of Head and
Health lines.
FEMALES ONLY.

MALE   yr ZA-15.4

Line is thin and a
star is on crossing
of Head and
Health lines.
MALES ONLY.

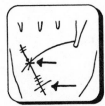

MALE   yr ZA-15.5

Line has crossbars,
dot and a star where
Head and Health
lines cross.

FEML   ZA-15.6

Star on Health and
Head lines.

FEML   yr ZA-15.7

Star on Health and
Head lines, crosses
on "F" Mount.

FEML   yr ZA-15.8

Star on Health and
Head lines, grille
on "F" Mount.

159

FEML ZA-15.8

Star on Head and
Health lines, island
on "F" Mount.

FEML yr ZA-15.8

Star on Head and
Health lines, dot
on "F" Mount.

FEML yr ZA-15.8

Star on Head and
Health lines,
imperfect star on
"F" Mount.

FEML yr ZA-15.9

Star on Head and
Health lines, Life
line sweeps wide
into the hand.

ZA-16 THE CROSS

ZA-16.1

Line ends in a cross.

ZA-16.2

Line ends in a cross,
grille on "F" Mount.

ZA-16.3

Line ends in a cross,
grille on "F" Mount
and a dot under
3rd finger.

yr ZA-16.4

A cross on the line.

ZB — THE NEUROSIS LINE

This line nearly always indicates an intense state of nervousness and, in a large majority of cases, great liability to hysteria. Neurosis means any of various mental functional disorders characterized by anxiety, compulsions, phobias, depression, and dissociation.

ZB-1.1

Neurosis line.

The Neurosis line starts between the 1st and 2nd fingers, deflects down and ends between the 3rd and 4th fingers. The line does not always run exactly over this path but sometimes starts under the 1st finger, ending under the 4th finger or on the outside of the hand. It is, in part, a Sister line to the Heart line; in some hands, when the Heart line is absent, it takes the place of the Heart line.

ZB-7 ITS CHARACTER

MNTL   ZB-7.1

A single deep line with multiplicity of lines in the hand.

MNTL   ZB-7.2

A single deep line with "G" Mount in excess, red hands and course texture.

ZB-7.3

A deep line with bony, thin hand.

ZB-7.4

A single deep line.

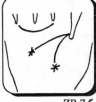

ZB-7.5

A deep line with thick fingers plus short Head and Life lines ending in stars.

ZB-7.6

Deep line cuts Career line, Fate line ends in a dot.

MNTL   ZB-7.7

Line cuts Affection line, with the other marks in the picture.

161

ZB-10 THE BREAK

ZB-10.1	ZB-10.2	ZB-10.3	ZB-10.4
Line is comprised of broken lines.	Composed of double or triple lines.	Made up of broken lines with multiplicity of lines in the hand.	Made up of broken lines, multiplicity of lines in hands, star on joining Head and Health lines.

MNTL   ZB-10.5

ZB-10.6

HLTH   ZB-10.7

Made up of broken lines, with any other defects on the Head line.

Made up of broken lines with Head line ending abnormally.

Made up of broken lines, cross under 2nd finger, island or dots on Head line, grille on "F" Mount, white spots or fluted nails.

ZC — THE WARRIOR LINE

This line's effect is to strengthen its Sister line (Life line) and to indicate a stronger constitution than is shown even by a good Life line.

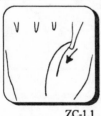

ZC-1.1

Warrior line.

The Warrior line starts on the lower "E" Mount and runs inside the Life line close to the thumb. The two lines are Sister lines to each other.

ZC-4 ITS LENGTH

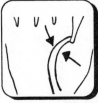

ZC-4.1	yr ZC-4.2
Line extends the full length of the Life line. Equal in strength without defects.	Line extends part way along Life line.

ZC-6 ITS TERMINATION

 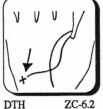  

ZC-6.1	DTH ZC-6.2	DTH ZC-6.2	DTH ZC-6.2
Line ends on the "F" Mount.	Line ends on the "F" Mount with a cross.	Line ends on the "F" Mount with a bar.	Line ends on the "F" Mount with a star.

ZC-6.3	DTH ZC-6.4	DTH ZC-6.5	DTH ZC-6.6
Line ends on the "F" Mount with a dot, star, bar or cross plus any mark on Head line.	Line ends on "F" Mount with a dot, star, bar or cross, Life line ends in a star under the 4th finger, Head line thin at the start, chained during deflection, ends in a star	Line ends on "F" Mount with a dot, star, bar or cross, Head line ends in a star on "F" Mount, a star or cross following a dot on Head line.	Line ends on the "F" Mount with a dot, star, bar or cross, Head line ends in a star on the "F" Mount, an island following a dot on Head line.

163

ZC-7 ITS CHARACTER

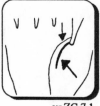

yr ZC-7.1

A strong line and a
thin Life line.

yr ZC-7.1

A strong line and a
broad and shallow
Life line.

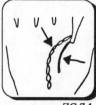

yr ZC-7.1

A strong line and a
chained Life line.

yr ZC-7.2

Strong Life and
Warrior lines.

ZC-9 THE SPLIT

yr ZC-7.3

A strong line runs
past any defect on
Life line.

ZC-7.4

Line is thinner than
Life line.

yr ZC-9.1

Split lines rise
from line and
cross Life line.

ZC-9.2

Line or lines rise and
merge into Head line.

yr ZC-9.3

Split line rises from
line and merges into
Career line.

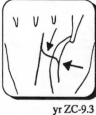

ZC-9.4

Split line cuts
Head line.

yr ZC-9.5

Split line cuts Head
line. Grille on "G"
Mount and a strong
Life line

yr ZC-9.6

Split line cuts Career
or Fate line.

yr ZC-9.7

Split line cuts Career
or Fate line that ends
in a dot.

yr ZC-9.7

Split line cuts Career
or Fate line that ends
in a crossbar.

yr ZC-9.7

Split line cuts Career
or Fate line that ends
in a cross.

yr ZC-9.8

Split line cuts Career
and Affection lines.

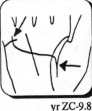

yr ZC-9.8

Split line cuts Fate
and Affection lines.

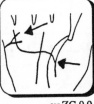

yr ZC-9.9

Split line cuts Career
line and a forked
Affection line.

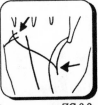

yr ZC-9.9

Split line cuts Fate
line and a forked
Affection line.

ZD — THE MYSTICAL LINE

*This line is an indication of a love for occult studies and of an ability to obtain
proficiency in them if other necessary Handology indications are present. In other
words, if you are basically a good person, your studies are religious; if you are not
a good person, occult studies win you over.*

ZD-1.1

Mystical line.

The Mystical line is a small line starting
between the 1st and 2nd fingers, running
downwards and encircling the Mount under
the 1st finger, and ending near the start of the
Life line.

ZD-1.2	ZD-1.3
The line is present.	Line is present with multiplicity of lines in the hand.

ZE — THE BALANCE LINE

This line shuts out the wisdom, seriousness and balancing qualities of life.

ZE-1.1

Balance line.

The Balance line starts between the 1st and 2nd fingers and ends between the 2nd and 3rd fingers, thus completely crossing the Mount under the 2nd finger. This makes the Mount under the 2nd finger defective.

ZE-1.2	ZE-1.3	MNTL ZE-1.4
The line is present.	Line consists of two lines.	Line consists of two lines crossing each other.

ZF — THE 1ST RASCETTE

The 1st Rascette adds additional confirmation to other indications of a strong constitution.

ZF-1.1

1st Rascette.

The Rascette, also known as bracelets, are the lines crossing the wrist at the base of the hand. We are concerned only with the 1st Rascette.

ZF-5 ITS COURSE

MALE   ZF-5.1

Rascette rises in the middle.

FEML   ZF-5.2

Rascette rises in the middle.

ZF-7 ITS CHARACTER

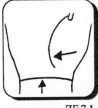

ZF-7.1

Line and Life line are deep and well cut, few lines in the hand.

ZF-7.2

Line and Life line are deeper than other lines, few lines in the hand

ZF-7.3

Line is poorly marked, strong Life line, few lines in the hand.

ZF-7.3

Line is chained, strong Life line, few lines in the hand.

ZF-7.3

Line is broad and
shallow, strong
Life line, few lines
in the hand.

ZF-7.4

Short lines rise from
the 1st Rascette.

ZG — THE TRAVEL LINES

The Travel lines are analyzed to indicate journeys. These lines increase restlessness and desire to travel. Travel lines can often be quite successfully used, long lines indicating more restlessness and longer journeys.

ZG-1.1

Travel lines.

Travel lines are the long branches which rise high into the "F" Mount from the 1st Rascette.

ZG-1.2

A travel line.

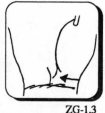

ZG-1.3

Split line from
Life line goes to
Travel lines.

168

ZH — THE INTUITION LINE

The presence of this line, if well marked, adds greatly to your intuitive faculty, though this may be only another name for your character's shrewdness. To those people with well-marked Intuition lines who are likely to become unbalanced from believing themselves to possess the powers of a medium or clairvoyant, an Intuition line is a poor possession. If they are devoted to luxury and sensuous pleasures, this line will be a menace to their careers. Such people seem to receive impressions for which they cannot account and to form accurate opinions which they are unable to justify. They seem to possess heightened faculties of sensitivity, of keenness in estimating people and of adroit shrewdness in arriving at correct opinions concerning many of their fellows. Some people with this mark are not conscious of these faculties and, upon being asked to justify certain statements, tell us that they "feel it in their bones." This faculty of receiving correct impressions from those we meet can be cultivated. If a person is not conscious of such powers and does not use them, he or she will experience many things concerning other people, but dismiss the impressions as fancies.

ZH-1.1

Intuition line.

The Intuition line lies at the side of the hand starting on the "F" Mount and, after making a curve towards the plain of the "E" Mount, ends on or just under the 4th finger. It can occupy the same position as the Health line but is distinguished from it by its curved formation.

ZH-1.2

Line with hard and square hands.

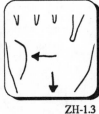

ZH-1.3

Line with long, spatulate fingers and a conic thumb tip.

ZH-1.4

Line cuts the Head line.

169

ZH-9 THE SPLIT

ZH-9.1

A split line goes to
1st finger.

ZH-9.2

A split line goes to
3rd finger.

ZH-9.3

A split line cuts the
Fate line.

ZH-9.4

A split line merges
into Career line.

ZH-10 THE BREAK

ZH-10.1

Line consists of
many broken lines.

ZH-13 THE ISLAND

yr ZH-13.1

Island on the line.

ZH-15 THE STAR

ZH-15.1

Line ends in a star.

ZH-15.2

Line ends in a
star with a puffy
"D" Mount.

ZH-15.3

Line ends in a star
with a person who is
a poor business type.

170

ZH-16 THE CROSS

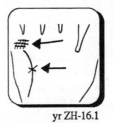

yr ZH-16.1

Cross on the line
and a grille under
4th finger.

ZI — THE LASCIVIA LINE

Such people will likely expend their surplus energy in the sphere of activity indicated by their hands. A fine hand (intellectual) shows greater results; in a low animal hand, poorer results. Lascivious means lewd, lustful and immoral.

ZI-1.1

Lascivia line.

The Lascivia line is seldom seen but should run so as to form a Sister line to the Health line. It generally occupies a slanting position starting from the outside of the Health line and ending before the Heart line.

ZI-7 ITS CHARACTER

ZI-7.1

Line deep and well cut or marked.

ZI-7.2

Deep and well cut plus soft hands.

ZI-7.3

Deep and well cut with any defect on Head line.

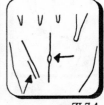

yr ZI-7.4

Deep and well cut with an island on Career line.

171

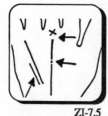  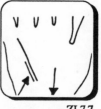

ZI-7.5

Deep and well-cut line, Fate line has a dot and ends in a cross.

HLTH   ZI-7.6

A deep line, well marked Warrior line, deep lines on "G" Mount, long 3rd phalange or short 1st.

ZI-7.7

A deep line, with a thick thumb or a clubbed thumb.

ZI-9 THE SPLIT

ZI-9.1

Forked Affection line is cut by a split from the Lascivia line.

ZI-9.2

Split line cuts the Fate line.

ZI-9.3

Split line cuts the Career line.

ZI-9.4

Split line cuts the Life line.

 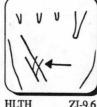  

HLTH   ZI-9.5

Split line cuts Life line, Life line becomes defective.

HLTH   ZI-9.6

Split lines cut Health line.

ZI-9.7

Split lines cut Health line, Warrior line ends on "F" Mount.

HLTH   yr ZI-9.8

Chance line runs to a dot on Life line.

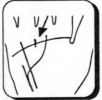

HLTH   yr ZI-9.9

Split line cuts
Head line.

HLTH   yr ZI-9.10

Split line cuts Head
line, a dot after cut
on Head line.

HLTH   yr ZI-9.10

Split line cuts Head
line, a deep bar after
cut on Head line.

HLTH   yr ZI-9.10

Split line cuts Head
line, a break after
cut on Head line.

HLTH   yr ZI-9.10

Split line cuts Head
line, a cross after
cut on Head line.

173

ZI-17 SISTER LINES

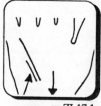

yr ZI-17.1

Line is a Sister line to Health line.

yr ZI-17.2

Line is a Sister line to a wavy Health line.

ZI-17.3

Line is a Sister line to a broken Health line.

ZI-17.4

As a Sister line, runs part way along Health line.

ZI-17.5

As a Sister line, runs part way along Health line, which ends under 4th finger.

Part 3

Interpreting Description Codes

In this section, look up the Description codes you selected from the Character Styles (Part 1) and Future Projection (Part 2) sections.

Information from Part 1 describes traits of character you:

a) express now,
b) have expressed in the past,
c) are capable of expressing.

They are not necessarily the traits you display all the time. Different emotional situations warrant different expressions. The traits you uncover are those you possess now.

Information from Part 2 concerns events that:

a) have occurred in the past,
b) may occur if you continue on the same course,
c) may be changed if you desire it.

Remember, not all future events will occur. Therefore, statements about what will happen should only be interpreted as insights. If your age is 30 at the time of analysis, for example, statements following this age are future projections only, not statements of fact.

Also keep in mind that lines change weekly, monthly and yearly and that future analyses could produce different projections if your lifestyle has changed substantially.

Some statements may at first appear to be in error, but keep in mind that it is the overall impression that is important, not one particular statement.

A

DESCRIPTION "A": TEXTURE OF SKIN — *Holds the key to knowledge of a person's natural refinement.*

A-1   EFFECT OF FINE TEXTURE
Coarseness offends you, and it is not possible for you to do things in a coarse, common or brutish way. You are a refined, sensitive person, influenced by these qualities in everything you do.

A-2   EFFECT OF COARSE TEXTURE
You lack refinement, delicate sensibility, or fine quality of nature.

A-3   EFFECT OF MEDIUM TEXTURE
Shows refinement. If male, you do not have more feminine qualities than are suitable; if female, you have fineness without idealism.

A-4   EFFECT OF 1ST PHALANGES, FINGERTIPS
You are keenly alive to all your surroundings, easily wounded when slighted by others and, knowing how such things jar upon yourself, you are most careful of the feelings of other people. You would suffer intensely yourself rather than wound another.

B

DESCRIPTION "B": CONSISTENCY OF THE HAND— *This is the embodiment of healthful energy, evenly distributed. Shows the activity of intelligent energy and force. Well-directed energy, "sensibly energetic."*

B-1 EFFECT OF FLABBY CONSISTENCY

You dream but do not act; you love, but your love finds expression only in words, not deeds. You desire ease, both mental and physical. You also desire luxury and beautiful surroundings, but will not work to gain them. You prefer to live in squalor, so long as there is plenty of rest and no exertion, rather than to enjoy better living, if labor is the price of the improved condition. You are an idle, luxurious, sensitive dreamer who will not work or exert; like a ship at sea without wind, you are content to drift.

B-2 EFFECT OF SOFT CONSISTENCY

You are an idle, luxurious dreamer who will not work, will not exert; like a ship at sea without a wind you are content to drift. However, your faculty of energy can be developed and increased.

B-3 EFFECT OF ELASTIC CONSISTENCY

Puts vitality into all human qualities. You have life, energy, push, vim and vigor. You do no more work than is necessary, but you do enough; you do not over-exert, but rather occupy the plane of a happy medium. Your life, action and energy is a moving force in the world today. You are the most active kind; manual labor is not a burden, but is expected.

B-4 EFFECT OF FLEXIBILITY, HARD HANDS

The most active kind; manual labor is not a burden, but is expected. You do not receive and assimilate impressions and ideas quickly or readily.

C

DESCRIPTION "C": FLEXIBILITY OF THE HAND — *Shows the degree of flexibility of mind and nature and the readiness with which the mind has power to unfold itself to "see around the corner."*

C-1 EFFECT OF STIFF HAND, HARD TO OPEN

Indicates that the mind is cautious, immobile, closed, inclined to narrowness and stinginess, lacking pliability or adaptability. You are afraid of new ventures, new ideas; your manner of dress and the mode of living of your ancestors satisfies you; you have the practical and religious faith of your fathers and will not be changed.

You are exceedingly closed-mouthed and can safely keep a secret, not from your desire to do so but because nothing gets away from you; the secret will be held as avariciously as a dollar.

C-2 EFFECT OF FLEXIBILITY, NORMAL DEVELOPMENT
Balanced, even in action, up-to-date and in control. Thoughtful, broad, earnest, sympathetic, yet all within bounds. Well balanced, not extremist. Life is serious and much time is spent trying to understand it.

C-3 EFFECT OF EXTREME FLEXIBILITY
You readily adapt to surroundings, are versatile and do not need a diagram with every statement. Because you possess the highest degree of versatility and are able to do many things, you are likely to diversify your talents and concentration in any direction, thus becoming a jack-of-all-trades.

You are extremely sympathetic and generous, and money to you is only a means of securing what is needed; nothing is to be hoarded for itself alone. Yours is the hand of a dreamer, but you are full of life and action, though often too versatile for your own good. Your mind works rapidly, ideas are absorbed quickly, and there is a tendency to go too fast. These brilliant hands are capable of the most wonderful achievements.

C-4 EFFECT OF FLEXIBILITY, 1ST PHALANGE
You have flexibility in your mental qualities.

C-5 FLEXIBILITY, HAND COMPARISON
Shows whether you are improving in mentality or going in the opposite direction.

   C-5.1 PASSIVE HAND STIFF, ACTIVE HAND FLEXIBLE
   You are high-minded, improving mentally, your mind elastic.

   C-5.2 PASSIVE HAND FLEXIBLE, ACTIVE HAND STIFF
   You have become more stingy, careful, less versatile, and your qualities of vim and vigor are changing to caution and immobility.

D

DESCRIPTION "D": COLOR OF HANDS — *Indicates temperament, health or disease.*

D-1 EFFECT OF COLOR: WHITE
Indicates a corresponding lack of force and strength in nature. You are dreamy, unenthusiastic, unemotional, selfish, unimaginative. You are not sensual, for the vital force of strong health, which gives force to passion, is absent; you are cold in love and, while often very clever, do not seek the society of others.

Such people are good poets and prose writers; they do not find great enjoyment in gratification of the senses. The mind may be active and at work, though not spurred on by marital fire or love. In the business world you make few friends; you do not enter the social world when it can be avoided. In religion you are mystical.

D-2 EFFECT OF COLOR: PINK
Pinkness is health. You find life pleasant, bright and attractive. Pink indicates the nearest approach to normal conditions in temperament.

D-3 EFFECT OF COLOR: RED
Red shows good physical strength; your nature is ardent and intense, you do not mince words but use strong, short sentences. If you love, it is with no feeble flame, but a withering blast of strength. If you are angry, you are violent and find the greatest difficulty in exercising self-control.

Your difficulty lies in being so much stronger than most people that you overshadow others and wear them out by your intensity. You cannot do things by halves. You have so much vitality that it may be called an excess of health and strength. Thus, instead of nursing a physical pain or delicacy, you are impelled to great exertions to work off or use up the super-abundance of vital energy with which you are charged.

D-4 EFFECT OF COLOR: YELLOW
Yellow shows biliousness. You are held down by a weight that seems about to crush you; moody and melancholy, you take a dark view of life and have "the blues." You constantly cross the bridge before you get to it. You become morose and silent, and form the habit of shunning society and happiness in every form.

Your brain is clogged by bilious poisoning, and your views become poisoned. You see no bright side to anything, but revel in gloom, mystery and superstition. You take a sickly, distorted point of view and are soon inclined to seek seclusion and give way to gloom and despondency. The bile irritates the nerves, so you are cross, irritable.

D-5 EFFECT OF COLOR: BLUE OR PURPLE
Blueness or purplishness is caused by improper circulation of the blood, not necessarily a poor quality. You must take one day at a time and keep excitement to a low level. If you feel sluggish or slow, see your doctor for a check-up.

E

DESCRIPTION "E": NAILS—*These are windows through which we look into the interior organization of the human being. Nails show quality, as does skin.*

E-1   EFFECT OF NAILS, GENERAL DATA
        The great nerve centers under the nails, when operating in a healthy manner, allow the texture to be seen; when the nerve center in the quick is impaired, it affects the nail texture by changing the quality of the nail itself.

E-2   EFFECT OF COARSE NAILS AND FINE SKIN
        You are out of proportion and the normal balance has been disturbed. Something is bothering you.

E-3   EFFECT OF NAILS, WHITE SPOTS OR FLUTING
        Your nails indicate a beginning of the loss of vitality — nature's first warning of trouble ahead. White spots appearing on the nails are the first indication that you are under pressure of some sort or are not at peace with your environment.

E-4   NAILS MANIFEST THEMSELVES
        Your nails show that your nerves are very delicate, that your vitality is being burned up. You are painfully aware of your problem and the reason for your nervousness.

E-5   EFFECT OF NAILS, RIDGED CROSSWISE
        Your nails show a poor disposition and that a serious problem has interrupted your health.

E-6   EFFECT OF NEW NAIL
        You show refreshed vitality and clear thought.

E-7   BADLY FLUTED NEW NAIL
        You still have a nervous disorder. Freedom from all excitement and problems is advised.

E-8   EFFECT OF NARROW NAILS
        Your nails show that you do not have robust muscular strength but are carried by nervous energy. These are psychic nails, and a delicacy of the psychic character is present.

E-9   EFFECT OF BROAD NAILS
        Your nails show muscular strength, either in physical appearance or in actual power in the muscles.

E-10 EFFECT OF SHORT NAILS
These nails show a critical turn of mind, or a quizzical or investigating disposition.

E-11 EFFECT OF EXTREMELY SHORT NAILS
These nails show pugnacity. You argue, not to prove you are right and not because you believe you are always right, but because you love contention.

E-12 EFFECT OF FLAT, BLUNT NAILS
These nails go with a vigorous composition, an active mind and a very critical, pugnacious, argumentative disposition. It shows you would rather argue than eat. You disagree when you know perfectly well the other party is right, simply for the delight it gives you to argue.

You criticize everything, for in this way you can best provoke contention and, while you do not want a fight with the other party physically, you love the battle of the mind and bring to bear on the argument all your physical energy until you tire out your opponent and win a victory even though you are not always right. Your critical mind is a factor in everything: love, business, art, eloquence, war, literature or music.

E-13 EFFECT OF OPEN AND FRANK NAILS
These nails indicate that you are a person with an open and frank nature to whom honesty of thought is natural. Their breadth reflects your broad ideas.

E-13.1 ADD FINE TEXTURE OR PINK COLOR
With this effect the open and frank nature in the above statements becomes more pronounced.

E-14 BLUE-COLORED NAILS
This nail shows heart trouble and is found mostly on people with heart problems. This is not always the case, however. It could indicate more of an organic difficulty than a lack of circulation.

E-15 FAINT, BLUE-TINGED NAIL
The deepest blue tinge at the base of any nail indicates poor circulation.

E-16 BULBOUS NAILS
This indicates an advanced stage of consumption or tubercular trouble. Medical authorities say it is caused by a lack of nourishment, and among physicians it is a well-known indication of tubercular trouble somewhere in the system.

E-17 LARGE NAILS
These nails indicate a delicacy of the bronchial tubes and throat. Sometimes it may signify a weakness of the lungs as well, but never a disease. It does show that you are susceptible to colds. Sudden changes of temperature can produce disturbances in your throat and bronchial tubes. This is a delicacy to be guarded against, and you should always use care to avoid colds.

E-18 CLUBBED NAILS
May signify emphysema, tuberculosis, cardiovascular disease, ulcerative colitis or cirrhosis.

E-19 SPOON NAILS
Associated with iron deficiency, anemia, syphilis, thyroid disorders and rheumatic fever.

E-20 BEAU'S LINES
These lines result from malnutrition or any severe illness that temporarily interferes with nail growth, including measles, mumps, heart attack and conditions such as carpal-tunnel syndrome.

E-21 TERRY'S NAILS
Cirrhosis of the liver may be indicated.

E-22 LINDSAY'S NAILS
This can be a sign of chronic kidney failure.

E-23 YELLOW-NAIL SYNDROME
Could include chronic respiratory, thyroid or lymphatic diseases.

E-24 SPLINTERING AND HEMORRHAGING
May be a sign of chronic high blood pressure, psoriasis or an infection of the lining of the heart, a potentially life-threatening condition.

E-25 IRREGULAR PITTING OR PITTING IN ROWS
Irregular pitting occurs in many cases of psoriasis. Pitting in rows sometimes occurs as a result of alapecia areata, a poorly understood auto-immune disease that results in partial or total hair loss.

E-26 BROWN OR BLACK DISCOLORATION
May signify malignant melanoma.

F

DESCRIPTION "F": HAIR ON THE HANDS—*Tells of the vigor and iron in your composition, how hardy you are. Hair shows strength.*

F-1   EFFECT OF NO HAIR ON THE HAND
You are a finely strung person, not physically strong, perhaps, but not necessarily weak in character.

F-2   EFFECT OF LIGHT OR BLOND HAIR
Shows you are even in temper, cool, phlegmatic, unexcitable, not over-amorous, less sensual than most, constant, energetic, intensely practical, common-sensical, frequently honest and matter-of-fact.

F-3   EFFECT OF BLACK HAIR
You have heat and vitality to spare, and love to expend your excess of health on pleasure. You have a warm, intense nature.

F-4   EFFECT OF WHITE HAIR
Your vital force has gone below the normal point.

F-5   EFFECT OF GRAY HAIR
Indicates a possibly worn-out, libertine person.

F-6   EFFECT OF RED HAIR
This is a color that indicates a hot temper, excitability of disposition, a certain tendency to engage in quarrels, and a liability to flare up at the slightest provocation.

F-6.1   ADD FINE TEXTURE
The fits of temper are momentary, though violent while they last.

F-6.2   ADD COARSE TEXTURE
Indicates brutality, violent temper and a tendency to sullenly nurse a fury and seek revenge.

F-7   AUBURN OR BROWN HAIR
Auburn hair is much praised. It is a combination of warmth and passion, of black hair with a touch of added fire from the red, a combination which tinges the hair with a golden auburn glow. A brilliant combination; but if you happen to have bad qualities, beware: a furnace is burning beneath the surface.

G

DESCRIPTION "G": HAND AS A WHOLE — *Indicates whether your mind is defined primarily by the intellect, by a desire for material possessions, or by baser instincts.*

G-1   LONG FINGERS
You live in the realm of ideas and are in need of constant encouragement and support.

> **G-1.1   ADD LONG 1ST PHALANGE, WELL-MARKED HEAD LINE**
> Sorry, this combination is still under investigation.

G-2   MIDDLE OF THE HAND IN EXCESS
Shows that business, practical life, everyday ideas and material success compose the world in which you live. Thus you are best fitted for commercial positions or for anything which is entirely practical. You have contempt for anyone who is all brains. Money-getting is your moving desire and you live in a world of material matters.

G-3   BASE OF THE HAND IN EXCESS
You can appreciate nothing high or elevating. If you acquire money you do not know how to make a refined use of it. You love beauty but are vulgar. You love eating, but with the gluttony of the gourmand, not the delight of the epicure. You have no mental recreations; mind is not a guiding force.

You are sometimes shrewd, but with the instinctive cunning of the fox, not the talent of a high and lofty mind. You love display and in your home will have profusion, not taste; glaring colors, not harmony. You are vulgar and common in all your tastes and among people of refinement and good breeding are a veritable bore. You do not see how ridiculous you appear to people of elevated thought. You see only from your earthly point of view.

G-4   A BALANCED HAND
A balanced hand indicates a balanced mind. This means you are wise, intelligent, prudent, practical, even-tempered and yet not unsophisticated, for you have enough of the base alloy to give you necessary knowledge. You are thus able to weigh all matters not from just a purely mental standpoint, but with the common sense needed to make life successful.

G-5   IF HAND IS SLIGHTLY OUT OF BALANCE
The portion of the hand which is larger than normal indicates a tendency which you lean towards, but perhaps not enough to follow it. Long fingers

indicate intelligence; large middle portion of hand indicates interest in material things; large base of hand indicates basic animal instincts.

G-6 EFFECT OF SMALLER BASE
With your well-developed mind and desire for material possessions, you can obtain financial results from mental strength.

G-7 EFFECT OF SMALLER FINGERS
You can gain riches, though they may be gained in coarse occupations.

G-8 FINGERS AND BASE LONGER
You have the supremacy of the mind and the predominance of the earthly without the leavening of common sense.

H

DESCRIPTION "H": FINGERS IN GENERAL — *This system of thoroughly analyzing fingers gives the ability to minutely assess character and to estimate future success.*

H-1 1ST FINGER SET HIGH OR LONGER
You are an absolute tyrant if the 1st finger is longer than the 2nd. If the 1st finger is as long as the 2nd, your desire for power is great.

H-2 2ND FINGER SET HIGH OR LONGER
You have unusual endurance and staying power, a cautious approach, thoroughness of method, and patience to wait for the best time for everything. Things are well balanced and done in moderation. There is little danger of self-indulgence, waste or carelessness, for you have an enviable gift for self-control and discipline which usually leads to considerable achievement.

H-3 3RD FINGER SET HIGH OR LONGER
If the 3rd finger is longer than the 1st finger, artistic or business tastes are in the ascendancy. If the 3rd is as long as the 2nd, or nearly so, you take great chances in everything; you will risk life, money and reputation in carrying out your enterprises. You tend to plunge in; you are a speculator or gambler. If the 3rd is longer than the 2nd, you are a foolhardy gambler, unable to restrain yourself.

H-4 4TH FINGER SET HIGH OR LONGER
You are particularly strong in terms of quickness, shrewdness, industriousness and business abilities. Actually, you are strong in anything you wish to accomplish.

H-5 1ST FINGER SET LOW OR SHORTER
If the 1st finger is shorter than the first joint of the 2nd finger, you lack the ability to lead. In this case, ambition, religious beliefs and honor remain high.

H-6 2ND FINGER SET LOW OR SHORTER
You allow personal ambitions or desires to hold sway over reason and then often lack the self-discipline to achieve those goals. There is also a tendency towards self-indulgence and a definite lack of staying power. However, there is a relaxed sort of adaptability that sometimes leads to knowledge and awareness, even achievement, through many varied experiences.

H-7 3RD FINGER SET LOW OR SHORTER
This indicates a person whose life may lack creativity and expression of the real self in an effort to win the approval of others by meeting their needs and living up to their standards and expectations. However, there can be a sincere and truly unselfish quality here as well.

H-8 4TH FINGER SET LOW OR SHORTER
This element creates an unusually long-distance approach to learning. You see things first as a whole rather than a sum of many parts. In other words, you see the forest instead of the trees.

H-9 NORMALLY SET FINGERS
This shows that you are very well balanced and could well be successful.

H-10 THUMB AND 1ST FINGER ARE WIDE
You are generous, love freedom and independence, and are tolerant of restraint.

H-11 1ST AND 2ND FINGERS ARE WIDE
You have great independence of thought; you are not bound by the views of others, but form your own opinions.

H-12 2ND AND 3RD FINGERS ARE WIDE
You are careless of the future, unconventional in ideas, and entirely devoid of stiffness and love of formality.

H-13   3RD AND 4TH FINGERS ARE WIDE
You are independent in action. You do what you wish without caring what others may think.

H-14   ALL EQUALLY SEPARATED
You are unconventional in thought and action. You have difficulty making the aquaintance of people of a similar nature.

H-15   ALL EQUALLY TOGETHER
You are difficult to get acquainted with, are stiff and lack independence in thought or action. You are a slave to formality, and to make your acquaintance one must approach you in a respectful manner. You are also stingy, for you are self-centered and constantly looking to the future.

H-16   THE THREE FINGER PHALANGES
These tell whether mental quickness, business abilities or common instincts rule you.

H-17   LONG 1ST PHALANGES
Mental matters greatly absorb your attention, indicating mental strength.

H-18   LONG OR THICK 1ST PHALANGES
You are more domineering and less religious than most.

H-19   SHORT 1ST PHALANGES
Enjoyment of mental occupations is lacking, and qualities more material absorb your attention.

H-19.1   ADD PINK COLOR
This indicates a coldness in religious beliefs.

H-20   EXCESSIVELY SQUARE 1ST PHALANGES
Shows a domineering spirit which in family, business and every walk of life marks the tyrant and the despot.

H-21   LONG OR THICK 2ND PHALANGES
The money-making side is uppermost. These phalanges tell of an ambition that makes even weak natures advance.

H-22   SHORT 2ND PHALANGES
Your practical ideas are diminished.

H-22.1   ADD PINK COLOR
Makes business abilities and ambitions cold.

H-23 LONG OR THICK 3RD PHALANGES

Shows that sensuality and the gratification of appetite are the pleasures you seek. The extreme thickness of the third phalange shows a great love for eating and drinking. There are medical problems which cause people to be obese. If this is the case, ignore interpretations in this book which are associated with obesity. This phalange indicates an increased sensuality in the qualities indicated by your fingers.

H-23.1 ADD RED COLOR

Gluttony is further fired by ardor and strength of blood current; apoplexy is certain.

H-23.2 ADD COARSE TEXTURE

This means miserliness. If your third phalanges are thick, you are less studious.

H-24 NARROW 3RD PHALANGES

Shows you eat to live and do not live to eat. You expend your strength in either the mental or business worlds, not in the sensual. You do not care for money except for what it will buy and the pleasure it can bring. It slips through your fingers for whatever suits your fancy. You have an inquiring mind.

H-24.1 ADD FLABBY CONSISTENCY

This shows the third phalanges were thick but have shrivelled, that you were an over-eater, have ruined your stomach and become a dyspeptic, suffering from stomach disorders of various kinds.

H-25 SHORT AND NARROW 3RD PHALANGES

Your baser world is diminished; this makes you more positive.

H-25.1 ADD PINK COLOR

Decreases your enthusiasm.

H-26 1ST PHALANGES SHORT, 2ND NORMAL, 3RD THICK

You do not care for mental pursuits at all, but desire only to make money and to have plenty to eat and drink. This does not indicate the sexual sort of sensuality, but rather the sensuous gratification of appetite and a love of luxury and comfort.

H-27 1ST PHALANGES SHORT, 2ND NORMAL, 3RD MODERATE

Your desire for sensuous gratification of appetite and love of luxury and comfort is excessive.

H-28   ADD LONG FINGERS AND WIDE CHINKS
You are not an investigator, merely curious. You pry into the affairs of everyone from innate curiosity.

I

DESCRIPTION "I": FINGERTIPS — *Shows what kind of a machine you are, whether there is water in your boiler and fire to turn it into steam. Shows whether the machine is acting in its intended fashion.*

I-1   SPATULATE FINGERTIPS
In your daily life you are constantly on the go; you inspire all about you with your wonderful enthusiasm and activity. You are fond of horses, dogs and, in fact, all animals. You are a strong lover, constant and true. There is little that is vacillating about you. You are real, earnest, practical and show great originality. You do not do things by any well-ordered system or by established rules.

You like to think of new ways in which to expend your energies, so you invent new methods, always with something practical in view. You follow no creed, but have your own ideas. You love independence and pursue your active way through life caring little what people say. In whatever you undertake you are skillful, for it is not your intention to be in the rear. A power in activity, originality and enterprise.

I-1.1   ADD SOFT CONSISTENCY
You are a lover of action.

I-2   SQUARE FINGERTIPS
Square fingertips indicate that you seek regularity, order, system and arrangement in everything. You see disorder, whether in the home or in the store or shop, as an abomination. You can be happy only when everything is well ordered, systematically arranged and done according to rules.

I-3   VERY SQUARE FINGERTIPS
If your fingertips are very square then the attributes stated in Description code I-2 are more pronounced.

I-4   SLIGHTLY CONIC FINGERTIPS
You are less tied down by such absolute regularity.

I-4.1   ADD SOFT CONSISTENCY

This lessons the vigor implied by your square fingertips.

I-5   CONIC FINGERTIPS

You are an artistic, impulsive, quick, intuitive person, to whom the beautiful and harmonious in all things appeals most strongly and who is very impressionable.

I-5.1   ADD SOFT CONSISTENCY

Adds idealism to your basic character.

I-6   POINTED FINGERTIPS

You have no part or place in the materialistic operations of business, nor can you be held down to any set way of doing things.

You are highly inspirational, idealistic in the extreme and dwell in the clouds, mentally far from the bustle of a practical money-seeking world. To you beauty is all; dreams and visions take you through a vista of imaginings and life is happy or unhappy in proportion to your ability to indulge in these beautiful fancies.

I-6.1   ADD SOFT CONSISTENCY

Adds idealism to your basic character.

I-7   FINGERTIPS AND THEIR PHALANGES

The effect phalanges have on fingertips.

I-7.1   ADD LONG 1ST PHALANGES, CONIC FINGERTIPS

Shows that idealistic, intuitive qualities are added to mental qualities. You are a strong, high-minded person and your artistic qualities are more pronounced.

I-7.2   ADD LONG 1ST PHALANGES, SQUARE FINGERTIPS

Shows a tendency towards practical application. You are more common-sensical, will reason and take less for granted.

I-7.3   ADD LONG 1ST PHALANGES, SPATULATE FINGERTIPS

Adds mental activity and originality.

I-7.4   ADD LONG 2ND PHALANGES, CONIC FINGERTIPS

Indicates that you have an artistic, impulsive turn. You keep your place attractive and, wherever you go, have artistic things around you. You are fond of pleasure.

I-7.5   ADD LONG 2ND PHALANGES, SQUARE FINGERTIPS

This indicates practicality and common sense. You have strength in business and are likely to be productive as a money-maker.

I-7.6   ADD LONG 2ND PHALANGES, SPATULATE FINGERTIPS
Shows an active, ambitious, original person sure to force a way in the world, especially along practical lines.

I-7.7   ADD LONG 3RD PHALANGES, CONIC FINGERTIPS
You idealize everything and are visionary and impractical.

I-7.8   ADD LONG 3RD PHALANGES, SQUARE FINGERTIPS
You are less liable to carry things to excess; common sense and practical ideas dominate.

I-7.9   ADD LONG 3RD PHALANGES, SPATULATE FINGERTIPS
You are active and original in devising ways for expending your efforts.

J

DESCRIPTION "J": KNOTTY FINGERS — *Analysis, reasoning, investigation and thoughtfulness are the ever-present tendencies of those with knotty joints. They also have diminished enthusiasm and spontaneity.*

J-1   BOTH KNOTS DEVELOPED
For you to accept anything as truth means you first hear it, think about it and digest it. You examine every statement with your systematic mind and assess it from the standpoint of common sense and practical reasoning. You are not carried away by enthusiasm or impulse, but bring to bear on everything the light of thorough investigation and thought.

You are seldom emotional, not easily led by sentiment; reason, not impulse, is your guide. You cannot be suddenly rushed into anything. Whichever side you are on, you honestly believe it is right. You are philosophical and honest; a reasoner, investigator, preacher of truth; energetic, hard to change, a thinker, doubter, slow to arrive at conclusions, patient and systematic.

J-1.1   ADD SPATULATE OR SQUARE FINGERTIPS
You are a severe taskmaster who, whether husband, wife or employer, is almost fanatical about discipline. You are bound by materialism. You do not believe in what you cannot see and touch. A skeptic.

J-1.2   ADD CONIC OR POINTED FINGERTIPS
You possess analytical doubting qualities combined with a little idealism. Of those with knotty fingers, these are the only ones willing to take anything for granted.

191

J-2 1ST KNOTS DEVELOPED
You have immense thoughts; you are careless to an extreme in your personal appearance. Mental development entirely displaces the material. You are out of balance.

> *J-2.1* ADD SPATULATE FINGERTIPS AND SOFT HANDS
> You are an obstinate kind of person, cranky in the extreme. Realism in the greatest degree is indicated.

J-3 2ND KNOTS DEVELOPED
You want your home neat and well kept, your place of business clean and orderly; in all material matters you are careful and systematic. You are neat in appearance, though your clothing may be old and worn. You are methodical in your daily life and habits.

K

DESCRIPTION "K": SMOOTH FINGERS — *Quickness of thought, inspiration, impulse and spontaneity are the guiding forces indicated by smooth fingers.*

K-1 EFFECT OF SMOOTH FINGERS
You do not delve into every subject but rely on the impressions which come to you, without stopping to consider all "whys and wherefores." You are not by nature a reasoner, though you often grow into a habit of analyzing; if these tendencies increase, knots appear on your fingers. You are mostly guided by your first impressions and seldom are wrong in your intuitive deductions.

> *K-1.1* ADD HARD HANDS
> Your impetuosity gives you a strong tendency to fail. Only an extraordinarily straight and strong head can keep you from continual blunders.

> *K-1.2* ADD RED COLOR
> Your impetuosity gives you a strong tendency to fail. Only an extraordinarily straight and strong head can keep you from continual blunders.

> *K-1.3* ADD SPATULATE FINGERTIPS
> Your force is strongly augmented by the originality, activity and independence indicated by your fingertips. Such a combination needs most careful handling to prevent you from becoming a crank and, due to an excess of good qualities, from having ill success.

K-1.4 ADD SQUARE FINGERTIPS
Your quickness and inspiration operate in practical ways and you are less idealistic.

K-1.5 ADD CONIC FINGERTIPS
You are sympathetic, emotional, often easily led; as a consequence, such people are not constant lovers. The eye, ear and senses are all trained to respond to beauty, harmony and artistic surroundings. You appreciate beauty, even when it fades, because you understand the finer points. You are a poetic, lovable, attractive type.

You think quickly; thus it is quick, instinctive intuition that guides you rather than slow methods of thought. You are more inclined to idealism than to real things in life. With these artistic tendencies you seek occupations where there is a good opportunity to use your intuitive powers and where your love of beauty and art can find fuller expression.

K-1.6 ADD POINTED FINGERTIPS
You are the most artistic of those with smooth fingers; they stand for idealism and true art.

K-1.7 ADD KNOTTY SECOND JOINTS
Impulse, inspiration and artistic ideals guide you. You act on first impressions rather than by the slower, analytical methods of thought.

L

DESCRIPTION "L": LONG FINGERS—*These tell of your irresistible propensity for detail, for dealing with minutiae, for observing little and trifling things. They also tell of a tinge of suspicion and, if the shape bears it out, of selfishness and hypocrisy.*

L-1 EFFECT OF LONG FINGERS
You have a mind which goes into the minutiae of everything, seeks every detail and accepts nothing as a whole until first separated into its parts. You are particular, especially about small things. You engage yourself with some small detail and allow a larger one to escape you. You are suspicious and do not feel quite sure that friends are true.

L-1.1 ADD SQUARE FINGERTIPS

Your regularity and attention to detail make you almost infallible as an accountant. You check accounts for a month to discover a penny which has destroyed your balance. Your long fingers indicate that you are slow.

L-1.2 ADD KNOTTY FINGERS

This means love of detail and analysis. Plodder you are, not achieving success by brilliance or quick spurts, but by slowly and carefully laboring to keep abreast of the times. Patient you are, for you see many pass you on the roadway of life and it requires patience to see oneself outstripped and not get moody.

L-1.3 ADD SMOOTH FINGERS

It does not take you long to grasp an idea.

L-1.4 YOUR PROFESSIONS:

IF A MUSICIAN, you achieve success from careful and close observation of detail. You do not depart from the composer's concept but adhere strictly to every notation and mark of expression.

IN CONVERSATION, you are apt to be tiresome for, in telling a story or describing anything, you go into every detail with wearisome accuracy.

IN LITERATURE, you are exact and active in style. You tend to pay too much attention to detail and to give long and tiresome descriptions. Your work in literature, as everywhere else, has the stamp of painstaking carefulness. You can describe natural scenery and not a tree or a leaf will escape you.

IF A NOVELIST, you describe minutely every character and incident. In business you are accurate but more careful than usual for your type.

IF AN ARTIST, you give every detail of the scene you are drawing. If a portrait painter, you reproduce every button, every hair and every eyelash. If a sculptor, nothing escapes you.

IF A PAINTER, you create an imaginative scene and do not omit a detail in your treatment of the subject. In conversation you are fanciful and tiresome.

IF A SPEAKER, you describe every detail of any subject.

IF A LAWYER, you hunt every bit of testimony that can bear on your case and prepare your petitions and papers with the greatest care. You keep the records in your cases exact, with every exception noted, so that you can appeal if ruled against.

IF A DOCTOR, you do not neglect detail in the treatment of your patients. You attend to their diet, hygiene, and the air in their room, and in everything you are most careful.

IF A BUSINESS PERSON, you are constantly going over everything in your place of business. Not a thing escapes you and no detail is omitted that can add to the results you wish to accomplish. With the extra suspicion and neatness implied by your long fingers, you are a most pronounced example of this type.

IF A SOLDIER, you plan campaigns with the utmost care, look after equipment and ensure that people are amply provided with proper food, noting details that can add to efficiency. You are neat in dress and require other soldiers to keep equipment constantly bright. You are suspicious of those with whom you deal and do not implicitly trust anyone; therefore you see to it yourself that your instructions are carried out. Your long fingers show a fondness for minutiae and detail.

IF A SCHOLAR, you are prone to sacrifice strength to detail in your writing; as a teacher you tend to prolong your lectures to unwise lengths.

L-1.5 YOUR FAULTS

Long fingers indicate slowness and tediousness. You are often boring and, worse than this, are frequently selfish. This comes from the fact that your suspicious way of looking at things causes you to draw within yourself and not push out among people, nor do you love to mingle with others. In this way you acquire habits of selfishness which grow with years.

L-2 LONG HANDS

These hands reveal the slow-going, slow-talking person who enunciates each syllable of every word. While you do not drawl, you are slow in forming and speaking your words. Anyone who is quick in thought knows, after the first few words, just what you will say and wishes you to hurry and finish.

Long hands also indicate slow-acting minds. You are slow in movement, dignified, and unable to rush. You are often the fine engraver who can trace the most delicate lines and tracery on jewelry. You handle the smaller parts of machinery and in general do the minute and fine-detail work in mechanics and mechanical art.

L-3   THIN, LONG FINGERS

Thin, long fingers indicate that long-fingered qualities are accentuated. You are not bold and fearless, but inclined to be cowardly and consequently servile. You are not always true to people. You are suspicious, often nurse feelings of resentment and become hypocritical.

L-3.1   ADD 2ND KNOTS DEVELOPED

You go into detail. You are suspicious and distrustful even of your own supporters, are neat in appearance, and have all the other long-fingered qualities.

L-3.2   ADD EXTREMELY SHORT NAILS

This accentuates long-fingered qualities (see L-1).

L-4   LACK OF THUMB AND 3RD FINGER MOUNTS

You are inclined to be selfish. You acquire habits of selfishness which grow with years.

L-5   A STRONG "F" MOUNT

You acquire habits of selfishness which grow with years.

L-6   LONG AND THICK FINGERS

You are true to your friends. These fingers indicate that you are less prone to pushing long-fingered qualities to excess than to seeking pleasure, so they indicate fewer of the disagreeable qualities than do thin, long fingers.

L-6.1   ADD SQUARE FINGERTIPS

Regularity, practical matters, business or common-sense duties attract you.

L-6.2   ADD SPATULATE FINGERTIPS

Activity and originality are your moving forces; you make the most remarkable inventors, careful explorers. There is also a fondness for minutiae.

M

DESCRIPTION "M": SHORT FINGERS — *You abhor detail and have great distaste for doing anything slowly. You have quickness of thought and action, but impulse and hasty conclusions are a danger.*

if the fingers are normally short, like a flash if they are very short, and you act as quickly as you think. No analysis, no detail, no minutiae for you. Things as a whole are what you deal with, and this without delay.

You are impulsive, act on the spur of the moment and do many hasty things for which you are later sorry. You are in danger of falling into error through jumping to conclusions. While you possess brilliant possibilities, you often ruin them by impetuosity. You are hot-headed and, once started, push ahead with extreme diligence at any enterprise undertaken. You are never satisfied to be doing any but big things. Those with short fingers are dashing, impetuous, quick, and full of big plans; they look down on small matters. You are not always careful of appearance, and are too occupied with large matters to attend to the trifles of etiquette or society.

You quickly digest what is said in order that you may determine what people are driving at. Short fingers do not indicate hypersensitivity; as a rule, you are happy and lively companions. Your letters are marvels of brevity, as you have a great facility of saying much with little. This facility makes for excellent newspaper reporters or short-story writers. Such pronounced attributes need to be accompanied by great strength in order to give success. Short fingers are a fine possession if the proper qualities are behind them.

There is nothing little or mean about you. You are not cramped or dwarfed in your views. But with your abhorrence of detail, quickness of thought and action with impulse, hasty conclusions and great distaste for doing anything slowly, you are in constant danger of making mistakes as a result of a lack of deliberate and careful thought.

M-1.1 ADD FLABBY CONSISTENCY
You are lazy, which reduces the force of your qualities. You think quickly but, being lazy, do not act with the same speed. Only the mental indications of short fingers are called into play.

M-1.2 ADD SOFT CONSISTENCY
You are lazy, which reduces the force of your qualities. You think quickly but, being lazy, do not act with the same speed. Only the mental indications of short fingers are called into play. You are more active than those in M-1.1, but not intense.

M-1.3 ADD ELASTIC CONSISTENCY
Brings out fully the force of short-fingered qualities. Because an elastic hand implies intelligent energy, this is not a bad combination.

M-1.4 ADD HARD HANDS
Shows that the energy of an unelastic brain is pushing short-fingered qualities, but perhaps pushing them too much.

M-1.5   ADD FLEXIBILITY IN THE EXTREME

Adds elasticity of mind to short-fingered qualities, indicating a great adaptability to a large range and variety of subjects. This adds much to keenness but is likely, on account of the versatility and predisposition to extreme views that go along with short fingers, not to be a good combination. The boiler will surely burst.

M-1.6   ADD SPATULATE FINGERTIPS

Adds great activity and originality. Adds more calmness and common sense than any of the other elements.

M-1.7   ADD SQUARE FINGERTIPS

Short-fingered impetuosity is directed into more practical channels, making you less impressionable and less likely to "go off half-cocked."

M-1.8   ADD CONIC OR POINTED FINGERTIPS

The impractical view indicated by pointed fingertips lead you to be much more impulsive and quick, in which case you are in danger from an excess of your short-fingered qualities. Conic fingertips do not lead you into quite so great a danger, but still emphasize these qualities.

M-1.9   ADD KNOTTY FINGERS

These reduce the short-fingered qualities of quick thought and are in consequence excellent companions. The knotty qualities of analysis, if possessed by you, and the faculty of always having a reason for everything, check the impulsiveness that usually goes along with short fingers.

M-1.10   ADD 1ST KNOTS DEVELOPED

Adds to quickness of thought.

M-1.11   ADD 2ND KNOTS DEVELOPED

You are not so careless in your dress and surroundings.

M-1.12   ADD LONG 1ST PHALANGES

Adds quick thought to your mental world; possibly an early nervous problem. Common errors also result.

M-1.13   ADD SHORT 2ND PHALANGES

Quickness in assuming ideas and restlessness in the business field could cause social problems with employees. Quick answers could cause poor judgment.

M-1.14 ADD SHORT AND NARROW 3RD PHALANGES
Quick in thought; you misjudge common sense and get wrong impressions.

M-2 SHORT FINGERS WITH A CLEAR, DEEP AND WELL-CUT HEAD LINE
Does more to bring short fingers to perfection than any other factor.

N

DESCRIPTION "N": THE THUMB — *This is the fulcrum around which all the fingers revolve; in proportion to its strength or weakness, it maintains, enhances or detracts from the strength of other elements. The thumb alone can strongly contradict the other elements and can overpower or cancel some of them.*

N-1 LARGE THUMB
This shows that your mental strength and head guide you and that something pronounced may be expected. You naturally rule, and this is more certain if the thumb is at all coarse. It also indicates a love of history. You seek and enjoy useful, necessary and practical things.

N-1.1 ADD ANY KIND OF NAILS
This thumb adds determination to critical nails and makes them more critical. A strong thumb makes any type of nail stronger.

N-1.2 ADD KNOTTY FINGERS
Your desire to be analytical is increased and you are more painstaking in searching for truth.

N-1.3 ADD SMOOTH FINGERS
This thumb strengthens the indications of smooth fingers.

N-1.4 ADD SPATULATE OR SQUARE FINGERTIPS
This thumb pushes you to greater activity along practical lines.

N-1.5 ADD CONIC OR POINTED FINGERTIPS
This thumb decreases artistic qualities by making you more practical and more likely to accomplish something by exerting yourself.

N-1.6 ADD SHORT FINGERS
The large thumb adds quickness and determination to your short-fingered qualities.

N-1.7 IF A WOMAN

Women with this thumb love as truly as any but have regard for the bread-and-butter supply as well. The man you marry must be able to support you; if adversity comes you make the best of it, put on a brave front and help overcome the difficulty. You are ruled by your head and are strong.

N-1.8 ADD LONG FINGERS

You are more determined in the application of your qualities. You are a great lover of detail.

N-2 SMALL THUMB

Your thumb shows a weak character. You are guided by the heart and possess a lack of force. Your heart and sentiments rule; you are certain to be led. It also shows a love of romance. You appreciate only the beautiful, poetical, sentimental side; consequently you are not able to go into the world and hold your own.

N-2.1 ADD ANY NAIL TYPE

A weak thumb makes the effect of your nails weaker.

N-2.2 ADD KNOTTY FINGERS

Decreases other effects and allows many things to be taken for granted.

N-2.3 ADD SPATULATE OR SQUARE FINGERTIPS

You are a talker, not a doer.

N-2.4 ADD CONIC OR POINTED FINGERTIPS

You are a dreamer and averse to effort.

N-2.5 ADD SMOOTH FINGERS

Makes you act more by impulse; lends added artistic qualities.

N-2.6 ADD LONG FINGERS

You love detail but do not trouble to secure it.

N-2.7 ADD SHORT FINGERS

Reveals quickness and inspiration but not the force and practical application of your qualities.

N-2.8 IF A WOMAN

You marry for love and do not stop to think whether your lover can support you. You brave poverty and will marry a drunkard, thinking you can reform him. You are ruled by heart and sentiment.

N-3   THE THUMB AS A WHOLE
The thumb's indications are divided into mental and abstract worlds, indicated by the first and second phalanges.

N-4   HIGH-SET THUMB
You are bright and shrewd, but in an animal way.

N-5   LOW-SET THUMB
Your thumb indicates a nature full of the highest human qualities. It speaks of generosity, independence, love of liberty for yourself and others, sympathy for all who are in distress and a readiness to share with less fortunate brethren. While liberal and generous, you do not throw money away.

You are filled with the greatest strength of sympathy and generosity and are fired with warmth which, while it may not mean passion, reveals one who is not cold-blooded. If asked a favor, you grant it if at all possible. You do not give the cold response of a selfish person; having a feeling of common humanity, you do all you can.

N-6   THUMB IS LOW-SET AND LONG
Reveals power, determination and reason, which intensifies generous and sympathetic qualities.

N-7   THUMB IS LOW-SET AND SHORT
The setting of the thumb is good, but the thumb itself reveals selfishness. The good quality it indicates is independence, which comes from selfish motives.

N-8   MEDIUM-SET THUMB
You have well-balanced views, not prodigal yet not stingy and mean. You always listen to a reasonable appeal and respond in a sensible way. You are balanced, properly cautious, reasonably generous, dignified and responsive to approaches coming in sensible and reasonable ways. You do not overflow with sentiment, nor do you shut yourself off from your fellows; but in business, religion, love, home life, in fact, everywhere, you are a balanced, sensible person.

N-9   A STRAIGHT THUMB
You are a cautious person who will be afraid to say much because you fear people may presume on your acquaintance and ask some favor. You are closed and not easy to approach. You surround yourself with a wall which is difficult to scale.

You hold people at arm's length and are entirely lacking in independence,

201

narrow in your views, bigoted, and set in your ways. You do not impress others as being open or frank. You are secretive, neither giving nor inviting confidences; consequently you do not make many friends, nor do you seek them. You lack flexibility.

N-9.1 ADD SHORT, EXTREMELY SHORT OR FLAT BLUNT NAILS
You are mean and petty. Your thumb indicates a want of warmth and sympathy. You show caution, secretiveness, narrowness and unresponsiveness.

N-10 THUMB, SHAPE AS A WHOLE
Shows upon which plane the thumb qualities operate.

N-11 HEAVY, ELEMENTARY THUMB
Everything about this thumb speaks of heaviness, coarseness; the animal brute force in will, brute force in reasoning and brute passion in love. There is nothing elevating or uplifting about it; all is heavy, coarse and common, blunt, tactless and ignorant.

You walk over everyone you meet and care nothing for refinement of manner or speech, nor for the feelings of others. You are boorish and clownish even among those as coarse as yourself. You are the personification of ignorant obstinacy, operating in an unreasoning way.

N-12 A FLAT THUMB
You are nervous and show people the nervous force and energy which is proving too strong for you.

N-12.1 ADD SHORT FINGERS
Adds nervous excitement to a set of forces already too great, producing bad results.

N-13 A BROAD THUMB
Your thumb indicates a determination that accomplishes its objective and, rising over every obstacle, is pushy and aggressive but may easily be turned into violent obstinacy; often you need guidance to keep it within bounds.

N-14 ONE-THICKNESS THUMB
You will not wound the feelings of others, nor will you walk roughshod over anyone. With diplomatic mind and firm determination, instead of knocking people down you slip by them so easily that no one wishes to check you. You are refined, intelligent, with a kindly nature filling the lives of all around with beauty, yet having ample firmness of purpose. This thumb shows a refinement of will, intelligent reason, tact and perseverance.

N-15 THUMB, PHALANGES
The 1st phalange should generally be a little shorter than the 2nd. These two phalanges are called will and reason (logic).

N-16 THUMB, FIRST PHALANGE
Shows will, decisiveness and ability to command others.

N-17 THUMB, LONG 1ST PHALANGE
You are obstinate, tyrannical, despotic and, if crossed in the operation of your plans, will, with unreasoning stubbornness, fly into a temper. You are set and determined in your ways and make mistakes because you have allowed these qualities to rule reason. You are stubborn and cannot see that it is better to acknowledge and correct an error than to suffer the consequences of unreasonable obstinacy.

N-18 THUMB, EXTREMELY SHORT 1ST PHALANGE
You may be ruled by any person, no matter how ignorant. You are "weaker than water," easily discouraged, and stand no chance of being anything but a server. You sometimes show great stubbornness, especially if on your guard, but this display of will is spasmodic and weak.

N-19 THUMB, 2ND PHALANGE
Shows perception, judgment and reasoning faculties.

N-20 THUMB, LONG 2ND PHALANGE
You lack power to carry out ideas, determination to live up to intentions. You are always saying how government, business, religion and so on should be run, but do nothing to have your ideas carried out. You are a planner, not a doer. You must have some special ability if your determination is to bring success.

N-21 THUMB, 2ND PHALANGE MUCH LONGER THAN 1ST
You may be ruled by any person, no matter how ignorant, and go through life in easy toil for anyone who chooses to command you. You are "weaker than water," easily discouraged, and stand no chance of being anything but a server. You sometimes show great stubbornness, especially if on your guard, but this display of will is spasmodic and weak.

N-22 THUMB, BOTH PHALANGES SAME LENGTH
Your will and reason are strong, consequently your determination is the quiet strength that comes from good judgment; no bullying or tyranny. You have as much firmness and determination as is necessary, but it is controlled and operated by logic and reason. There is some weakness or fickleness present, but also the intelligent strength that marks a natural leader.

N-23 THUMB, LARGE 3RD PHALANGE
Shows love, sympathy and passion.

N-24 THE THUMB TIP
Shows an increase or decrease in strength, following the same formula as the tips of the fingers.

N-25 THE CONIC THUMB TIP
You are impressionable and do not have a strong will.

> *N-25.1* ADD LONG 1ST THUMB PHALANGE
> Your willpower is lessened by impulse, love of beauty and idealism. You are less tyrannical and despotic, and more easily influenced.

> *N-25.2* ADD EXTREMELY SHORT 1ST THUMB PHALANGE
> Your are hopelessly weak, shifting with every change of the wind; instability is your leading characteristic.

N-26 CONIC THUMB TIP BUT NO CONIC FINGERTIPS
Shows you are an artistic, impulsive, quick, intuitive person, to whom the beautiful and harmonious in all things appeals strongly, and who is very impressionable.

N-27 A SQUARE THUMB TIP
Shows that strength is added to a deficient will, common sense is added to normal development, and excessive will is more pronounced. If you have an excessive will, you are fanatical in your obstinacy.

N-28 SQUARE THUMB TIP BUT NO SQUARE FINGERTIPS
Your square thumb tip indicates regularity, order, system and arrangement in everything. To you, disorder, whether in the home, store or shop, is an abomination. You can be happy only when everything is well ordered, systematically arranged, done according to rules. "A place for everything and everything in its place" is your motto.

You think by rules, eat by rules, are never late to dinner, always on time at the office and insist that everyone else must be. You do the same things at the same hour each day and keep every appointment you make.

You retire and rise at an appointed time, and everything you do is governed by rules and systems. You are polite and a strict observer of social customs, and you resent people who break away from accustomed forms. You are skilled in games, perhaps a good shot, are careful in dress and methodical in everything you think or do.

N-28.1 ADD THUMB, LONG 1ST PHALANGE
Your willpower is strong and practical and you have common sense.

N-29 SPATULATE THUMB TIP
Reveals action, independence and originality.

N-30 SPATULATE THUMB TIP BUT NO SPATULATE FINGERTIPS
Reveals action, independence and originality. In your daily life you are constantly on the go. You inspire all about you with your wonderful enthusiasm and activity. You are fond of horses, dogs, in fact of all animals. You are a strong lover and are constant and true. There is little that is vacillating about you. You are real, earnest and practical.

N-30.1 ADD SHORT 1ST THUMB PHALANGE
Adds great strength to your will.

N-31 NORMAL 1ST THUMB PHALANGE
Adds originality and action to a normal will.

N-31.1 ADD LONG 1ST THUMB PHALANGE
Fire, action and ingenuity are added to an excessive will. This is a menace; it always endangers success.

N-32 WEAK OR STRONG 1ST THUMB PHALANGE
This is a benefit to those with a weak phalange and adds to the excesses of those with a strong phalange.

N-33 PADDLE-SHAPED THUMB
This thumb shows an exceedingly strong determination which, in the case of excessive development, degenerates into tyranny and obstinacy. An indication of a person with a strong mental will, who goes boldly through a trying emergency and then collapses after the strain is over.

N-34 CLUBBED THUMB
This thumb shows great obstinacy; on a poor hand it is a common grade of obstinacy, coupled with a violent temper. Whether these coarse and disagreeable qualities have, or ever will be, brought out is another question. We must not, however, ignore the fact that a mine lies beneath which takes only a match properly applied to explode it. These thumbs are largely hereditary and their presence, on any hand, can be traced back to some parental influence. There are cases in which they have been transmitted from generation to generation without harmful results.

N-34.1 ADD HARD HANDS, LONG 2ND PHALANGES AND SHORT FINGERS

This formation is not often seen on this type and is not normal. There is no fierceness or bloodthirsty desire for murder in this good character. If this person kills it is in a fit of jealousy or thwarted passion; such a person is a low specimen of the type.

If this thumb is seen on a refined subject, that person will find that the brutal tendencies are inherited, sometimes from generations back, and often never display themselves. These people never commit murder; they have too much kindness and sympathy. On low-type people there will be a strong secondary characteristic present, nearly as strong as this one, and it is from this secondary characteristic that comes the nerve and brutality to commit murder. The thumb supplies the passion and jealousy, the secondary characteristic the instinct to kill.

N-34.2 ADD SHORT FINGERS

Short fingers add obstinacy; the thumb increases the short-fingered qualities to an intolerable extreme.

N-34.3 ADD BIG "G" MOUNT, ETC.

This thumb undoubtedly indicates the brutal obstinacy, violent temper and low qualities characteristic of a murderer. Such a person is a danger, always shows terrific obstinacy if aroused, and has a brutal temper and a furious rage.

N-35 A LARGE THUMB JOINT

Indicates dilation of thought.

N-35.1 ADD LONG 1ST THUMB PHALANGE

Adds to analytical strength; also, there is less impulse.

N-35.2 ADD A CONIC THUMB TIP

Greatly strengthens willpower.

N-35.3 ADD ANY THUMB TIP

Adds force, originality, independence, action, common sense and willpower.

N-35.4 ADD VERY LONG 2ND THUMB PHALANGE

Adds to reasoning, making hasty decisions unlikely until thought and consideration have had a chance.

N-36 2ND THUMB PHALANGE
Indicates reasoning qualities, perception and judgment, plus logic and prudence.

N-36.1 ADD A STRAIGHT THUMB
Adds caution or prudence. In this case, prudence comes from a stingy tendency.

N-37 LONG 2ND THUMB PHALANGE
Shows strong powers of logic, quick perception and prudence. With these qualities you act from well-defined motives, know what you are doing, are sure of your opinion and expend yourself in beneficial ways. With this phalange there is never unreasoning obstinacy, but willpower guided by a reasoning brain.

N-37.1 ADD CONIC THUMB TIP
Strengthens impulsive ways, makes one less impressionable.

N-37.2 ADD SQUARE THUMB TIP
Adds sound practical judgment.

N-37.3 ADD SPATULATE THUMB TIP
You direct your energy into well-thought-out channels.

N-38 SHORT 2ND THUMB PHALANGE
You have an excess of ill-directed will, modified in cases where the second phalange is exceedingly waistlike.

N-38.1 ADD SHORT FINGERS
Your reasoning qualities are not less than those indicated by short fingers.

N-39 2ND THUMB PHALANGE SHORT AND THICK
You are stubborn and headstrong, acting without careful thought and making many mistakes which you are too stubborn to correct even though it is to your advantage to do so.

N-39.1 ADD CONIC THUMB TIP
Reveals weakness; an impressionable will, with lack of logic behind it, lessens your good thumb qualities.

N-39.2 ADD SQUARE THUMB TIP
You are a martinet who makes a poor attempt to show strength when there is only weakness.

N-39.3 ADD SPATULATE THUMB TIP

You are fussy without producing tangible results; you worry as well as irritate yourself by foolish restlessness. Your deficient logic will ruin you.

N-40 2ND THUMB PHALANGE EXCEEDINGLY SHORT

Reveals a weakening of all qualities.

N-40.1 ADD LONG 1ST THUMB PHALANGE

Your will, if strong, runs rampant for want of direction.

N-40.2 ADD SQUARE OR CONIC THUMB TIP

You spend all of your force in brushing clothing, dusting the room or cleaning up the desk. You would rather see things in order than see much accomplished; you become the plaything of anyone who chooses to lead you.

N-41 FLAT AND FLABBY 2ND THUMB PHALANGE

This thumb indicates weakness of constitution and vitality. You may have knowledge, but not the physical strength required to make logic operative. There is a lessening of all qualities.

N-41.1 ADD HEAVY ELEMENTARY THUMB

Shows elementary reasoning, the brutal, common point of view.

N-41.2 ADD FINE TEXTURE

You have refined logic; you think in a fine, delicate way, and lose no element of strength by this fineness. You reason and plan how to gain your ends tactfully.

N-42 NEGATIVE THOUGHTS

A poorly shaped thumb is much more to be feared than the elementary thumb, not because of any physical danger, but because of the clever and adroit direction it can give to your will. In this case it indicates the crafty, fox-like, designing villain.

N-43 POSITIVE THOUGHTS

If the shape of your thumb is pleasing, this is one of the best indications to be found.

N-44 WAIST-LIKE 2ND THUMB PHALANGE

This is the sign of a brilliant, tactful nature. You do everything in an adroit and diplomatic way and have the faculty of approaching people in the right manner. You never "rub people the wrong way" but seem to know how to gain ends by pleasant means. You are pleasant to meet because you do not always step on people's toes.

N-45 SHAPES OF THUMB PHALANGES
Shows good muscular strength and robustness of reasoning faculties.

N-46 A MERELY BROAD THUMB PHALANGE
You have healthy views and, while vigorous and strong, are not coarse.

> *N-46.1* ADD WAIST-LIKE 2ND THUMB PHALANGE
> Shows great determination coupled with tactful reasoning qualities, reducing the brutality of an aggressive person but not lessening aggression; willpower will be just as great but is governed by good reasoning, power and tact.

> *N-46.2* ADD SQUARE THUMB TIP
> You are practical and, with a good first phalange, determined.

> *N-46.3* ADD CONIC THUMB TIP
> This shape is a rarity, indicating a healthy outlook in all ways.

N-47 THE SUPPLE THUMB
You are a spendthrift, brilliant, versatile, easily adapting yourself to changing circumstances. You are at home anywhere, sentimental, generous and sympathetic, will give your last cent to a beggar, are improvident, and do not lay up for a "rainy day."

You are emotional, consequently extremist; you are up one day, in the depths the next. This comes from great versatility and from the fact that your brilliant qualities enable you to do so many things. You are a plodder but, by brilliant dashes, achieve your successes. Never satisfied to be led, you aspire to surpass your brethren and as a rule you find no trouble in doing so. You are talented and versatile.

> *N-47.1* ADD SQUARE THUMB TIP AND GOOD HEAD LINE
> Does more than any other combination to hold you in balance.

> *N-47.2* ADD SPATULATE THUMB TIP
> Spatulate originality will not help you; you need sobering qualities.

> *N-47.3* ADD CONIC THUMB TIP
> Conic impulse will not help you; you need sobering qualities.

N-48 THE STIFF THUMB
You are practical, have common sense, are economical, stingy, and weigh everything carefully. You possess a strong will and stubborn determination, are cautious and reserved, and do not give or invite confidence. You save your money and plod along.

You are steady, not extremist, do not expect a great deal, and are consequently not disappointed when you do not receive much. You enjoy life in a quiet fashion. You cannot do many things, but what you do attempt is done well. You are not erratic but stick to one thing, commanding respect by your strength of purpose.

You have a sense of justice and great self-control. You are quiet, cautious, economical, practical and reliable, not attracting attention, yet possessing many qualities which command respect.

N-48.1 ADD COARSE TEXTURE
Lowers the quality of all of the stiff thumb's attributes and produces a mean, stingy, hard-hearted person.

P

DESCRIPTION "P": FINGER STANCE—*Every finger leaning towards another gives up some of its strength to the finger towards which it leans.*

P-1 1ST (INDEX) FINGER IS ERECT
Reveals an efficient and confident person.

P-2 1ST FINGER LEANS TO 2ND
Ambition denoted by the 1st finger combines with wisdom to help you reach a new high, decreasing your tendency to sadness.

P-3 2ND FINGER IS ERECT
Denotes constant awareness of responsibilities.

P-4 2ND FINGER LEANS TO 1ST
You are wise and cautious as a leader.

P-5 2ND FINGER LEANS TO 3RD
Some soberness is drawn towards this character type, making you quiet and careful.

P-6 3RD FINGER IS ERECT
Emphasizes qualities needed for success, for good health, for a happy disposition and to be dashing.

P-7 3RD FINGER LEANS TO 2ND
Gives off some of its brightness and happiness to the melancholy person. Thus you are less somber, sad and severe.

P-8   3RD FINGER LEANS TO 4TH
Tinges you with love of beauty, artistic sense and brilliance.

P-9   4TH FINGER IS ERECT
You possess business skills, shrewdness and a scientific turn of mind.

P-10   4TH FINGER LEANS TO 3RD
You are shrewd in business and have abilities in the sciences.

Q

DESCRIPTION "Q": THE APEX—*These are the swirls under each of the fingers in the palm of the hand.*

Q-1   1ST APEX IS CENTERED
The qualities of ambition, leadership, religious beliefs, love of nature, good health and happy disposition are evenly distributed.

Q-2   1ST APEX LEANS OUTWARDS
Your qualities are directed towards seeking purely selfish, personal advancement.

Q-3   1ST APEX LEANS TO 2ND
Sobriety, sadness and wisdom hold ambition in check and make it safer, for you are guided by the 2nd apex. This decreases sadness and gives your life meaning.

Q-4   1ST APEX NEAR THE TOP
Your may have an ambition to gain distinction in a literary career. You tend towards mental work but you show your love of rule and leadership even in the choice of subjects for your writings. Intuition and religion are strong.

Q-5   1ST APEX NEAR THE BASE
You lead in business and the affairs of the commercial world. You pay practical affairs much attention, for you want to lead in money-making areas.

Q-6   1ST APEX NEAR THE HEART LINE
Your ambition and pride is for those whom you love.

Q-7   1ST APEX NEAR THE HEAD LINE
Your ambition is for intellectual success.

Q-8   2ND APEX IS CENTERED
All interest is centered in yourself and you are not influenced by other characteristics.

Q-9   2ND APEX LEANS TO 1ST
Wisdom is added to your ambitions, pride, and love of command, and the severity of your morbidness is diminished, for you give yourself over to other characteristics.

Q-10 2ND APEX LEANS TO 3RD
The severity of your morbidness is diminished, for you give yourself over to other characteristics. This lends soberness and wisdom to your qualities, making you more grave and serious, and less spontaneous.

Q-11 2ND APEX NEAR THE TOP
You are not business-minded. You write learned books, make a good teacher, but are not a money-maker.

Q-12 2ND APEX NEAR THE BASE
Grosser qualities are added to this character type and could make you a bad person.

Q-13 3RD APEX IS CENTERED
Your focus is on making other people feel comfortable.

Q-14 3RD APEX LEANS TO 2ND
Brightness and happiness is added to a melancholy character. Thus you are less somber, sad and severe, but your brightness and happiness could diminish as soberness and sadness dampen your spirits.

Q-15 3RD APEX LEANS TO 4TH
Brightness and happiness is added to shrewdness, tinging you with a love of beauty, artistic sense and brilliance.

Q-16 3RD APEX NEAR THE TOP
Your mind rules, whether it be in literature, art, poetry, drawing, architecture or kindred subjects.

Q-17 3RD APEX NEAR THE BASE
You are ruled by the baser instincts, are commoner in your tastes, and are fond of show.

Q-18 4TH APEX IS CENTERED
You develop normally and you have true business ideas in any sphere of life in which you are placed.

Q-19 4TH APEX LEANS TO 3RD
You are shrewd in business and scientific endeavors. Your love of art and beauty is great and you give up some of your qualities to enjoy them. Your life is less dominated by shrewdness and more given over to instincts (to be dashing, successful, and to have good health and a happy disposition).

Q-20 4TH APEX LEANS OUTWARDS
You employ your aptitudes for your own advantage and are selfishly inclined.

Q-21 4TH APEX NEAR THE TOP
Your mind rules and your quickness and shrewdness make you a winner in anything you do, with lots of enemies, for you do not recognize anything that is material.

Q-22 4TH APEX NEAR THE BASE
You do not appreciate anything you do for yourself, nor anything anybody does for you.

Q-23 4TH APEX CENTERED; 1ST, 2ND AND 3RD LEAN TO 4TH
You are shrewd in business and scientific endeavors.

R

DESCRIPTION "R": THE MOUNTS — *These help us to determine the strongest character traits.*

R-1 A LARGE "A" MOUNT
A large Mount under the 1st finger. Indicates generosity, enthusiasm, desire for power and ambition.

R-2 A LARGE "B" MOUNT
A large Mount under the 2nd finger. You are able to use the stabilizing influence of your character without being weighed down or slowed to a stop. There is prudence and earnestness in matters undertaken, and a taste for those pursuits connected with the earth and the study of curious sciences.

R-3 A LARGE "C" MOUNT
A large Mount under the 3rd finger. This indicates a person with a large ego, one who seeks constant reassurance and encouragement from others. In

situations where there is an audience or large group to supply this feedback, such as teaching or performing, this trait may inspire constant growth and improvement.

R-4 A LARGE "D" MOUNT

A large Mount under the 4th finger. One of your chief elements is success based on your ability to judge human nature and character. You have a love of study, especially scientific investigation. You are a born mathematician and no problem is so intricate that you cannot solve it. You are, of all the character types, the most successful as a physician. Energy, studiousness and scientific aptitude, combined with keenness in judging human nature, can make you an excellent diagnostician and practitioner.

R-5 A LARGE "E" MOUNT

All or some of the "E" Mount is large. This indicates the two kinds of fighters: aggressors who force the issue and those who act in self-defense or resist the pressure brought to bear upon them. The upper "E" Mount indicates resistance and the lower "E" Mount shows aggressive spirit. Often, one of these Mounts is large and the other small, in which case you have either great aggression or great resistance, according to whichever Mount is larger. Sometimes both Mounts are highly developed. In this case there is a large supply of both aggression and resistance.

Such people push forward with great persistence and resist vigorously all attempts to impose upon them. People with both Mounts large surmount every obstacle and stubbornly resist any attempt to force them down. They never know when they are beaten and permit no one to think that their defeat is a possibility. The plain of the "E" Mount, if greatly developed, indicates a sudden temper. This development, with the other two Mounts large, makes for a dangerous combination, for it adds inflammability to an already great aggression and resistance.

The hollow palm is to be found in the hands of very successful people. A person with only the upper "E" Mount developed will not force a conflict, will not hunt strife, but will resist opposition and overcome oppression. Under all circumstances such people are cool, collected, calm, do not lose their heads, are equal to emergencies and do not get discouraged if things go against them. They do not give up fighting even when their chances seem slim, and when knocked down they rise again, seemingly unaware of the possibility of defeat. This power often produces success despite all obstacles.

Those with a larger lower "E" Mount push their plans to the fullest extent, not stopping to consider other people; they force themselves over and through all opposition, with "hammer and tongs" if necessary. They seek and enjoy strife and are full of aggression. A person with the lower Mount strong and the upper Mount absent will be a great bluffer but, not having resistance, will back down easily if pressed. The typical character is either the aggressor, the resister, or a combination of the two.

R-6   A LARGE "F" MOUNT
You express yourself well and enjoy the pleasures of imagination. If your "E" Mount is excessive, you easily become flighty, imaginative to a dangerous degree, and even lose control of the mind entirely, becoming insane. These are two well-developed and excessive characters.

R-7   A LARGE "G" MOUNT
Denotes strong passions for the opposite sex, inconstancy, and love of material pleasures.

R-8   A SMOOTH, ORDINARY "A" MOUNT
Your "A" Mount is normal or ordinary in its effect.

R-9   A SMOOTH, ORDINARY "B" MOUNT
Your "B" Mount is normal or ordinary in its effect.

R-10   A SMOOTH, ORDINARY "C" MOUNT
Your "C" Mount is normal or ordinary in its effect.

R-11   A SMOOTH, ORDINARY "D" MOUNT
Your "D" Mount is normal or ordinary in its effect.

R-12   A SMOOTH, ORDINARY "E" MOUNT
You say what is on your mind, even if you know it will provoke a fight. You are aggressive and go after what you want in life.

R-13   A SMOOTH, ORDINARY "F" MOUNT
Shows the presence of a healthy imagination, one which lifts the world above the plane of materialism into the realm of fancy.

R-14   A SMOOTH, ORDINARY "G" MOUNT
Indicates a love of flowers, music, form, color, paintings, etc., but not a strong sexual passion. It also indicates affection, sympathy and benevolence, a desire to be agreeable, a love of the beautiful and of melody in music; always found in the hands of talented singers and artists.

R-15   A DEPRESSED "A" MOUNT
Shows selfishness and want of self-respect.

R-16 A DEPRESSED "B" MOUNT
Could indicate an insignificant life. Shows selfishness and want of self-respect.

R-17 A DEPRESSED "C" MOUNT
Could indicate a material existence. Shows selfishness and want of self-respect.

R-18 A DEPRESSED "D" MOUNT
Shows selfishness and want of self-respect.

R-19 A DEPRESSED "E" MOUNT
Denotes want of power of resistance, both in body and mind. Absence of the lower "E" Mount allows those much inferior in ability to push past you by sheer force of aggression. Absence of the upper "E" Mount and side of the hand indicates that you are easily discouraged, give up quickly when hard pressed, and lack resistance.

In moments of danger you become excited and, when knocked down, do not rise, believing it is no use to try anymore. Absence of the middle "E" Mount shows that you seek peace at all costs. You may have many talents, but avoid competitive situations. If you are to succeed, you need a push.

R-20 A DEPRESSED "F" MOUNT
Tells of the presence of a healthy imagination, one which lifts the world above the plane of materialism into the realm of fancy.

R-21 A DEPRESSED "G" MOUNT
Indicates coldness, apathy, selfishness and want of self-respect.

R-22 1 TO 3 VERTICAL LINES ON A BIG "A" MOUNT
Indicates success as a leader.

R-23 1 TO 3 VERTICAL LINES ON A BIG "B" MOUNT
Success is derived later in life from serious studies and applied talent.

R-24 1 TO 3 VERTICAL LINES ON A BIG "C" MOUNT
Denotes success in the creative arts in later life.

R-25 1 TO 3 VERTICAL LINES ON A BIG "D" MOUNT
These are the marks of success in business.

R-26 1 TO 3 VERTICAL LINES ON A BIG "E" MOUNT
Indicates success as a leader. Vertical lines reinforce the Mounts. One vertical line is stronger than three vertical lines. Aggressive courage.

R-27 1 TO 3 VERTICAL LINES ON A BIG "F" MOUNT
Indicates success as a leader, but you could be influenced to become evil-minded. Vertical lines reinforce the Mounts. One vertical line is stronger than three vertical lines.

R-28 1 TO 3 VERTICAL LINES ON A BIG "G" MOUNT
Indicates success as a leader; you are greatly dependent on affection.

R-29 A TRIDENT ON A BIG "A" MOUNT
This is a reinforcing sign at all times. A rare mark, and always a good one. It must be perfectly formed in order to give its full meaning.

R-30 A TRIDENT ON A BIG "B" MOUNT
You are lucky in career matters, reaching personal goals, gaining special attention and consideration, and accomplishing big things. You are fortunate in games of chance.

R-31 A TRIDENT ON A BIG "C" MOUNT
Adds strength, increasing your brilliance and chance of success.

R-32 A TRIDENT ON A BIG "D" MOUNT
This is a reinforcing sign at all times. A rare mark, and always a good one. It must be perfectly formed in order to give its full meaning.

R-33 A TRIDENT ON A BIG "E" MOUNT
You are lucky in career matters, reaching personal goals, gaining special attention and consideration, and accomplishing big things. You are fortunate in games of chance.

R-34 A TRIDENT ON A BIG "F" MOUNT
Your destiny may include an inheritance, public appearances, profits related to the sea, and luck in matters having to do with homes and property.

R-35 A TRIDENT ON A BIG "G" MOUNT
You receive many gifts and favors, are considered beautiful and attract money (the Midas touch).

R-36 A PERFECT STAR ON A BIG "A" MOUNT
Wherever placed, this is a reinforcing sign at all times. It is sometimes a good indication, sometimes bad, depending entirely on its location.

R-37 A PERFECT STAR ON A BIG "B" MOUNT
This is a negative sign. The fatalism indicated becomes very pronounced since the star is a strengthening mark. You are a leader, but fate opposes you.

Your genius is ultimately destroyed. This could also indicate a fatality in connection with a crime.

R-38   A PERFECT STAR ON A BIG "C" MOUNT
Shows a life ending in brilliance. Tells of wealth without satisfaction.

R-39   A PERFECT STAR ON A BIG "D" MOUNT
Tells of brilliance and success in science, late in life. You achieve success in business, science or eloquence, but such success is most often the result of chance, a prominence through lucky accidents. This mark is found on great scientists who ultimately gain recognition. These people are always appreciated within their circle, but universal recognition comes late.

R-40   A PERFECT STAR ON A BIG "E" MOUNT
Could show danger or military honors late in life. This is positive (aggressive) if the lower "E" Mount is large, passive (defensive) if the upper "E" Mount is large.

R-41   A PERFECT STAR ON A BIG "F" MOUNT
This is a sign of excessive or supreme imagination. The star denotes the border line between imaginative genius and insanity. In a literary hand it is the sign of a great fiction writer; in a musical hand it is the sign of a great composer.

R-42   A PERFECT STAR ON A BIG "G" MOUNT
This is the star of conquering love. The greatest lovers, the sex conquerors, the unopposed Don Juans, women who seduce all men, bear this mark. This power is devastating in a bad hand; the toll is in human souls and lives.

R-43   A TRIANGLE ON A BIG "A" MOUNT
The character mark of the great organizer, the highly successful leader. Tells of lofty ambitions in the mental realm.

R-44   A TRIANGLE ON A BIG "B" MOUNT
You are lucky in career matters, reaching personal goals, gaining special attention and consideration, and accomplishing big things. You are fortunate in games of chance. Indicates talent for mystical work.

R-45   A TRIANGLE ON A BIG "C" MOUNT
Tells of well-directed artistic abilities.

R-46   A TRIANGLE ON A BIG "D" MOUNT
Your destiny may include an inheritance, public appearances, profits related

to the sea, and luck in matters having to do with homes and property. Indicates great skills in science, business or politics.

R-47   A TRIANGLE ON A BIG "E" MOUNT
You have great courage and knowledge of warfare and exploration. A large lower "E" Mount indicates generosity to one's enemies; you achieve success by bravely surmounting difficulties. If the plain of the "E" Mount is large, you have an aggressive character; if small, you go with the tide.

R-48   A TRIANGLE ON A BIG "F" MOUNT
Shows brilliant imagination used practically.

R-49   A TRIANGLE ON A BIG "G" MOUNT
You receive many gifts and favors, are considered beautiful and attract money (the Midas touch). Shows great prudence and calculation in matters of the affections.

R-50   A CIRCLE ON A BIG "A" MOUNT
Indicates that you are protected by people in high places, or held back and limited because of your choice of friends or associates.

R-51   A CIRCLE ON A BIG "B" MOUNT
Indicates support, encouragement, even special assistance from others concerning career matters or social position.

R-52   A CIRCLE ON A BIG "C" MOUNT
Shows that you could have increasing difficulties with the eyes. The circle could also mean success in life.

R-53   A CIRCLE ON A BIG "D" MOUNT
Indicates strong resistance to illness and disease. You may be involved with storing, withholding or compiling information. You are associated with names, titles, methods of identification.

R-54   A CIRCLE ON A BIG "E" MOUNT
Such marks emphasize a tendency towards trouble with the eyes, but they are not seen on the hands of all who are blind, have poor vision or weak eyes.

R-55   A CIRCLE ON A BIG "F" MOUNT
You are associated with homes and dwelling places, containers, enclosures, protective coverings.

R-56   A CIRCLE ON A BIG "G" MOUNT
Shows that you could have increasing difficulties with the eyes.

R-57   A SQUARE ON A BIG "A" MOUNT

Indicates that the poor qualities of the Mount do not predominate. A square is always a mark of preservation, but when placed on a Mount it indicates that you were or will be in danger of ruin, but will pull through.

R-58   A SQUARE ON A BIG "B" MOUNT

A square is always a mark of preservation, but on a Mount it indicates that you were or will be in danger of ruin, but will pull through. Generally a safety mark against fatality.

R-59   A SQUARE ON A BIG "C" MOUNT

A square is always a mark of preservation, but on a Mount it indicates that you were or will be in danger of ruin, but will pull through. A protection against failure.

R-60   A SQUARE ON A BIG "D" MOUNT

Indicates preservation from danger brought on by the restlessness of your temperament.

R-61   A SQUARE ON A BIG "E" MOUNT

Indicates preservation from danger and protection from anger.

R-62   A SQUARE ON A BIG "F" MOUNT

Indicates preservation from danger.

R-63   A SQUARE ON A BIG "G" MOUNT

Denotes preservation from trouble brought on by passion.

R-64   A CROSS ON A BIG "A" MOUNT

Shows difficulties concerning education or advancement. You may be manipulated or taken advantage of by people in high places. A cross on the Mount can also indicate marriage.

R-65   A CROSS ON A BIG "B" MOUNT

Indicates an association with matters related to violence, cruelty or extreme hardship (but not necessarily as perpetrator or victim). Because of its reputation as a warning of violence, this has been referred to as the "mark of the scaffold."

R-66   A CROSS ON A BIG "C" MOUNT

Indicates complications in the presentation of personal products, reaching personal goals, self-expression and self-satisfaction. Denotes disappointment in carrying out an artistic career without success.

R-67 A CROSS ON A BIG "D" MOUNT
Indicates difficulties concerning legal matters. There is the possibility of confusion or misinformation concerning medical care or diagnosis, and an association with gossip or slander.

R-68 A CROSS ON A BIG "E" MOUNT
Indicates danger or difficulties caused by a reckless or careless attitude, or danger from your quarrelsome nature.

R-69 A CROSS ON A BIG "F" MOUNT
Could indicate kidney trouble, possibly threatening your life. Also indicates exaggeration, no respect for the truth.

R-70 A CROSS ON A BIG "G" MOUNT
Indicates misfortune caused by greed or vanity. There may be an attack on your public image.

R-71 A GRILLE ON A BIG "A" MOUNT
Denotes snobbery or excessive pride.

R-72 A GRILLE ON A BIG "B" MOUNT
Gives a strong indication of a gruesome or morbid outlook.

R-73 A GRILLE ON A BIG "C" MOUNT
Indicates conceit. This is a hindrance to all forms of success, not only in the arts. It shows folly and the vain desire for glory and show.

R-74 A GRILLE ON A BIG "D" MOUNT
A block to an active, extroverted character. You have a volatile, pseudo-businesslike manner. You cheat yourself and others, usually involuntarily.

R-75 A GRILLE ON A BIG "E" MOUNT
This is not a good sign. It indicates health defects, depending on your character. Denotes superstition, egotism and overbearing pride.

R-76 A GRILLE ON A BIG "F" MOUNT
Could indicate kidney trouble, possibly threatening your life. Shows a worrying tendency, discontent.

R-77 A GRILLE ON A BIG "G" MOUNT
Indicates passion. If you are a woman, you are strongly attracted to the opposite sex, even as much as a man would be with a similar Mount. If you are a man, you possess a grade of femininity equal to that of women, resulting in this character type becoming dangerous in his tendencies, for he

has the power to attract without a woman's ability to resist. Not a good sign, denoting lasciviousness and morbidity.

R-78 A CROSSBAR ON A BIG "A" MOUNT
This indicates a blocked condition in which leadership qualities are negated. It indicates a character trait that makes leadership unwanted or impossible. It is also seen in the hands of people who do not want to follow a political or religious dictum.

R-79 A CROSSBAR ON A BIG "B" MOUNT
Brings out the bad side of a character, such as health defects.

R-80 A CROSSBAR ON A BIG "C" MOUNT
Indicates health defects.

R-81 A CROSSBAR ON A BIG "D" MOUNT
Indicates health defects.

R-82 A CROSSBAR ON A BIG "E" MOUNT
Indicates health defects.

R-83 A CROSSBAR ON A BIG "F" MOUNT
Indicates health defects.

R-84 A CROSSBAR ON A BIG "G" MOUNT
Indicates health defects.

R-85 AN ISLAND ON A BIG "A" MOUNT
Indicates that you are protected by people in high places, or held back and limited because of your choice of friends or associates.

R-86 AN ISLAND ON A BIG "B" MOUNT
Indicates support, encouragement, even special assistance from others concerning career matters or social position. It can also show misfortune due to illness.

R-87 AN ISLAND ON A BIG "C" MOUNT
Could show increasing difficulties with the eyes.

R-88 AN ISLAND ON A BIG "D" MOUNT
Shows strong resistance to illness and disease. You may be involved with withholding, storing or compiling information. You are associated with names, titles, methods of identification.

R-89 AN ISLAND ON A BIG "E" MOUNT
Could show increasing difficulties with the eyes.

R-90 AN ISLAND ON A BIG "F" MOUNT
Indicates an association with homes and dwelling places, containers, enclosures, protective coverings.

R-91 AN ISLAND ON A BIG "G" MOUNT
Could show increasing difficulties with the eyes. Also shows a person who is very susceptible to love affairs.

R-92 DOTS OR SPOTS ON A BIG "A" MOUNT
A bad sign, bringing out the bad side of your character. If blue or dark, it denotes a bad matrimonial choice. A misfortune, loss of name or position.

R-93 DOTS OR SPOTS ON A BIG "B" MOUNT
A blue or dark dot on the Mount denotes a bad matrimonial choice.

R-94 DOTS OR SPOTS ON A BIG "C" MOUNT
A bad sign, bringing out the bad side of your character. Shows loss of position. If blue or dark, it denotes a bad matrimonial choice.

R-95 DOTS OR SPOTS ON A BIG "D" MOUNT
A bad sign, bringing out the bad side of your character. Shows loss of position. If blue or dark, it denotes a bad matrimonial choice. Trouble in business.

R-96 DOTS OR SPOTS ON A BIG "E" MOUNT
A bad sign, bringing out the bad side of your character. Shows loss of position. If blue or dark, it denotes a bad matrimonial choice. Accidents through fights.

R-97 DOTS OR SPOTS ON A BIG "F" MOUNT
A bad sign, bringing out the bad side of your character. Shows loss of position. If blue or dark, it denotes a bad matrimonial choice. An ailment of the nervous system.

R-98 DOTS OR SPOTS ON A BIG "G" MOUNT
A spot, dark blue or black, shows disease of a nervous character; blue denotes poisoning of some kind. The dot is also a bad sign, bringing out the bad side of your character. Shows loss of position. You are deserted in love or have unhappy love affairs.

R-99 AN IMPERFECT STAR ON A BIG "A" MOUNT
Shows difficulties concerning education or advancement. You may be manipulated or taken advantage of by people in high places.

R-100 AN IMPERFECT STAR ON A BIG "B" MOUNT
Indicates that you are associated with matters related to violence, cruelty or extreme hardship (but not necessarily as perpetrator or victim). Because of its reputation as a warning of violence, this has been referred to as the "mark of the scaffold."

R-101 AN IMPERFECT STAR ON A BIG "C" MOUNT
Shows complications in the presentation of personal products, reaching personal goals, self-expression and self-satisfaction.

R-102 AN IMPERFECT STAR ON A BIG "D" MOUNT
Shows difficulties concerning legal matters. There is a possibility of confusion or misinformation concerning medical care or diagnosis, and an association with gossip or slander.

R-103 AN IMPERFECT STAR ON A BIG "E" MOUNT
Tells of danger or difficulties caused by a reckless or careless attitude.

R-104 AN IMPERFECT STAR ON A BIG "F" MOUNT
Could indicate kidney trouble, possibly threatening your life.

R-105 AN IMPERFECT STAR ON A BIG "G" MOUNT
Could tell of misfortune caused by greed or vanity. Your public image may be attacked.

R-106 MORE THAN 3 VERTICAL LINES ON A BIG "A" MOUNT
Your hopes will be realized.

R-107 MORE THAN 3 VERTICAL LINES ON A BIG "B" MOUNT
Means a lack of success late in life.

R-108 MORE THAN 3 VERTICAL LINES ON A BIG "C" MOUNT
Means you may have too many ideas for your own good.

R-109 MORE THAN 3 VERTICAL LINES ON A BIG "D" MOUNT
Means a scheming nature, scientific tastes.

R-110 MORE THAN 3 VERTICAL LINES ON A BIG "E" MOUNT
Means you could have a violent temper.

R-111 MORE THAN 3 VERTICAL LINES ON A BIG "F" MOUNT
Means you are changeable in love, imaginative, and have a tendency to dream; you suffer insomnia or nightmares.

R-112 MORE THAN 3 VERTICAL LINES ON A BIG "G" MOUNT
Means you could have a passionate disposition.

S

DESCRIPTION "S": CHARACTER OF THE LINES

S-1.1 This refers to their clearness, depth and evenness, unspoiled by broad, shallow or poorly colored lines.

S-1.2 MULTIPLICITY OF LINES
You are an intensely nervous person who is prey to innumerable conflicting emotions which lead you aimlessly in all directions. You have great mental anxiety about your surroundings and self; a highly nervous temperament.

S-1.3 CLEARLY CUT AND DEEP LINES
These lines show vigor and strength, steadiness of purpose, evenness of temper. You are a person who, while you may encounter many difficulties, overcomes them.

S-1.4 SMALL HANDS, LARGE LINES
You have too much energy for safety.

S-1.5 BROAD, SHALLOW, POORLY COLORED LINES
Shows weakness, vacillation and discouragement. You generally achieve few results, gained only after great effort and with strong outside influences to spur you on.

S-1.6 LARGE HANDS WITH TINY, NARROW LINES
You are not capable of carrying any great responsibility or handling emotional problems. A disaster in some form could follow.

T

DESCRIPTION "T": THE HEART LINE

T-1.1   The Heart line reveals not only muscular, vital strength and the action of the heart itself but, as a result of these conditions, the strength and character of the affections.

T-2.1   HEART LINE ABSENT
This indicates a lack of sympathy. Such people are cold-blooded and selfish; they desire personal success even at the expense of others. It is a bad sign; such people move easily from mere selfishness into hypocrisy, deceit, lack of candor and dishonesty. If this does not describe you now, it will in your ending years.

T-3   HEART LINE: ITS STARTING POINT

T-3.1   Reflects early years in life. Your love is ideal, and love comes your way even if you live in poverty.

T-3.2   Reflects early years in life. You possess common sense and maintain a practical "middle ground" with the affections; you are not carried away with sentiment, but view love from a practical standpoint. You are not "soft" or "spongy," but are inclined to think that love in a cottage without plenty of bread and butter is a myth. You are never carried away by sentiment and, while strong in affection, are sensible and not foolish.

T-3.3   Reflects early years in life. This line shows sensuality in the affections; your feelings of love are tinged with the idea of pleasures from sexual relations. This indication is all the more certain if combined with a large "G" Mount. You have physical desires, and physical strength sufficient to satisfy them. You are not particularly demonstrative, but passionate and selfish.

T-3.4   Reflects early years in life. Resentment, common sense or passion is the strongest force. This always produces an affectionate person who has a warm heart and loves friends, relatives and mankind in general. Your danger is too much heart, and you do not always look after your own interests when considering those of others. This may also indicate an increased sentimentality. You are successful, for you have many friends.

T-3.5   Reflects early years in life. You allow your affections to rule your interests.

T-3.6   Reflects early years in life. Shows that head has control of heart and completely dominates it. This is especially true if other marks point this way.

T-3.7   Reflects early years in life. There is a continual struggle between the heart and head for supremacy, with the chances in favor of the head since the Heart line takes its source from the Head line. In this case, the Head line takes control of the Heart line.

T-3.8   Reflects early years in life. Indicates an added exuberance and generosity. You are an extremely affectionate, outgoing personality who basically loves people and enjoys making them happy. It is sometimes difficult for you to be tied to one love object, especially since you seem to remain attractive and sexually appealing even as you grow older. This also often indicates a great love of children and young people.

T-3.9   Reflects early years in life. You are very careful and selective when it comes to affairs of the heart. You are less sure of yourself emotionally and are not apt to take too many risks in this area. You tend to limit your own love nature, channeling all your love to a few chosen individuals and expecting whole-hearted devotion in return. Your nature is passionate and generous but also jealous and possessive. You are the "strong, silent type"; your feelings are intense, but you are hesitant to express yourself emotionally for fear of being thought weak or appearing vulnerable.

You are attractive sexually, with lots of animal magnetism or a certain mysterious aura. However, you are not always physically or emotionally responsive to others and certainly are not open or obvious about your feelings.

T-3.10   Reflects early years in life. You remain tied to your family and early beginnings, rarely (if ever) developing an independent personal life. The early objects of your affection remain prominent throughout your life. While your personality is not lacking in warmth and affection, it often tends to be emotionally immature.

T-3.11   Reflects early years in life. You were prone to serious illnesses or accidents in your early years.

T-3.12   Reflects early years in life. You have too much pride, too much enthusiasm. You are blind to the faults of others and, though you can be trusted, you are not able to help yourself or others in the event of a real problem. You get hurt easily.

T-3.13 Reflects early years in life. This is a sign of extreme and brutal jealousy caused by excessive passion; a potentially violent person.

T-3.14 Reflects early years in life. You have an advantage, promising happiness and worldly success.

T-3.15 Reflects early years in life. This mark denotes good luck.

T-4 HEART LINE: ITS LENGTH

T-4.1 This abrupt termination of the Heart line means either that the heart will stop beating or that from this age onwards you have little heart or affection for others.

T-4.2 You have too much heart and allow sentiment to guide you in everything. In business you do not choose employees because they are best fitted to do their work but because "they need a job." You are easily jealous, love much and suffer if you do not get much in return.

T-5 HEART LINE: ITS COURSE

T-5.1 Reflects middle years in life. You are attracted to the type of person who has the qualities of soberness, wisdom, sadness, superstition, gloom, balance and brilliance, who has artistic tendencies, is dashing and successful, and has good health and a happy disposition. The Heart line indicates the age at which this occurs.

T-5.2 Reflects middle years in life. You are attracted to a person who has the qualities of soberness, wisdom, sadness, superstition and gloom, and is balanced.

T-5.3 Reflects middle years in life. You are attracted to a person who is brilliant, artistic, dashing, happy and successful, with good health and a happy disposition.

T-5.4 Reflects middle years in life. You are attracted to a person who is shrewd and industrious, has a scientific turn of mind, has business abilities and is quick.

T-5.5 Reflects middle years in life. At the time of this deflection the head exerted a powerful influence over the heart. During such a period you are indifferent to others, avaricious, selfish and cold-hearted. The point at which the deflection begins indicates the age at which this tendency begins.

T-5.6 Reflects middle years in life. The qualities indicated by the Head line have swallowed all further independent action of the affections. You are henceforth dominated by the head.

T-5.7 Reflects middle years in life. You still possess a portion of your former affectionate disposition; head and worldly interests have not entirely overcome heart and sentiment. However, your characteristics will always be tinged strongly with much head and little heart.

T-5.8 Reflects middle years in life. In this case serious injury and damage to the head are indicated; at the time the incident takes place there is either an unbalancing of mental faculties, serious emotional trauma or death. Such a mark cannot take place without disaster. Apoplexy is most to be feared, followed by an impairment of the brain or paralysis if the attack is survived.

T-5.9 Reflects middle years in life. Since the heart is much more indicative of intuitive actions than the head, the emotions (sometimes intuitive actions) influence thought. Your family or loved ones may interfere with cool, logical business decisions.

T-5.10 Reflects middle years in life. This is a sign that you are always logical even in affairs involving the emotions.

T-6 HEART LINE: ITS TERMINATION

T-6.1 Reflects ending years in life. Indicates that your heart, which began with the right sort of affections, soon changed; coldness and dislike of humankind quickly altered your nature. Philosophical qualities have taken possession of your affections.

T-6.2 Reflects ending years in life. If there are other marks at the same age of 25-30 on other major lines, your life will be short: not over 30.

T-6.3 Reflects ending years in life. If there are other marks at the same age of 50-55 on other major lines, your life will be short: not over 50.

T-6.4 Reflects ending years in life. Shows that artistic ideas of beauty and art strongly attract you. You are not satisfied in marriage except with an artistic type of person or one approaching that type.

T-6.5 Reflects ending years in life. Shows that the affections are largely influenced by finances. Shrewdness guides this Heart line; there must always be money in sight before love is recognized.

T-6.6 This is not a true Heart line; your Heart line has never run in its proper channel. You are cold and heartless, are very ambitious and consider the welfare of no one when furthering your ambitions.

T-6.7 This is not a true Heart line; your Heart line has never run in its proper channel but, in a modified way, has run longer. You are cold and heartless, are very ambitious and consider the welfare of no one when furthering your ambitions.

T-6.8 Reflects ending years in life. You love ardently and with brusqueness and strength. This line also produces a narrow quadrangle and consequently a secretive disposition.

T-6.9 Reflects ending years in life. You are extremely jealous, for there is too much Heart line which, backed by the imagination of this character type, magnifies every act of a loved one into some form of unfaithfulness. This formation is a most unhappy one.

T-6.10 Reflects ending years in life. There may be a serious threat to your life. This could be confirmed by other marks on Life and Health lines.

T-6.11 Reflects ending years in life. Shows that you are exceedingly irritable, changeable in affections, constantly seeking excitement and difficult to get along with.

T-6.12 Reflects ending years in life. Your head has been damaged and your life could be in danger.

T-6.13 Reflects ending years in life. Your affections are largely influenced by love, sympathy and passion. Shows that ideas of grace, music, good health and generosity strongly attract you.

T-6.14 Reflects ending years in life. Indicates insane jealousy and subsequent violent action against yourself or others.

T-7 HEART LINE: ITS CHARACTER

T-7.2 Indicates that you are reliable in love but not frivolous or sentimental. You are brave, courageous and fearless. You love ardently and remain constant but do not make a display of your feelings; neither do you enjoy it when others are extremely demonstrative. You are consequently sometimes thought to be cold and distant. This is incorrect; you love devotedly but do not "wear your heart on your sleeve." With this Heart line you have fewer love affairs, but those you do have are strong. You have confidence in those you love, and disappointments affect you severely.

T-7.3   You have little caring for others, are narrow-minded, cowardly, timid, unsympathetic, and have no real affection for anyone. Any display of love which you might make is from a desire to further selfish ends.

Note: If the character of the line changes, your qualities will change. When this statement follows an age indicator, its effect is good only until the age indicated.

T-7.4   You fall violently in love but quickly transfer your affections to the next attractive person who comes along. Your affections are broad and shallow. You like to be told how much you are loved. Those who love you are often people who do so during prosperity but turn their backs in times of trial. There is in your nature no true ring of deep, strong affection.

Note: If the character of the line changes, your qualities will change. When this statement follows an age indicator, its effect is good only until the age indicated.

T-7.5   Shows a constant uncertainty in your affections. You think one day that you are in love and change your mind the next. You rush up to others and smother them with a great demonstration of affection but, the next time you meet them, you hardly speak. You vacillate and change, are cowardly, uncertain and weak.

Note: If the character of the line changes, your qualities will change. When this statement follows an age indicator, its effect is good only until the age indicated.

T-7.6   Indicates sterility as you get older.

T-7.7   This shows inconsistency both in love and friendship.

T-8   HEART LINE: ITS COLOR

T-8.1   WHITE HEART LINE
When this color is present in the Heart line, even if the line is otherwise good, the heart's action is weaker than normal and the affections colder.

T-8.2   PINK HEART LINE
Makes a deep line operate properly; all the warmth, steadfastness and reliability of this good line is accentuated. When found on warm types, it makes them strong. When found on cold types, it warms them up. This color makes those with weak heart lines less selfish

231

and narrow, less fickle; often this color will save such people from being entirely inconsistent.

T-8.3 RED HEART LINE

This color is the intensity of rich, even, warm blood and, when present in the Heart line, makes intense all the fires of affection.

T-8.4 YELLOW HEART LINE

Tinges the affections with morbidness and makes even those with a good, deep line suspicious of loved ones. Bile spoils everything and adds its pessimistic view even to love. Leads to distortion in one's manner of looking at things.

T-8.5 BLUE OR PURPLE HEART LINE

Tells of the congestion, the sluggish movement, of the physical heart.

T-9 HEART LINE: THE SPLIT

T-9.1 Shows a weakened condition of the heart, with impaired circulation.

T-9.2 Indicates that either the characteristics of that Mount, or someone belonging to that type, strongly attracts you.

T-9.3 At the age indicated, ambition guides love and the person who attracts you is someone of the leadership order. You do not necessarily have to have money, but you must be prominent or give promise of rising.

T-9.4 At the age it begins you are attracted by someone with philosophical qualities. You realize the need to have a relationship with a person who has this type of character. In any case, you like best one who has the soberness, caution and wisdom that belong to this type of person.

T-9.5 You are attracted to an artistic, dashing, happy and successful person. Note the year.

T-9.6 You love the qualities of an industrious, scientific, quick and businesslike person. In the latter case you prefer money to love. Note the year.

T-9.7 Indicates a part of the conflict between heart and head. At the time these lines fall, the head exerts a very strong influence.

T-9.8 There is constant conflict between heart and head for mastery. This indicates an effort by the head to control sentiment.

T-9.9 This shows that the heart has surrendered to the head completely, and is thereafter ruled by it. It indicates the age at which this begins.

T-9.10 This indicates constant heart irritations or illness. It could also tell of palpitation and valvular difficulties. Note the year.

T-9.11 Indicates constant heart irritations and worries in the affections. It may also indicate heart disturbance of a functional character and constant jars to the affections.

T-9.12 Indicates an extremely nervous nature.

T-9.13 Denotes unusual interest in the opposite sex.

T-9.14 Indicates minor disappointments in your sex life.

T-9.15 Indicates interference in the affections.

T-9.16 Indicates that attempts to change the natural course of the affections of the heart have failed. While these splits show attempts to change, they also show by their shortness that those attempts did not succeed.

T-9.17 This is an excellent mark if small. It denotes absolute honesty and decency with a warm character.

T-9.18 This is a weakening sign. It adds uncertainty and gloom to the emotional outlook; this makes for a person who is difficult to live with.

T-9.19 This mark denotes widowhood.

T-9.20 An indication of parental affection.

T-9.21 An indication of crossed parental affection.

T-9.22 A friendship has caused sorrow.

T-10 HEART LINE: THE BREAK

T-10.1 This is due to a disturbance of the heart brought about by a tendency to overeat. This produces functional heart disturbance, which can be overcome by removing the cause. Note the year.

T-10.2 These qualities attract you at the age marked: ambition, leadership, religion, love of nature, good health, happy disposition. This mark has been caused by too much ambition or pride.

T-10.3 The same mark on any other line in precisely the same year. In this case gout and rheumatism could be the trouble with the heart's action; rheumatism of the heart is often diagnosed using this mark. Your type's characteristics show how much your health is likely to be influenced.

T-10.4   Shows that you have been influenced by a person with some or all of these qualities: soberness, wisdom, sadness, gloom, superstition, balance. Note the year.

T-10.5   This is nearly conclusive proof that there is a health defect, if the same mark occurs on any other line at precisely the same year. While this break is natural to those with heart problems, it does not always indicate heart disease. It may indicate another health problem not associated with the heart.

T-10.6   Tells of the affections being influenced by a person who is brilliant, artistic, dashing and successful, with good health and a happy disposition. Note the year.

T-10.7   This mark occurring under the 3rd finger is at age 43. If a successful, dashing, artistic person has caused strong attraction at an earlier age, it is shown elsewhere in the hand.

T-10.8   With the same mark on any other line in precisely the same year. This is probably not a health defect; the position of the 4th finger registers 60 years on the Heart line, and the heart's action generally gets weaker at this age and is likely to become disturbed.

T-10.9   A shrewd business-type person has caused strong attraction at an earlier age, which will be shown elsewhere in the hand. At this age (63) it is not likely that an affection causes this mark, for the age of youthful love has passed.

T-10.10 You have a constant recurrence of weakness in the heart's action.

T-10.11 You have had a constant recurrence of broken love affairs.

T-10.12 The head strongly influences you at the time the marks occur, and cold reason fights against warm sentiment. If the marks show other deviations, the head does not rule completely.

T-10.13 Reasoning wins out over sentiment. You may or may not get over this problem but, if you do, you will be unhappy at the approximate time indicated.

T-10.14 The problem which caused this mark is related to health or affection. It seriously impairs the head at the approximate time indicated.

T-10.15 An interruption could or has occurred on the Head line, caused by whatever made the mark on the Heart line (health or affection); emotional trauma or death may ensue at the approximate time indicated.

T-10.16 Indicates a delicacy of the head which lasts a few years after the delicate condition develops.

T-10.17 Shows that the heart never fully recovers from whatever caused the mark at the approximate time indicated.

T-10.18 Indicates a delicate period during the time occupied by these marks.

T-10.19 Death comes suddenly or there is a very serious attack of heart disease at the approximate time indicated.

T-10.20 Sudden death by heart failure occurs in 95% of these cases. Repair marks could alter the ending of life at the approximate time indicated.

T-10.21 Death from heart disease occurs in 99% of these cases. Repair marks could alter the ending of life at the approximate time indicated.

T-10.22 At the approximate time indicated there could be great danger, but a Sister line shows a healing process.

T-10.23 There is a serious impediment to the heart at the time this mark occurs.

T-10.24 This indicates a serious attack of heart disease. A very large, deep mark indicates a probable fatality; a small mark indicates a serious illness which may be overcome.

T-10.25 The danger here is serious but not insurmountable. Reflects early years in life.

T-10.26 A small problem is associated with the physical heart.

T-10.27 A serious check to your affections has occurred or will occur.

T-10.28 There is a decided check to the operation of the affections or physical heart, but this is not serious.

T-10.29 There is a decided check to the operation of the affections or physical heart, but this is not serious.

T-10.30 There is a decided check to the operation of the affections or physical heart, but this is not serious.

T-10.31 Loss of affection.

T-10.32 Indicates a fatality.

T-10.33 Fatality by folly.

T-10.34 Fatality by avarice, caused by hopes of obtaining a better venture.

T-10.35 Denotes great anxiety concerning the affections and, to a certain extent, self-preservation.

T-11 HEART LINE: THE TRIDENT

T-11.1 Reflects ending years in life. Denotes gradual lessening of affection in old age.

T-11.2 Reflects ending years in life. Denotes gradual lessening of energy in old age.

T-12 HEART LINE: THE DOT

T-12.1 Signifies heart disease. If no indication is seen elsewhere, it can be assessed as mild heart trouble.

T-12.2 Indicates constant irritations, worries and jars to the affections. It could also indicate heart disturbance of a functional nature.

T-12.3 This mark is not serious and usually follows severe illness, generally of a febrile nature.

T-12.4 This mark is not serious and usually follows severe illness, generally of a febrile nature.

T-13 HEART LINE: THE ISLAND

T-13.1 Shows a serious problem with the physical heart. How serious it is depends on the nature of the mark and how much you are aware of it.

T-13.2 Indicates that an impeding object has affected the course of your affection.

T-13.3 Indicates that external conditions forced the termination of a relationship. The love partner made excessive demands, causing you great emotional and personal loss.

T-14 HEART LINE: THE CIRCLE

T-14.1 Indicates a delicacy of the eyes. Note that this mark is not seen in the hands of all who are blind, have poor vision or weak eyes.

T-15   HEART LINE: THE STAR

T-15.1   Indicates heart disease. A severe attack is indicated if the mark is small or badly formed.

T-15.2   Your affections have been hurt badly. You recover if the mark is small or badly formed.

T-15.3   This mark means sudden heart failure at the age at which the mark appears.

T-15.4   Your affections have been hurt badly but you are strong and recover. The cause could be sorrow or a love who is lost because of an act by another party.

T-15.5   You have a serious attack of heart disease from which you never fully recover.

T-15.6   Indicates a severe attack on the affections from which you never fully recover.

T-15.7   You have a severe attack of heart disease with delicacy afterwards, more pronounced and severe during the periods covered by the marks.

T-15.8   Your affections are hurt badly, followed by delicacy, more pronounced and severe during the periods covered by the marks.

T-15.9   Tells that the illness shown by the mark destroys the vigor of the heart, which is always weak afterwards, and that the affections become cold and views become selfish and narrow.

T-15.10   Tells that the hurt affections, shown by the mark, destroy the vigor of the affections, which are always weak afterwards, and that the affections become cold and views become selfish and narrow.

T-16   HEART LINE: THE CROSS

T-16.1   Indicates a small problem associated with the physical heart.

T-16.2   Your affections have been hurt but you recover.

T-17   HEART LINE: SISTER LINE

T-17.1   Indicates an ongoing relationship. Long and happily married individuals have this mark.

U

DESCRIPTION "U": THE HEAD LINE

U-1.1 The Head line is an important line indicating clearly your degree of mental prowess, your power of mental concentration and your ability to exert self-control. The importance of this line will be recognized when considering what a tremendous part mental attitude plays in the shaping of destiny.

U-3 HEAD LINE: ITS STARTING POINT

U-3.1 Reflects early years in life. The sooner the Head line separates from the Life line, the younger you were when you began to think for yourself.

U-3.2 Reflects early years in life. The longer the Head line is tied to the Life line, the less self-confidence you have and the more you rely on the advice of others. The longer the period covered by this union of the two lines, the later in life you began to rely on yourself. The Head line is not often bound to the Life line past the 12th year of age.

U-3.3 Reflects early years in life. You are sensitive, your feelings easily hurt.

U-3.4 Reflects early years in life. Self-confidence began later in life.

U-3.5 Reflects early years in life. Shows you to be somewhat indifferent to slights by others.

U-3.6 Reflects early years in life. Indicates elementary heaviness of intellect. You are cautious, noncommittal, dependent on others, lacking ability to command, unoriginal, blunt, tactless.

U-3.7 Reflects early years in life. You are original, not bound by the views of others, act for and depend upon yourself, can plan well. You are guided by your own judgment and are independent and courageous in your views.

The wider the separation, the greater the degree of self-reliance, to the extent that with a very wide separation you become foolhardy and not a safe counsellor. You are very confident of your ability, but your feelings are hurt when others do not have the same degree of confidence in you.

U-3.8   Reflects early years in life. You are extremely vacillating, starting many things with enthusiasm and making innumerable changes. Such people are shifters who constantly alter their opinions and do not continue in the same way of thinking, are always intense in their views, make very strong resolutions, and change their minds easily but always with vigor.

Such people are rarely successful, for they do not stick to anything long enough to win. They are always aggressive; consequently they are frequently in trouble, always picking quarrels, and are avoided by those who do not want contention. Their shifting minds and quarrelsome dispositions make a poor combination, for one can never tell which track these people may take next.

U-3.9   Reflects early years in life. Shows fine capability for leadership, a person who can handle people with ease and get the most out of them, one who is self-confident; this source of the Head line is always an indication of strong mentality. There is diplomacy present which enables you to dictate without being harsh, to rule when you seem to be ruled, to appear dependent when you know everything depends on you; you are brainy, brilliant and successful.

U-3.10   Reflects early years in life. Shows fine capability for leadership, a person who can handle people with ease and get the most out of them, one who is self-confident; this source of the Head line is always an indication of strong mentality. There is diplomacy present which enables you to dictate without being harsh, to rule when you seem to be ruled, to appear dependent when you know everything depends on you; you are brainy, brilliant and successful.

U-3.11   Reflects early years in life. Shows that ambition and the desire to be great or famous rule you. If the hand is purely mental, your ambitions are for mental fame. If the hand is purely artistic, your ambitions are for fame in that direction. If the hand is purely material, your ambition is for riches. You always strive to rise, and your life generally follows an upward grade.

U-3.12   Reflects early years in life. Denotes a creative, unusual way of thinking; a person of extremes. Your thinking is narrow in some ways but expansive in others. Such people enjoy mystery and intrigue and have good heads for games and puzzles. You may also have a great deal of psychic ability. Such people usually become lonely too easily to enjoy independent lifestyles, but neither do they respond well to a routine lifestyle or being closely supervised.

U-3.13 Reflects early years in life. Indicates duality and an unconventional way of thinking, a person who leads a "double life" with two distinctly different lifestyles going on simultaneously. There is a very fertile imagination and flair for the unusual as well as a need for what is conventional and mundane. Such a person has the desire to be different, to stand apart, yet also to be easily accepted by all.

U-3.14 Reflects early years in life. Denotes good common sense and a practical way of looking at things.

U-3.15 Reflects early years in life. Indicates want of confidence in self and oversensitiveness.

U-3.16 Reflects early years in life. Shows that home life was against you, preventing the development of capabilities (you were chained by circumstances).

U-3.17 Reflects early years in life. You have great difficulty in surmounting the disadvantages of early life. The result is a disappointing career unless the Career and Fate lines are good, in which case you get through, but only with a struggle.

U-4 HEAD LINE: ITS LENGTH

U-4.1 Indicates you are not very "long headed" or, in other words, you do not have a strong mentality.

U-4.2 A pronounced indication of small mentality. Shows a person who is easily led, weak in mentality, the servant and creature of others, never the leader.

U-4.3 The death of this person is almost certain between the ages indicated. Caution must be taken at this age if the fatality is to be avoided.

U-4.4 Shows a sudden end, but one which could be avoided if cautious. The larger, better formed the mark, the more certain the indication.

U-4.5 Fatality may be predicted confidently if this is present in the active hand (right hand if right-handed, left if left-handed, right if ambidextrous) or seen as a threat if present in the passive hand. The larger and better formed these marks, the more certain the indication.

U-4.6   Shows a depressed state, possibly leading to death. Other marks may indicate the cause.

U-4.7   Shows the preponderance of the head; you are out of balance in this respect. You are avaricious and view all things from the mental standpoint; sentiment is subservient to interest. You are practical in all things and more interested in whatever is capable of producing direct results than in beautiful things which please the eye or appeal to the heart.

U-4.8   The head is under constant strain and must not be overworked or the brain will be wrecked.

U-4.9   You have developed your mentality.

U-4.10 You have regressed mentally, or else there is danger of fatality or accident.

U-4.11 You have regressed mentally, to the point where an accident could be induced. A severe case of being accident-prone.

U-4.12 Indicates a sensible, practical way of thinking, a person who goes straight to the heart of a matter and always seeks the simplest, most direct solution to any problem. You have sound judgment and a careful way of thinking that requires proofs. You are more apt to stick with tried-and-true methods than to try new ideas.

U-5   HEAD LINE: ITS COURSE

U-5.1   The less its course changes, the more fixed are your ideas, the more evenly you are balanced mentally, and the more practical are your views. This shows that you pursue an even course and that outside influences have very little effect.

You gauge everything by a practical standard and accept what you choose, allowing the balance to pass by. You can be too unimpressionable, too inflexible, too sordid, to allow any adaptability. You do not make many friends, because you want everyone to come over to your way of thinking. Everything is subjected to plain common sense; often you have narrow views, and you see anything speculative or ideal as an abomination.

U-5.2   Reflects middle years in life. It shows you are strongly tinged with the qualities of soberness, wisdom, sadness, superstition, gloom and balance. The greater the deflection of the line towards the finger, the more these qualities are pronounced.

U-5.3 Reflects middle years in life. Your mind turns towards these qualities: brilliance, artistic endeavors, happiness, success, good health, a happy disposition. The greater the deflection, the greater the degree of influence exerted by these qualities.

U-5.4 Shows that your qualities of shrewdness, industriousness, scientific ability, business and quickness are very strong.

U-5.5 Shows you have had no permanent fixedness of ideas. There is a lack of continuous mental effort in any one direction, changeability of purpose and consequent vacillation. A person with such a Head line is never self-reliant. As counsellors and advisers these people are not safe, for their opinions are not sound, their ideas not stable.

U-5.6 Reflects middle years in life. Shows that the heart is a stronger factor than the head and that you are largely influenced by sentiment.

U-5.7 Shows the heart is a stronger factor than the head, which began to develop later in life, and that you are largely influenced by sentiment.

U-5.8 Reflects middle years in life. The heart influences but it does not entirely rule.

U-5.9 Reflects middle years in life. Sentiment guides and reason gives way.

U-5.10 Reflects middle years in life. Reason asserts itself, often producing mental distress because the dictates of the heart cannot be followed.

U-5.11 Reflects middle years in life. Your mental attitude has been lowered during the period covered by this deflection, and departure from practical lines of thought occurs. If the deflection is short, you are pulled in that direction only for a time; the return of the line to a straight course indicates that your ideas have been drawn back into the more practical world. Psychic powers are usually the result.

U-5.12 There have been conflicts between practical ideas and a desire to indulge in imaginative endeavors. However, as the line returns to a straight course, practical ideas prevail.

U-5.13 Reflects middle years in life. In your character the influence of sentiment predominates over mind. This is a good sign in human terms, and a bad sign for a business person or politician.

U-5.14 Reflects middle years in life. Your head and heart do not communicate as much, resulting in cold, calculating thoughts. This strengthens abstract thought in mathematical and psychic types.

U-5.15 Reflects middle years in life. Shows a change away from the practical and the mathematical towards the theoretical and the imaginative.

U-5.16 Reflects middle years in life. Indicates an extremely cold, calculating nature which takes any chance. Such people are potentially quite harmful.

U-6 HEAD LINE: ITS TERMINATION

U-6.1 Your mental attitude causes early death. Other marks on other lines confirm this. Mental stamina is not especially strong. Your head has been overcome by feelings.

U-6.2 Shows you have an attitude problem; death due to a brain problem results. Other marks on other lines confirm this. Mental stamina is not especially strong.

U-6.3 The sudden termination of life is certain. Mental stamina is not especially strong.

U-6.4 Paralysis followed by paresis is indicated; the mark shows the gradual dissipation and diffusion of mental powers. Mental stamina is not especially strong.

U-6.5 Reflects ending years in life. Shows you are strong in the qualities of art. Mental stamina is not especially strong and your head has been overcome by feelings.

U-6.6 You allow feelings to overcome judgment. When emotions are aroused, you lose self-control and could commit crimes in response to your passions. You are not necessarily criminal, though you may be weak. Your head is not strong enough to control the passions raging within.

U-6.7 Indicates a complication of the heart and some disorder in mental health, most probably brain illness.

U-6.8 The danger is very grave. Heart failure or disorder in mental health is likely.

U-6.9 The illness at this point permanently weakens the mind; brain illness is indicated.

U-6.10 Reflects ending years in life. Indicates shrewdness, quickness and business ability. There is a love of, and talent for, making money. You love bargains and go miles to save a few pennies. Everything is measured by its value in money.

U-6.11 Reflects ending years in life. Indicates special aptitude for medicine.

U-6.12 Reflects ending years in life. Your bilious tendency, stomach disorder and nervousness affect the head and produce vertigo, though serious results are not often encountered. The age of the line, when it has reached this point, is about 70; at that time the end, naturally, is not far distant.

U-6.13 Reflects ending years in life. Sudden death is indicated at approximately 70.

U-6.14 Reflects ending years in life. Indicates that you have practical common sense and that your mental qualities are not pulled out of balance. If your qualities of resistance are developed then you are cool, calm, brave and warlike and defend yourself when attacked; if not, then you are easily discouraged, are unable to resist strong attacks, and lack confidence.

U-6.15 Reflects ending years in life. You are somewhat influenced by imagination and are not practical to the exclusion of everything. You are not entirely material in your ideas, but have the power of imagination.

This is an essential quality for writers, speakers, linguists and poets, and in varying degrees this mark is often seen in the hands of such people. When this line is seen on a poor type of person or when the Head line is thin or defective, it is unfavorable. An excess of imagination is one type of insanity.

U-6.16 Reflects ending years in life. You are somewhat influenced by imagination and are not practical to the exclusion of everything. You are not entirely material in your ideas, but have the power of imagination.

This is an essential quality for writers, speakers, linguists and poets, and in varying degrees this mark is often seen in the hands of such people. When this line is seen on a poor type of person or when the Head line is thin or defective, it is unfavorable. An excess of imagination is one type of insanity.

U-6.17 Reflects ending years in life. This mark, with unfavorable signs, indicates mental derangement. A star on the end indicates insanity.

U-6.18 Reflects ending years in life. This mark, with unfavorable signs, indicates mental derangement. A chain on the end indicates mental impairment.

U-6.19 Reflects ending years in life. This Head line, with unfavorable signs, indicates mental derangement. The line ending in a cross indicates an impairment of mentality.

U-6.20 Reflects ending years in life. There is a danger of mental disturbance. The size of the island or dot at the end of the line tells how serious.

U-6.21 Reflects ending years in life. There is a danger of mental disturbance. The size of the island or dot at the end of the line tells how serious.

U-6.22 Reflects ending years in life. Indicates mental disturbance. These marks are more dangerous because of the character of the line and its position; imaginative tendencies make it a fertile place for trouble.

U-6.23 Reflects ending years in life. You have always been imaginative, not practical to the exclusion of everything.

U-6.24 The practical plane at the beginning is changed to a tendency towards imaginative ideas later in life. Such violent changes are not good.

U-6.25 Reflects ending years in life. Indicates versatility, a union of practical and imaginative ideas which makes you see things from a double point of view. Theatrical people and those who appeal to the public in other ways have this type of Head line.

U-6.26 Reflects ending years in life. You have a strong, practical set of ideas and a strong set of imaginative ones. You can see things from both the practical and fanciful sides and, with this double point of view, are less inclined to be narrow-minded and one-sided. The upper line is practical, the lower line imaginative.

Which side (practical or imaginative) prevails can be determined by noting which of the two forked Head lines is deeper and stronger. This is a fine mark on a good hand.

The double line, however, with its double point of view, often leads people into the habit of falsifying. They are not always intentional liars; often they are not sure whether they are telling a true story or an imagined one. Their imagination is vivid and they sometimes make themselves think they are telling the truth when they are not. When seen on an otherwise poor hand, the forked Head line produces the liar, sometimes from pride or vanity, for vicious ends; this applies to habitual falsifiers, not occasional "story tellers."

U-6.27 Reflects ending years in life. Your imagination is so vivid that you tend to stretch everything and describe things better when lying than when telling the truth; you possess such an enlarged imagination that you magnify everything to double the original size.

U-6.28 Reflects ending years in life. It is almost certain that the enlarged imagination will produce insanity from over-imagination and from mental disease shown by the marks at the end of the line.

U-6.29 Reflects ending years in life. This is a splendid mark, showing great diversity of intellect, adaptability and versatility. The Head line's three terminations unite business, resistance and imagination. This combination generally produces a successful career unless laziness, lack of ambition or some other defect intervenes.

U-6.30 Reflects ending years in life. Indicates that love, sympathy, music, grace, passion, good health and generosity are some of the qualities attracting your uppermost mind. The mental is a strong feature of this person.

U-6.31 A sure sign of early death due to mental disorder if it appears in both active and passive hands.

U-6.32 Indicates that you are not so "long headed" or, in other words, your mentality is weak.

U-6.33 Reflects ending years in life. Indicates a combination of practical and imaginative ideas. A very successful sign in a hand that indicates willpower (in other words, a hand with a strong thumb).

U-6.34 Reflects ending years in life. This strengthens imaginative qualities. In a good hand, this is the strongest mark of the greatest fiction writers.

U-7   HEAD LINE: ITS CHARACTER

U-7.1   You are impelled by the following qualities: soberness, wisdom, sadness, gloom and balance.

U-7.2   Shows that a vigorous mind has started at the age indicated.

U-7.3   Shows that the mind becomes less vigorous at the age indicated.

U-7.4   Shows that your mind has become impaired.

U-7.5   Indicates one who is self-contained, does not lose his or her head, is not flighty or erratic, but is dignified, even-tempered, evenly balanced, and has the ability to make and carry out his or her plans.

U-7.6   The length of your Head line shows great mentality and its depth shows strength. You do not always make up your mind quickly, but weigh and consider things carefully. Once reaching a decision, you are firm in execution; you can concentrate your ideas, pursue a single aim in life and bring to bear great strength based on information drawn from many sources. You are cool, collected, and possess a great degree of self-control.

U-7.7   Your brain-power is not vigorous, but delicate. You are clever if the line is long, but lack mental vigor. You have good ideas but are easily talked out of them, for the conflict tires you. You cannot pass through trials without headaches and, whenever possible, avoid severe mental tensions and great brain effort.

You have little self-control, but give way to your feelings: temper, low appetite, laziness, or whatever. You possess mental inertia, a lack of desire and ability to operate with vigor, a lack of firmness, aggression and strong mental concentration. Such people never do great things requiring continued mental exertion, but do bright things which come by intuition and do not require much mental exertion. It is dangerous to surpass these people, for they cannot stand it.

U-7.8   You are a typical mental specimen of your particular character.

U-7.9   Great care must be used. No mental over-excitement must be allowed, no loss of sleep, no narcotics, no stimulants, no excess of any kind. You must care for the stomach and when fatigued must rest; any other sort of living produces mental discomfort.

U-7.10   Shows you were impaired by whatever caused this mark and that it ends tragically; this mark indicates either insanity or death.

U-7.11   Pressure has been too great, and if it continues the brain will collapse, producing paralysis or nervous prostration. Such lines are often seen on active business or professional people; the warning to "ease up" must be given.

U-7.12   Yours is not a vigorous brain but is liable to aches and deterioration. You are not firm, resolute and courageous, but are without determination, vacillating, uncertain; you lack self-reliance and boldness.

You may be bright but are weak in mental aggression. There is a lack of force or intensity in your mental attitude; you are not usually assertive, but may be if you have a large thumb. However, this is merely a veneer. Such people have poor control, little power to influence others, little concentration of mind, and poor memory. They are easily influenced and yield to temptation. They are not suited for mental occupations and do not often seek them. They are mentally lazy, do little thinking and are satisfied to have others think for them.

U-7.13   The age at which this change occurs indicates the time that this person energetically took up life's battle and really began to think for himself or herself. This mark is often seen on the hands of women who have been "spoiled" and who have never had to do anything until suddenly thrown upon their own resources, when they have had to take up life's struggle in earnest. As this person rises to the occasion, strength is developed.

U-7.14   Your mentality is weak and labored, utterly lacking in concentration, vacillating, timid, sensitive and changeable. No reliance can be placed on your promises; you do not remain faithful. You have poor memory, poor judgment, and are continually subjected to headaches and various mental problems.

If your Heart line is strong you are ruled by sentiment and are impractical. You should not attempt mental vocations, should not choose literature, scientific studies or brain-exerting occupations, but should take outdoor positions where labor with the hands or legs is required. You are not be able to direct your own efforts, but rely on being directed.

U-7.15   You change your mental weakness into mental vigor. This is a very good sign.

U-7.16   Gradual progress from mental weakness to strength.

U-7.17 The mentality changes: weak for a period of years, then strong, then weak, with as many changes indicated as there are uneven places on the line. At the time this mark occurs there is no doubt that great concentration of thought takes place and the pressure on the brain is very great.

This is a dangerous line, for at this point the line may be crowded. Such people alternate between enthusiasm and despair, are changeable and not reliable counselors or guides. The greatest care, plenty of sleep and no excitement is the prescription for this person.

U-8 HEAD LINE: ITS COLOR

U-8.1 This white color shows a poor blood supply to the brain and consequent weak operation of that organ, making you low in mental strength.

U-8.2 Pink color gives more force and eliminates some of the weakness of this line.

U-8.3 A red line makes you more intense and less subject to absolute weakness.

U-8.4 In addition to being weak mentally, you are cross, nervous, despondent, fault-finding and of a mean disposition if the line is very yellow. It is a weak and mean line.

U-8.5 Blue shows congested circulation in the brain. While it is primarily a heart indication, it also shows that mentality may be cut off at any moment by sudden heart failure.

U-9 HEAD LINE: THE SPLIT

U-9.1 You are aspiring to rise and to improve and seek all opportunities for advancement.

U-9.2 Indicates that your head is influenced by too many things, making you vacillate. You never have good mental concentration; your thoughts wander too much. If the Head line droops toward the "F" Mount, it indicates that you are a dreamer.

U-9.3 You are easily discouraged and do not fight the battle of life with vigor, but are prone to say, "I'm not lucky." Such people start every enterprise by saying that they know it will fail; because they believe this, it generally does. They must resist more and not give way so easily.

U-9.4   Ambitious thoughts fill your mind. You wish to rise and to achieve fame and notoriety. This is a mark of great ambition and pride if found with a large development of the "A" Mount.

U-9.5   Wisdom, soberness, studiousness.

U-9.6   Success rewards your ambitions and desires.

U-9.7   You possess the quality of pride, a love of display and beauty, a desire for wealth and fame, and a fascination with art and celebrity.

U-9.8   Prognosis is favorable. You will be successful.

U-9.9   A very good chance of success.

U-9.10   You love the business side of life; you possess shrewdness, industriousness, scientific interests, business abilities and quickness.

U-9.11   Sentiment, love and affection occupy your thoughts. You are less sordid and mercenary and more given to helping others. Also, you are more sympathetic and humane.

U-9.12   The head is powerfully guided by the heart.

U-9.13   Sentiment interferes with business success.

U-9.14   Head disorder: maybe fever, maybe only headaches, the severity of the attack depending upon the type of person you are.

U-9.15   You have mental worries and a predisposition to severe headaches, but these do not become a head illness. This mark is usually seen on the hands of hyper-nervous people.

U-9.16   Adds pride, ambition and leadership to your qualities.

U-9.17   Depresses your thinking because it adds a sense of gloom and fatalism.

U-9.18   Denotes an overpowering wish for fame. It is a good mark with a good thumb and directed hand, indicating that goals can be achieved. In a weak hand it indicates a wish to be noticed at any cost and can be found among the most infamous criminals.

U-9.19   Denotes a strong sense in business and science. With a negative, weak hand it denotes deceit.

U-9.20   Indicates a person near to being schizophrenic.

U-9.21   Indicates frequent headaches.

U-9.22 Indicates head illness, nervous prostration or paralysis.

U-9.23 Indicates a danger to your mental life that must not go unheeded. Shows that blockages occur unless care is used at the age indicated.

U-9.24 Indicates business, financial and mechanical aptitude.

U-9.25 Indicates an aptitude in philosophy and leadership.

U-9.26 Indicates an aptitude in philosophy and art.

U-9.27 Indicates an aptitude in art and business.

U-10 HEAD LINE: THE BREAK

U-10.1 Irregular action and consequent lack of concentration, firmness and self-control.

U-10.2 Could indicate an illness; often seen on the hands of flighty, nervous, changeable people.

U-10.3 An utter lack of stability; you are fickle and shifting. You have continuous headaches, poor health, visions and fantasies. Unless cared for by someone else, you will go insane or border on it from nervousness. Such people fly off on tangents, always seeking the impossible.

U-10.4 You have a constant recurrence of weakness of mind.

U-10.5 A period of great strain occurs.

U-11 HEAD LINE: THE TRIDENT

U-11.1 Reflects ending years in life. This mark denotes gradual loss of memory in old age.

U-12 HEAD LINE: THE DOT

U-12.1 Head disorders are indicated and great care should be taken.

U-12.2 The trouble indicated is an illness, but not of great importance.

U-12.3 Mental vigor has decreased.

U-12.4 Head sickness has greatly impaired the mind, which never fully recovers. Some mental disturbance precedes the illness.

U-12.5 You have a head sickness for a short period of time, then fully recover.

251

U-12.6   Great delicacy of the head follows a severe illness. This is a grave indication that you will be greatly unbalanced after the illness.

U-12.7   Death is caused by a severe illness.

U-12.8   A severe head illness occurs, followed by a period of delicacy, ending fatally.

U-12.9   Brain illness occurs, followed by a period of delicacy, ending in insanity.

U-12.10 Indicates a danger to mental life that must not go unheeded.

U-12.11 Indicates an injury from shock, a fall or a blow to the head.

U-12.12 Denotes a nervous illness.

U-13   HEAD LINE: THE ISLAND

U-13.1   Mental strength operates with diminished force. During this period the mind does not possess full health and power; if there is undue excitement or mental strain, it becomes unbalanced.

U-13.2   The trouble is brain fever, or possibly female trouble, delirium or other fevers, hyper-nervousness, severe mental strain, or sometimes the embracing of a new religion which produces the loss of mental equilibrium. The person who has hands free from lines (which shows them to be cold, reserved and without nervous strain) may avoid this danger by their naturally calm, even temper.

U-13.3   It might be impossible for you to avoid a mental disorder of some kind.

U-13.4   The brain was forced too much and produced the mental disturbance shown on the Head line.

U-13.5   Denotes danger to the lungs.

U-13.6   Reflects ending years in life. Death will ensue due to mental weakness of some sort.

U-13.7   Tells of trouble, the result of an illness.

U-13.8   Tells of danger to the brain, a warning not to overstrain the nervous system.

U-13.9   This shows indecision, want of stability of ideas.

U-14   HEAD LINE: THE CIRCLE

>   *U-14.1*   This is an extremely negative mark predicting inevitable tragedy and dire misfortune.
>
>   *U-14.2*   Indicates a danger to sight.

U-15   HEAD LINE: THE STAR

>   *U-15.1*   May mean a sudden collapse, head illness or insanity.
>
>   *U-15.2*   Indicates a danger to mental life that must not go unheeded.

U-16   HEAD LINE: THE CROSS

>   *U-16.1*   May mean a sudden collapse, head illness or insanity.
>
>   *U-16.2*   Indicates a danger to mental life that must not go unheeded.

U-17   A SISTER LINE TO HEAD LINE

>   *U-17.1*   A sign of good fortune.

V

DESCRIPTION "V": THE LIFE LINE

>   *V-1.1*   The Life line indicates health during the various periods of life, physical strength in general, and whether the primary energy of life has been nervous force or muscular strength. It records many events and provides a basis to fall back on when seeking confirmation or explanations of indications found elsewhere in the hand. It shows whether the course of life is upward or downward and fixes the year when the zenith of a person's power is reached.

V-2   LIFE LINE ABSENT

>   *V-2.1*   You have little muscular strength and vitality, living on nervous energy. You are subject to many nervous collapses and must constantly husband strength, get plenty of sleep and avoid excitement. Life hangs only by a hair; death is a visitor who may come at any moment. Such people have never lived in a robust condition but have always been delicate.

V-3   LIFE LINE: ITS STARTING POINT

V-3.1   Reflects early years in life. This is a normal source and marks the beginning of a life with leadership qualities.

V-3.2   Reflects early years in life. This shows that your life is a most ambitious one, filled with desire for wealth, success and fame, and that you take every opportunity to become acquainted with people of note. You are extremely proud.

V-3.3   Reflects early years in life. Indicates an achievement-oriented person. Even in early years, this person displays definite leadership qualities and the ability to make quick decisions. You need constructive goals and projects to channel these talents towards meaningful results. If these needs are not met, your personality may be frustrated and overly competitive.

V-4   LIFE LINE: ITS LENGTH

V-4.1   May indicate a chronic illness or susceptibility to functional problems. It often should be interpreted as a warning to look ahead and prepare for major decisions or significant changes that are likely to occur in later years when you are least expecting them.

V-5   LIFE LINE: ITS COURSE

V-5.1   Reflects middle years in life. Indicates a person who is cold, unsympathetic, lacking sexual desire and attraction for or to the opposite sex. Shows one who repels advances from the opposite sex instead of courting them.

This is also an indication of a diminished probability of long life, as it shows an abnormal dryness; such conditions are not compatible with the health and vigor of those full of desire and warmth. Coldness indicates nearness to death, either of the physical body or of some necessary emotion.

V-5.2   Reflects middle years in life. You are ardent, full of desire and warmth, passionate, generous, sympathetic, and attract others. You are also attractive, marry early, and in 90% of cases the union is fruitful. This also indicates long life and a strong vitality and constitution.

V-6 LIFE LINE: ITS TERMINATION

V-6.1 Reflects ending years in life. Indicates that you remain strong till the end of life and die of no lingering or wasting disease.

V-6.2 Strong will and determination to live prolong the life of many people with such a mark.

V-6.3 Reflects ending years in life. There is no great impediment at the end. Care and determination can keep you going.

V-6.4 The abrupt termination of the Head line tells that some affliction of the head will be the cause of death.

V-6.5 Reflects ending years in life. The abrupt termination of the Heart line shows heart failure will be the cause of death.

V-6.6 A sudden attack of bilious fever is the trouble. The Health line shows a chronic tendency, with an individual mark indicating an acute attack.

V-6.7a Head illness could be the cause of death.

V-6.7b Paralysis could be the cause of death.

V-6.7c Heart failure could be the cause of death.

V-6.7d Liver failure and paralysis in the upper extremities of the body could be the cause of death.

V-6.7e Blood disorder and intestinal inflammation could be the cause of death.

V-6.7f Bladder and kidney failure could be the cause of death.

V-6.7g Pulmonary troubles could be the cause of death.

V-6.8 Reflects ending years in life. Shows that vitality becomes less with age until it almost disappears, leaving you weak and feeble. You will not die from sudden disease; death will come from exhaustion. You are liable to develop some chronic ailment.

V-6.9 Reflects ending years in life. There is only half a chance that life will be continued past this mark; an indication that vitality wanes rapidly.

V-6.10 Reflects ending years in life. Vitality wanes; encouragement to live should be given.

V-6.11 Reflects ending years in life. A better indication of long life than 6.10, but vitality wanes and encouragement to live should be given.

V-6.12 Reflects ending years in life. There is only half a chance that life will continue past this mark; an indication that vitality wanes rapidly.

V-6.13 Reflects ending years in life. A complete dissipation of vitality.

V-6.14 Reflects ending years in life. There could be a new lease on life.

V-6.15 Reflects ending years in life. A complete dissipation of vitality at death. Such marks are frequently seen from age 60 to 65. In those cases they indicate the natural end of life. If the mark appears early, it indicates a premature dissipation of vitality and death at the age of the mark.

V-6.16 Reflects ending years in life. Ambition, leadership, religion and honor are present in your ending years.

V-6.17 Reflects ending years in life. Soberness, wisdom, sadness, superstition, gloom and a balanced personality are present in your ending years.

V-6.18 Reflects ending years in life. Brilliance, artistic tendencies, happiness, success and good health are present in your ending years.

V-6.19 Reflects ending years in life. Shrewdness, industriousness, scientific and business endeavors, and quickness of mind are present in your ending years.

V-6.20 Reflects ending years in life. Resistance, courage, coolness, calmness and the warrior spirit are present in your ending years.

V-6.21 Reflects ending years in life. Imagination, fancy, mysticism, coldness and selfishness are present in your ending years.

V-6.22 Reflects ending years in life. Love, sympathy, music, grace, passion, good health and generosity are present in your ending years.

V-6.23 Reflects ending years in life. Death at the age given. No lingering illness.

V-6.24 Reflects ending years in life. Death at the age given. No lingering illness.

V-6.25 Reflects ending years in life. Death at the age given. No lingering illness.

V-6.26 Reflects ending years in life. Death at the age given. No lingering illness.

V-6.27 Reflects ending years in life. Shows you have altered your life course to avoid its natural termination.

V-6.28 Reflects ending years in life. Indicates a fatal danger.

V-7 LIFE LINE: ITS CHARACTER

V-7.1 You are strong, vigorous, full of vitality; you resist disease and have few illnesses. This line is found most often on cold, reserved people, for these people live on muscular strength, not nervous energy.

You have the least sensitive nerves and consequently the fewest lines; life is more even, for you worry little and are not burdened with delicacy and poor health. You are capable of great exertion physically. You also have more ability to throw off worry and remain calm in moments of excitement. You are endowed with self-confidence and inspire it in others. You are intense in everything you do, in work and play.

V-7.2 Vitality and robustness continue during your entire life, but become weak at the end when vitality naturally wanes.

V-7.3 Indicates less vitality, less robustness and greater liability to various health problems. This line does not necessarily indicate that you are delicate or sickly; you resist major diseases as well as most people, but often suffer from colds and other minor ailments.

V-7.4 You go through life with less worry and fewer nervous spells.

V-7.5 Indicates a lack of robust, muscular vitality and endurance. You should never go beyond your strength.

V-7.6 You are continually under strain, and your health suffers. You are apprehensive, feeling instinctively that the stress on your health is great.

V-7.7 An utter lack of vitality. You have no ability to resist disease, no robustness, no physical vigor, no muscular power. You are easy prey to all kinds of disorders. Your system is in a flabby, weak condition; you have no endurance, no stamina, no confidence. Not to be taken as an indication of inherent laziness; such people are conscious of labored effort whenever they undertake physical exertion, and from this kind of Life line we get the chronic complainers and those who never feel well.

These people are very dependent; they lean on friends and relatives and soon fall into the habit of being looked after. They do not often

257

achieve great success, for they have not the strength to breast the tide of competition and the hustle of the age. They lack aggression and strength and must be taken care of or they go under. This line is an indication of great nervousness; these people are carried purely by their nervous force. Often, when necessity forces them to make strong efforts, they work when they can hardly put one foot in front of the other.

Only positions where the work is routine, easy and does not require much responsibility are suited to people with such a Life line. When forced into vocations requiring greater physical exertion and the shouldering of responsibilities, they do not hold out very long.

V-7.8   Health is unstable and intermittent; not only are you delicate but you have repeated illnesses, all of more than ordinary severity.

V-7.9   An intensely nervous state of health, great delicacy, and a tendency towards general weakness.

V-7.10   You are delicate and suffer repeated, annoying illnesses.

V-7.11   The first few years of life are filled with childhood diseases. If the beginning of the line is bad for a considerable distance, the child did not pass the danger point until late.

V-7.12   You have a strong constitution which asserts itself as soon as the delicacy of childhood is passed and which continues for as long as you live.

V-7.13   You do not have a vigorous constitution.

V-7.14   You were never strong.

V-7.15   Indicates a female change of life but shows it is not too serious.

V-7.16   The change of life greatly weakens your constitution.

V-7.17   Your original strength is never regained after the change of life.

V-7.18   Complications often ensue during the change of life. The marks on the Head line indicate that your mental strength is weak during this time.

V-7.19   Complications often ensue during the change of life. The marks on the Heart line show that the heart's action could be obstructed.

V-8   LIFE LINE: ITS COLOR

V-8.1   White diminishes the power of this Life line and you do not have much robustness or vitality.

V-8.3 Red is too intense and you are liable to febrile disease; you are ardent in everything, as well as having a strong appetite.

V-8.4 Yellow indicates chronic biliousness which aggravates defects of health and character induced by bile. You are cross, nervous, liable to fits of blues and, if any of the bad side of this type is indicated, you may be vicious, even criminal.

V-8.5 A blue or purple Life line with a marked and badly colored Heart line indicates an advanced state of heart trouble.

V-9 LIFE LINE: THE SPLIT

V-9.1 Indicates reduced strength of constitution during the period of the mark; while this may not result in delicacy, vitality is diminished.

V-9.2 Indicates reduced strength of constitution during the period of the mark; while this may not result in delicacy, vitality is diminished.

V-9.3 Indicates excess of strength, a running over of vitality.

V-9.4 You are filled with ambition, pride and a desire to achieve success. You have your greatest earning capacity and command of your best brain power and strength. During this time you should accomplish the most important part of your life's work.

V-9.5 There is no strength during this period. Your enthusiasm, vital energy, ambition and capacity to accomplish begin to wane during the length of the mark.

V-9.6 This is your turning point, indicating the pinnacle of your capabilities, the period of greatest power, the zenith of your ability to perform great things, and you are never able to do afterwards what is possible before this point is reached. You must be ready to begin the descent of the hill of life.

V-9.7 Indicates that delicacy occurring at this time dissipates your powers in such a way that you never fully recover. When it is indicated that a decline will begin at the age of 50, this is a natural decline of physical power caused by increasing age.

V-9.8 Indicates great ambition and a constant struggle to win.

V-9.9 Indicates a great desire to succeed using the qualities of wisdom and business aptitude.

V-9.10 You are inclined to brilliance, artistic endeavors and success.

V-9.11   Indicates great desire to succeed in a shrewd business-type direction, or in industrial or scientific endeavors.

V-9.12   Indicates that you have a strong ambition which you pursue using your powers of resistance, coolness and calmness.

V-9.13   These qualities strongly influence you: imagination, fancy, mysticism and selfishness.

V-9.14   You have innumerable worries, the result of an intensely nervous condition; you are prone to numerous small illnesses which have kept you in a continual state of depression or ill health. These illnesses have not been serious, but annoying; there will be more, which will keep you depressed.

V-9.15   There have been severe illnesses, which continue, as estimated by the age on the Life line.

V-9.16   This illness is a health defect associated with gout or rheumatism.

V-9.17   This illness could be heart disease.

V-9.18   This illness could be jaundice or a severe bilious fever.

V-9.19   This trouble could be either a blood disorder or throat and bronchial trouble.

V-9.20   Bowel trouble or intestinal inflammation could be the difficulty here.

V-9.21   Rheumatism could be the difficulty here.

V-9.22   This mark could confirm that you have rheumatism.

V-9.23   This trouble could be with kidneys or bladder or, if a woman, with female difficulties.

V-9.24   This mark could confirm trouble with kidneys or bladder or, if a woman, with female difficulties.

V-9.25   You have a vigorous constitution and ability to resist and throw off disease; consequently your chronic trouble shows itself in a severe illness, not a prolonged period of delicacy.

V-9.26   Your constitution is not robust and cannot shake off the type of health problems that may ensue.

V-9.27   You are not naturally robust and could have a severe attack of head trouble which leaves a delicacy from which normal strength may never be regained. Your head remains delicate as a result.

V-9.28 Worry concerning the influence of other people could have caused an illness.

V-9.29 Shows a tendency towards suffocation, possibly attacks of asthma.

V-9.30 Illness could come from stomach trouble.

V-9.31 Could indicate throat and lung trouble.

V-9.32 Indicates that you achieve success in your personal ambitions. In the early years it means scholastic distinction; in later years, business achievement.

V-9.33 Indicates minor achievements.

V-9.34 Indicates major achievements.

V-9.35 Indicates a great desire to change.

V-9.36 Indicates interference in business and work.

V-9.37 Indicates a serious misfortune connected with close relatives; an accidental death in the family with serious financial repercussions.

V-9.38 Indicates a serious misfortune experienced in the affections: lost love, for example.

V-9.39 May indicate a broken bone.

V-9.40 Indicates an accident or misfortune to the person causing the interference.

V-9.41 Could indicate an accident of some sort.

V-9.42 Indicates an accident to, and sometimes the death of, a person who affects your life.

V-9.43 This is a common sign for the suicide of a person who affects your life.

V-9.44 Indicates you have been forced by close relatives into a restrictive position involving religion or the military.

V-9.45 Ambitions are realized. Religion is strong and it can be assumed that your leadership is in the church.

V-9.46 Restrictions for faith reasons: the convent, priesthood or close family may oppose your ambition.

V-9.47 Indicates a major achievement in the arts.

V-9.48 Indicates a mistake in your career.

V-9.49 Indicates a mistake in the affections.

V-9.50 Indicates a loss of money, usually caused by ill health.

V-9.51 A mental or physical wound of some sort will occur.

V-9.52 There could be danger to the head.

V-9.53 Some sort of danger to the head may occur.

V-9.54 There is interference with plans and ideas.

V-9.55 Denotes troubles, worries and great anxiety regarding the affections.

V-9.56 Denotes troubles and worries.

V-9.57 Denotes troubles, worries and loss of money or even loss of position; often a disgrace.

V-9.58 Indicates that troubles, worries and anxieties of a domestic nature could injure your health.

V-9.59 Denotes troubles and worries.

V-9.60 Denotes troubles and worries.

V-9.61 Your anxieties could cause an illness.

V-9.62 Indicates a disgraceful liaison.

V-10 LIFE LINE: THE BREAK

V-10.1 Indicates a check or obstruction to health, consequently a threat to life, these obstructions coming either from illness or accident. In a healthy hand, this mark should be interpreted as indicating an accident, the cause of which is difficult to diagnose.

V-10.2 Indicates an interruption in your life, one which is repaired almost immediately.

V-10.3 Indicates a menace to life.

V-10.4 Indicates a gravely serious situation.

V-10.5 Your vitality is diminishing but you are able to resist this problem after each attack. You gradually grow weaker until your vitality is dissipated. This line indicates constitutional weakness and special problems.

V-10.6 Your vitality is diminishing but you are able to resist this problem after each attack. You gradually grow weaker until your vitality is dissipated. This line indicates constitutional weakness and special problems.

V-10.7   In the first few years of life there is a gradual overcoming of difficulties.

V-10.8   The health problem or accident which caused this mark creates a period of delicacy.

V-10.9   The disease or accident which caused this mark creates a period of delicacy. There is little possibility of complete recovery.

V-10.10   At the approximate age of 50 there is a gradual waning of vital force until it runs out; a period of great weakness begins when there is not enough strength left to resist disease or accident, and an illness or an accident occurs. Health returns by degrees.

V-12   LIFE LINE: THE DOT

V-12.1   Could indicate an acute illness or an accident.

V-12.2   Indicates that an illness was of such severity that the constitution did not regain its strength.

V-12.3   Indicates that an attack of head fever undermined the constitution and complete recovery did not follow.

V-12.4   The illness was bronchitis or other throat trouble.

V-12.5   The illness could be inflammation of the bowels.

V-12.6   Indicates that the illness could be heart disease.

V-12.7   Indicates that the illness could be a bilious fever. The mark on the Health line indicates an acute attack, the Health line itself indicating chronic biliousness.

V-12.8   Indicates that the illness is a disease of the joints.

V-12.9   The chances of a disease of the joints are increased by a Chance line and a mark on the "B" Mount.

V-12.10   Indicates the attack to be kidney or bladder trouble of an acute nature.

V-12.11   Indicates an accident; this character type is predisposed to accidents.

V-12.12   Indicates poisoning, self-administered.

V-12.13   Indicates illness in the form of a fever.

V-12.14 Denotes danger from a wound.

V-12.15 An illness has left a nervous complaint.

V-13 LIFE LINE: THE ISLAND

V-13.1 Indicates a period of delicacy. The point where the mark begins is the beginning period of delicacy and the end of the island tells when it is over.

V-13.2 Indicates a single illness, the nature of which may be indicated by another part of the hand.

V-13.3 Indicates a succession of illnesses and delicacy, the cause of which may be indicated by other parts of the hand.

V-13.4 Indicates an illness and delicacy that is increasing.

V-13.5 The illness or delicacy is diminishing.

V-13.6 Indicates a chronic state of ill health rather than acute attacks. Primarily this indicates delicacy and gives warning to look for other problems.

V-13.7 Indicates great nervousness which is likely the cause of health troubles.

V-13.8 If no other health problem shows up, severe headaches are indicated.

V-13.9 If no other health problem shows up, a head disturbance of a more serious nature is indicated.

V-13.10 The Head line shows the cause of the delicacy indicated on the Life line.

V-13.11 Head problems could be the cause of the delicacy shown by this mark on the Life line.

V-13.12 Heart disease could be the cause of this delicacy. These marks on the Heart line indicate acute attacks; if many are present, the attacks come frequently.

V-13.13 General heart weakness could cause the delicacy shown by this mark on the Life line. This Heart line does not indicate acute attacks, but rather a general structural deficiency.

V-13.14 Biliousness is intense and could cause the delicacy shown by the Life line.

V-13.15 Dyspepsia, indigestion and all forms of stomach trouble could cause the delicacy shown by the Life line.

V-13.16 An acute attack is followed by a period of delicacy, the nature of which may be indicated by another part of the hand.

V-13.17 Could indicate joint disease as the cause of the delicacy; could be rheumatism or gout.

V-13.18 Indicates that paralysis is the trouble.

V-13.19 Could mean an apoplectic tendency is the cause of trouble.

V-13.20 Could mean extreme biliousness and indigestion is the cause of trouble.

V-13.21 Indicates that extreme biliousness and indigestion is the cause of trouble. Yellow confirms this. The other marks on the Head line could also indicate headaches.

V-13.22 A woman's change of life. The age is approximately 42 to 56.

V-13.23 A woman's change of life only causes delicacy during the period of change.

V-13.24 An indication that you never recover your full strength and vigor after the change of life.

V-13.25 Female weakness could be an added impediment to a successful change of life.

V-13.26 Female weakness could be an added impediment to a successful change of life. There is a Chance line that could confirm this mark.

V-13.27 Female weakness could be an added impediment to a successful change of life.

V-15 LIFE LINE: THE STAR

V-15.1 This mark has been verified many times as indicating sudden death. However, whether it means this or not depends very much on the type of person involved. A complete analysis should disclose the cause of this mark.

V-15.2 Could indicate the loss of a parent or close one by a fatal accident.

V-16 LIFE LINE: THE CROSS

V-16.1 This mark is generally the result of illness or accident.

265

V-16.2 Could indicate danger during childhood.

V-17 LIFE LINE: A SISTER LINE

V-17.1 Counteracts feeble health or danger to life. Shows you have the strength to overcome any problem.

W

W-1 INFLUENCE LINE

W-1.1 The Influence line tells about people who have strongly influenced your life, either for good or ill, generally representing members of one's own family or the closest of friends. If the latter, they are those who have grown into your life and have become a part of it. In all cases they have strong influence.

W-1.2 The more lines there are, the greater the number of people who have exerted strong influence. You are influenced by many.

W-1.3 In some hands few of these lines are seen. The fewer the number, the more self-contained you are; you make few close friends, and even blood relatives do not greatly influence you.

W-1.4 Indicates an increase of love, sympathy, grace, passion and generosity in your character, and particularly an increase in the sexual appetites. The more grilles there are, the higher your sexual desires.

W-1.5 The absence of a grille on the "G" Mount shows an absence of sexual desires; this calm Mount indicates that you expend your energy in a love of beauty.

W-3 INFLUENCE LINE: ITS STARTING POINT

W-3.1 Reflects early years in life. The Influence line which runs closest to the Life line is the closest influence. This may be mother, father, a brother or a sister. A line starting near the beginning generally refers to the mother, because a mother's influence begins earlier in life than that of anyone else. Next follows other relatives, grandparents being generally associated with the fourth line. In any case, you know who these people are.

W-3.2 Reflects early years in life. Tells of a new love affair.

W-3.3   Reflects early years in life. Tells of a new love that slowly drifts away.

W-3.4   Reflects early years in life. This generally refers to the husband or wife, because it is at this age that marriage occurs. This line becomes your dominating influence line from the time of its appearance if the marriage is happy, but it shows only faintly if the marriage has made no more than a passing impression on you.

W-3.5   The wife or husband has displaced the mother completely through force.

W-3.6   Shows that through the power of another the affections have been lost.

W-3.7   This influence is a disadvantage to you.

W-3.8   Reflects early years in life. Shows that you are under the influence of another for the duration of the mark, possibly under guardianship.

W-3.9   The wife or husband has displaced the mother completely through force.

W-3.10   This influence is bad; people with such a line can scarcely call their souls their own.

W-4   INFLUENCE LINE: ITS LENGTH

W-4.1   Reflects early years in life. The length of these lines shows the duration of the influences as factors in your life. In this case, either the immediate family or someone close has influenced you up to the approximate age indicated.

W-4.2   A relative has greatly influenced you.

W-5   INFLUENCE LINE: ITS COURSE

W-5.1   Reflects middle years in life. Indicates that the influence of some distant person is gradually coming nearer to your life and growing stronger.

W-6   INFLUENCE LINE: ITS TERMINATION

W-6.1   This mark indicates the ceasing of the influence of someone very closely connected to you.

W-6.2   This mark indicates the ceasing of the influence of a distant relative or friend.

W-7   INFLUENCE LINE: ITS CHARACTER

W-7.1   This influence is powerful.

W-7.2   This influence is not strong.

W-7.3   This influence is strong in the beginning but gradually grows weaker until its effect on you disappears.

W-7.4   This influence is strong in the beginning, but at the approximate age indicated it begins to fade and gradually gets weaker as the years progress.

W-7.5   The person who influences you gradually grows away from you and finally disappears. This is an indication of estrangement.

W-7.6   The person who influences you gradually grows away from you and finally disappears. This is an indication of estrangement.

W-7.7   This shows that a succession of relatives or other parties have replaced each other as the leading influence.

W-7.8   Indicates that while your health has been delicate, some close person has been your mainstay in life. The influence may have been a nurse.

W-7.9   During a time of weak mental condition in your early life, you were sustained by the strong influence of someone for as long as such help was needed; as you grew stronger, the influence declined.

W-7.10   The influence is strong, then weak, and exerts its power spasmodically.

W-7.11   Your spouse is under the domination of a mother — his or her own, or yours.

W-9   INFLUENCE LINE: THE SPLIT

W-9.1   Indicates an impediment to your career and a check to your upward tendency.

W-9.2   Indicates that the influence has caused an impediment to your career.

W-9.3   Indicates an impediment to your career.

W-9.4   Indicates that the death of a relative caused an impediment to your career.

W-9.5   These marks indicate people or events which crossed your life and impeded you. They both impede your influences and worry and harass them.

W-9.6   Thin and puny lines indicate minor annoyances.

W-9.7   The seriousness of these marks must be determined according to how weak you are. They indicate people or events which continuously cross your life and impede you.

W-9.8   Deep split lines indicate illnesses of a serious nature.

W-9.9   Many split lines indicate continuing worries.

W-9.10   The person who influences you has a life of continual worry and impediment.

W-9.11   Some disaster has happened to this influence which has brought on delicacy and ends in tragedy. The cause of the mark has often been verified as the father; the death or injury of the father so shocks the mother that she never recovers.

W-9.12   Your family life has in many cases been found to suffer constant interruption and causes grief.

W-9.13   There is something most unpleasant connected with this impediment. It will cast a shadow over your life owing to some fault not your own.

W-9.14   You are troubled by relatives or close persons.

W-9.15   Indicates that the influence could cause your life to come to a premature end.

W-9.16   Relatives or people close to you uplift you.

W-9.17   Indicates that you are continually pulled down by your own kin, or by a person close to you.

W-9.18   Indicates that this relative, or a person close to you, is most ambitious. This person could spur you on and increase your success.

W-10   INFLUENCE LINE: THE BREAK

W-10.1   The influence of this person disappears and returns several times in your life.

W-10.2   There is a very close but intermittent influence, and another strengthening influence. Often such influences heal and correct a poor marriage.

W-12 INFLUENCE LINE: THE DOT

W-12.1 The increasing delicacy of a relative or person close to you ends in death; worry brings on delicacy, ending in a serious illness to you.

W-12.2 The increasing delicacy of a relative or person close to you ends in death; worry brings on delicacy, ending in a serious illness to you. There is an indication on your Life line that you might not recover.

W-12.3 The increasing delicacy of a relative or person close to you ends in death; worry brings on delicacy, ending in a serious illness to you. There is an indication on your Life line that you might recover.

W-13 INFLUENCE LINE: THE ISLAND

W-13.1 Indicates a delicate condition of the influence.

W-13.2 A delicate influence dies at the approximate age indicated.

W-13.3 The delicacy of some relative or close person proves a constant worry to you.

W-13.4 Cares or worries about relatives or a close friend seriously affect your health. This probably involves the close nursing of some invalid person.

W-15 INFLUENCE LINE: THE STAR

W-15.1 The increasing delicacy of a relative or person close to you ends in death; worry brings on delicacy, causing a serious illness.

W-15.2 The increasing delicacy of a relative or person close to you ends in death; worry brings on delicacy, causing a serious illness. There is an indication on your Life line that you might not recover.

W-15.3 The increasing delicacy of a relative or person close to you ends in death; worry brings on delicacy, causing a serious illness. There is an indication on your Life line that you might recover.

W-15.4 The death of a relative or close person brings on a severe mental illness.

W-15.5 The delicacy and death of a relative produces a weakened mental condition.

X

X-1 AFFECTION LINE

X-1.1 The lines of Affection or Marriage, as they are commonly called, have been used by palmists as if they indicated marriage. However, to use the word "marriage" in connection with the lines of Affection is misleading, for in no sense can they always be interpreted to indicate a legal marriage contract.

These lines are often seen when no such contract has been entered into but when two people have loved as much as if joined in wedlock. In such people a line of union will appear as if the ceremony had been performed. Viewed from this standpoint, Affection lines are remarkably accurate.

It must be stated that the value of these lines in analysis is considerable if used to their full extent and in combination with others. However, when used by themselves as a hard-and-fast indication of marriage, they will lead to error.

X-2.1 LINE IS ABSENT: You are not likely to be powerfully impressed by anyone. If you are robust and belong to an ardent type then you may have strong desires towards the opposite sex, but when these are satisfied you will relapse into a state of indifference until your superabundance of vitality again turns your thoughts in this direction. You are undemonstrative.

X-2.2 Measure the year of one or all of your affections from the Heart line up to the base of the 4th finger. These marks indicate when you are most likely to experience deep affection.

X-2.3 How long an affection lasts can be determined by measuring the Affection line starting from the outside of the hand and going inwards parallel to the Heart line.

X-2.4 MANY LINES: You are susceptible in affairs of the heart, more or less seriously according to whether the lines are strong or weak.

X-2.5 You show an affection at this point in your life which could be love for a spouse, relative or friend.

X-2.6 PLEASE NOTE: In no case can absolute statements be made that an affair or marriage will occur at a certain time because, although there may be marks present indicating such things, willpower and attitude may be strong enough to overcome them.

X-3 AFFECTION LINE: ITS STARTING POINT

X-3.1 Reflects your early years in life. The affection is of unusual strength. Two people have united to form a single unit, producing the effect of two people in one, thus taking on double strength.

X-4 AFFECTION LINE: ITS LENGTH

X-4.1 Indicates the length of your deepest affection, be it marriage, a relative or a very dear friend.

X-4.2 You have two affections equally strong at the same time.

X-6 AFFECTION LINE: ITS TERMINATION

X-6.1 Reflects the ending years of your strongest affection. The affection ends explosively and suddenly.

X-6.2 Reflects the ending years of your strongest affection. The affection separates and becomes weak. This probably indicates interference in married life, but not always a divorce. It shows the beginning of the dissipation of the affection.

X-6.3 Reflects the ending years of your strongest affection. The estrangement is not serious if the dissipation of the affection is great.

X-6.4 Reflects the ending years of your strongest affection. This indicates either a separation or that your spouse dies first.

X-6.5 Reflects the ending years of your strongest affection. Your spouse dies first.

X-6.6 Reflects the ending years of your strongest affection. You probably do not marry.

X-7 AFFECTION LINE: ITS CHARACTER

X-7.1 Indicates that early love has never entirely disappeared.

X-7.2 Indicates you have married for convenience or money, not from strong love.

X-7.3 Indicates you have no really strong affection. You have a brotherly or sisterly affection; you marry, but love is not your absorbing passion. Such people, giving little demonstration of affection, are indifferent, cold and, if they have many marks showing affection, are apt to be flirts.

X-7.4   Indicates that you lead suitors on for the pleasure of disappointing them. You have no real affection and are selfish, cold and cruel.

X-7.5   Indicates that you lead suitors on for the pleasure of disappointing them. You have no real affection and are selfish, cold and cruel.

X-7.6   Indicates you have no real affection and could be selfish, cold and cruel.

X-7.7   Indicates you have no real affection and could be selfish, cold and cruel.

X-7.8   Such people show deep, lasting affection, love ardently and constantly, and make sacrifices for those they love. It is their pleasure and pride to be constant and true.

X-7.9   You pursue a life of ardent attachment, of reliability and steadfastness, from beginning to end.

X-7.10 You gradually lose the strength of your attachment.

X-7.11 Your attachment was weak in the beginning and gradually becomes weaker as the years go by.

X-9   AFFECTION LINE: THE SPLIT

X-9.1   You have an affection for someone brilliant and famous.

X-9.2   The affection in your life is full of sorrows and disappointments.

X-9.3   You are uplifted; the affection is a benefit to you.

X-9.4   Indicates that relatives or personal friends are interfering with your affections.

X-9.5   Your affections are interfered with by a near relative or personal friend. You could lose enjoyment of the marriage relationship because of this interference.

X-9.6   Your affections are interfered with by a near relative or close friend. You could lose enjoyment of your affectionate relationship because of this interference.

X-9.7   An interference with your affections results in some form of head illness.

X-9.8   The person you marry dies first. The death was, or will be, sudden.

X-9.9   Indicates an objection to the marriage or affection.

X-10 AFFECTION LINE: THE BREAK

    X-10.1 Indicates that the affection is interfered with or broken in some way.

    X-10.2 Your affections could be disturbed, but you recover.

    X-10.3 Indicates you could lose your affection and not regain it.

X-11 AFFECTION LINE: THE TRIDENT AND TASSEL

    X-11.1 Reflects ending years in life. Shows the complete dissipation and scattering of the affections.

    X-11.2 Reflects ending years in life. Shows the complete dissipation and scattering of the affections.

X-12 AFFECTION LINE: THE DOT

    X-12.1 Indicates an impediment to the course of the affection.

    X-12.2 Indicates an impediment to the course of the affection, which is dissipated.

    X-12.3 Indicates an impediment to the course of the affection, which disappears gradually.

X-13 AFFECTION LINE: THE ISLAND

    X-13.1 There is some unhappiness during the course of the affection.

    X-13.2 Indicates that you never have affection enough to marry or to have a close relationship.

X-16 AFFECTION LINE: THE CROSS

    X-16.1 There could be a serious impediment to your affection.

Y

Y-1 CAREER LINE

    Y-1.1 Career lines indicate the course of people's lives from the standpoint of material success and show whether they will have a difficult time, or whether things will come easily to them. It can also locate their most productive periods. All indications on the Career line refer to financial affairs.

Y-2   CAREER LINE IS ABSENT

Y-2.1   There are many successful people with an absent Career line; in other prosperous people only its beginning is present. These are "self-made people" who begin life in humble positions and only by dint of energy and application have made their way in the world.

These self-made people are not always brilliant to begin with but have determination and energy and educate themselves, even if it must be done at night after the day's work is over. They do not fail to seize every opportunity for progress and feel that everything depends upon their own efforts; no amount of labor is allowed to stand between them and success.

Y-3   CAREER LINE: ITS STARTING POINT

Y-3.1   Reflects early years in life. Indicates you have material success and that near relatives or friends assist you greatly.

Y-3.2   Reflects early years in life. Indicates you could achieve success, largely due to your own efforts.

Y-3.3   Reflects early years in life. Your success could be materially assisted by one of the opposite sex. This may either be by good advice or by rendering financial aid.

Y-3.4   Reflects early years in life. You have a negative existence for the first part of life, as this is the point when you were too young to accomplish anything by your own efforts, and such a beginning of the line indicates that you were not born with a silver spoon in your mouth. If other lines show problems in health or attitude, then this could also be the reason for the late start in life indicated by the Career line.

Y-3.5   Reflects early years in life. You did little during the beginning of your life, perhaps because of a delicacy. At the approximate age indicated, you begin a productive life.

Y-3.6   Reflects early years in life. You continue to do better in business as your strength increases.

Y-3.7   Indicates your start in life may be impeded by a head weakness; your fate does not improve until you get yourself together. This mark shows that you will.

Y-3.8   Reflects early years in life. Indicates that your career is hindered first by a head problem and then by a possible heart weakness. You cannot begin to do your best until these problems have passed. In this case, they pass.

Y-3.9 Reflects early years in life. The natural course of this line was favorable, but because the mark appears in the active hand, something has occurred to alter the original plan of things. This may be a health problem, laziness or influence from family, friends or outsiders. It can often be explained by some accident to the parents. As this early period covers childhood, it is not your fault that your start in life was not as it should be.

Y-3.10 Reflects early years in life. It is possible that the death of a parent or a very close person has prevented a good start to your life.

Y-3.11 Reflects early years in life. The influence of relatives and great ambition unite to further your career; you could be very successful.

Y-3.12 Reflects early years in life. The assistance of relatives and ambition help for a while but do not bring ultimate success.

Y-3.13 WITH INFLUENCE LINE: Reflects early years in life. The assistance of relatives and ambition help for a while but do not bring ultimate success. An unhappy affection, possibly of your spouse, has injured your prospects.

Y-3.14 Reflects early years in life. A creative and imaginative force in your early years could cause great success in leadership if applied properly.

Y-3.15 Reflects early years in life. A creative and imaginative force in your early years causes great difficulty in leadership.

Y-5 CAREER LINE: ITS COURSE

Y-5.1 Reflects middle years in life. It indicates that you follow a constantly changing course.

Y-5.2 Indicates that you could have increased difficulty in your journey through life.

Y-5.3 Shows a severe reversal of prosperity between the ages of 30 and 45, but you pull through. This is the critical time in most business careers and is the formative financial period in life.

Most people before this age have been cared for and guided by parents or relatives. As the time approaches when you are no longer as dependent upon these aids, you begin to be guided by your own ideas. If these are good, you succeed, but if you believe that the experiences of others do not apply to you, you have disappointments and must pay for your experience.

Y-6   CAREER LINE: ITS TERMINATION

Y-6.1   Indicates that your career is favorable up to the approximate age indicated, when errors of judgment cause problems; you must rely entirely on effort, not luck, and do the best you can to force your way. Your period of greatest production has passed. You have to make great effort to accomplish much.

Y-6.2   Reflects ending years in life. Indicates that your success is the result of great ambition.

Y-6.3   Reflects ending years in life. Indicates that you win success in art, business, or as an actor, according to which phalange of the 3rd finger rules.

Y-6.4   Reflects ending years in life. Indicates that you have shrewdness, business ability, power of expression and a scientific turn of mind to assist your endeavors.

Y-6.5   Reflects ending years in life. Indicates that you achieve success through leadership abilities and power of resistance because you are not discouraged easily.

Y-6.6   Reflects ending years in life. Indicates that you achieve success through hard work and that your abilities continue to be strong even into your retirement years. You will be very productive right to the end.

Y-6.7   Reflects ending years in life. Your career is uncertain and there are worries in old age. This may not mean poverty or even loss of money, but may mean financial checks to your career, disappointments in children, or similar troubles.

Y-6.8   Reflects ending years in life. Ill health in old age troubles your last days. This may not mean poverty or even loss of money, but may mean financial checks to your career, disappointments in children, or similar troubles.

Y-6.9   Reflects ending years in life. Financial difficulties due to ill health cloud your last days.

Y-6.10   Reflects ending years in life. You could suffer losses and trials in old age.

Y-6.11   Reflects ending years in life. This is an indication of troubles and worries in old age.

Y-6.12 Reflects ending years in life. This is an indication of troubles and worries in old age.

Y-7 CAREER LINE: ITS CHARACTER

Y-7.1 Indicates that your material success is secondary to your well-being.

Y-7.2 Indicates that you have exceptionally fine qualities and that with proper care you should be able to achieve great success.

Y-7.3 Favorable conditions continue during your entire life.

Y-7.4 Favorable conditions are present only during the age specified.

Y-7.5 You have your best period during childhood. At this age you really can't take advantage of this opportunity.

Y-7.6 Indicates that you have much in your favor in the way of natural advantages. While you have to exert yourself to bring forth great results, you succeed more easily than those with a defective line or no line at all.

Y-7.7 Indicates a condition in which you have a better attitude towards a career.

Y-7.8 Indicates that you have continual struggles when striving for success.

Y-7.9 Your career is difficult and you have continuous obstructions. Your life may be a labored one, full of disappointments.

Y-7.10 Your career is difficult but you begin to be successful at the approximate age indicated.

Y-7.11 Whatever the cause of the trouble at the beginning, it has been overcome. Such a line shows either that the improved condition arises from the removal of the cause or that you have risen higher than the obstacle.

Y-7.12 The death of a parent or someone very close clouded your early career.

Y-7.13 The death of a dear one has brought a check to the upward course of your life. This has affected your mental strength and thus checked and retarded your career.

Y-7.14 Indicates that you have intermittent periods of prosperity. One must be continually watchful so that, during the low periods, all that was gained is not lost.

Y-7.15 You have continuous financial difficulty from 30 years of age onwards.

Y-7.16 Indicates a continual financial difficulty from the beginning of your career to the end.

Y-9   CAREER LINE: THE SPLIT

Y-9.1 Indicates an obstruction to your career. Continual annoying interferences and impediments.

Y-9.2 Indicates obstructions to your career. They are serious and threaten to destroy your success.

Y-9.3 Indicates the upward tendency of your life. On whatever portion of the line these marks appear, that part of your life is filled with hope and ambition and is more successful than any other period. Physical powers are good.

Y-9.4 Your life is harder, filled with discouragements, and progress is difficult.

Y-9.5 The unfavorable condition of this line is caused by delicacy of health.

Y-9.6 This difficulty could be associated with problems with your health that affect your career.

Y-9.7 This difficulty could be head disease (mental stress, for example) affecting your career.

Y-9.8 This difficulty could be rheumatism or gout which could hinder your career.

Y-9.9 Indicates that your upward course is constantly interfered with. While these interferences may not destroy your upward trend, they hamper and annoy you.

Y-9.10 Each of these events, persons, illnesses or whatever in some way affect your career. This is particularly the case if you are nervous. Some of these events are detrimental; others strengthen and aid your advancement.

Y-9.11 These marks indicate weakening at the approximate age indicated, and impede your progress.

Y-9.12 Indicates that you suffer a career setback due to too much ambition. You endeavor to meet distinguished people who lead you to do foolish things which injure your prospects.

Y-9.13 Your dishonesty brings you grief.

Y-9.14 An influence from relatives or someone you know well causes a disaster in your career.

Y-9.15 The ambitions of your spouse or someone very close lead you to extravagances which you cannot afford. You may never recover from the reversals.

Y-9.16 Ill health bars your prospects.

Y-9.17 You never get over whatever caused this severe check to your career and your fate; financially you suffer.

Y-9.18 These lines indicate events or influences which were abortive attempts to damage your career; while they continue to threaten, they present no immediate danger.

Y-9.19 These lines represent events or influences which have become part of your life but, because the lines do not cut the Career line, your career is not checked.

Y-9.20 Indicates an increase in your prosperity and assistance in overcoming difficulties.

Y-9.21 The influence coming into your life improves your condition.

Y-9.22 The influence coming into your life improves your condition.

Y-9.23 The influence of close relatives improves your career.

Y-9.24 This influence has not been greatly beneficial to your career but was of some help.

Y-9.25 These lines exert a strong influence on your career; by helping and supporting, they act as sister lines and are beneficial to you.

Y-9.26 Good judgment comes to your aid and helps you through your difficulties.

Y-9.27 Your inner resistance, as indicated by the "E" Mount, does not permit discouragements to overthrow you; this saves you from trouble.

Y-9.28 Indicates that you encounter obstacles to your career between the ages of 30 and 45. You could have great difficulty in overcoming these obstacles. This is the critical time in most business careers and is the formative financial period in life.

Most people before this age have been cared for and guided by parents or relatives. As the time approaches when you are no longer as dependent upon these aids, you begin to be guided by your own ideas. If these are good, you get along all right, but if you believe that the experiences of others do not apply to you, you have disappointments and must pay for your experiences.

Y-9.29 Indicates that you encounter obstacles to your career between the ages of 30 and 45. You could have great difficulty in overcoming these obstacles. This is the critical time in most business careers and is the formative financial period in life.

Most people before this age have been cared for and guided by parents or relatives. As the time approaches when you are no longer as dependent upon these aids, you begin to be guided by your own ideas. If these are good, you get along all right, but if you believe that the experiences of others do not apply to you, you have disappointments and must pay for your experiences.

Y-9.30 Indicates that you encounter obstacles to your career between the ages of 30 and 45. You overcome these difficulties and benefit from doing so. This is the critical time in most business careers and is the formative financial period in life.

Y-9.31 Difficulties will arise from errors of judgment between the ages of 30 and 45. This is the critical time in most business careers and is the formative financial period in life. Most people before this age have been cared for and guided by parents or relatives. As the time approaches when you are no longer as dependent upon these aids, you begin to be guided by your own ideas. If these are good, you get along all right, but if you believe that the experiences of others do not apply to you, you have disappointments and must pay for your experiences.

Y-9.32 Indicates that you permit your affections to get the better of you. Sentiment in business is disastrous. This happens between the ages of 30 and 45. This is the critical time in most business careers and is the formative financial period in life. Most people before this age have been cared for and guided by parents or relatives. As the time approaches when you are no longer as dependent upon these aids, you begin to be guided by your own ideas. If these are good, you get along all right, but if you believe that the experiences of others do not apply to you, you have disappointments and must pay for your experiences.

Y-9.33 Ill health has obstructed your career between the ages of 30 and 45. This is the critical time in most business careers and is the formative financial period in life. Most people before this age have been cared for and guided by parents or relatives. As the time approaches when you are no longer as dependent upon these aids, you begin to be guided by your own ideas. If these are good, you get along all right, but if you believe that the experiences of others do not apply to you, you have disappointments and must pay for your experiences.

Y-9.34 The death of a relative obstructs your career between the ages of 30 and 45. This is the critical time in most business careers and is the formative financial period in life. Most people before this age have been cared for and guided by parents or relatives. As the time approaches when you are no longer as dependent upon these aids, you begin to be guided by your own ideas. If these are good, you get along all right, but if you believe that the experiences of others do not apply to you, you have disappointments and must pay for your experiences.

Y-9.35 The death of a relative checks the progress of your career. This is the critical time in most business careers and is the formative financial period in life. Most people before this age have been cared for and guided by parents or relatives. As the time approaches when you are no longer as dependent upon these aids, you begin to be guided by your own ideas. If these are good, you get along all right, but if you believe that the experiences of others do not apply to you, you have disappointments and must pay for your experiences.

Y-9.36 Indicates that your success is largely due to your ambition and ability to command people and obtain support. This is a fine line for a politician.

Y-9.37 Indicates that you win success in art, in business or as an actor, according to which phalange of the 3rd finger rules.

Y-9.38 You have an assured future of wealth and fame because of ambition and leadership attributes, wisdom and brilliance, art and business abilities, all united to assist you in reaping a rich harvest.

Y-9.39 You have shrewdness, business ability, power of expression and a scientific turn of mind which assist in your endeavors.

Y-9.40 You have the assistance of strong mental capabilities in the shaping of your career.

Y-9.41 In many hands this line does not reach the Mount under the 2nd finger, but ends somewhere below it. This indicates periods of productive capacity; it is not strange that it should be absent. The presence of a Mount without a line shows that no forces are working against you; if the line is good in its early course, it indicates that a productive life is behind you and you will enjoy the results of your labor.

Y-9.42 Indicates that you can be promised a productive period only during the time the line exists. The following period will be productive only if you make it so by effort.

Y-9.43 A strong indication that you will be wealthy in your old age.

Y-9.44 Marriage at the age indicated.

Y-9.45 Marriage at the age indicated does not take place.

Y-9.46 Your career is interrupted.

Y-9.47 Some new interests or advantages.

Y-9.48 Indicates partnership at the age the split leaves the Career line.

Y-10 CAREER LINE: THE BREAK

Y-10.1 Some force has been sufficiently strong to halt the progress of your career entirely; it takes on a new character, starts a new direction or does not start at all. A complete change in the course of your life's work.

Y-10.2 These impediments are the result of acquired habits, miscalculations, ill health or other problems. A great many of your trials are brought on by yourself.

Y-10.3 Indicates continuing reversals and a laborious and troubled life. Each mark represents a different misfortune.

Y-10.4 These impediments are the result of acquired habits, miscalculations, ill health or other problems. A great many of your trials are brought on by yourself.

Y-10.5 Indicates that you eventually fight your way to success after numerous disappointments. It is a continual fight, however, requiring great willpower to carry yourself along.

Y-10.6 These impediments are the result of acquired habits, miscalculations, ill health or other problems. A great many of your trials are brought on by yourself.

Y-10.7   You have repeated reversals between the ages of 30 and 45.

Y-10.8   Indicates a situation in which you are personally honored.

Y-10.9   Indicates a change of position, with attendant success. The change is by choice.

Y-10.10 Indicates a change of career into the arts. The change comes by personal choice, with attendant success.

Y-10.11 Indicates that you change careers and enter the sciences. The change comes by personal choice, with attendant success.

Y-13 CAREER LINE: THE ISLAND

Y-13.1   These marks have generally been interpreted as indicating a check to the career, arising from marital infidelity or moral laxness. Indicates a period of financial difficulty lasting the length of the mark.

Y-13.2   This mark usually indicates infidelity, but if it's near the beginning of the Career line then you were too young. Possibly indicates financial difficulty if the mark is higher up on the Career line.

Y-13.3   Prolonged delicacy of health causes difficulty in early life.

Y-13.4   Poor mentality impedes your career.

Y-13.5   The death of a parent or guardian causes financial difficulty during your early years.

Y-13.6   The death of a relative intensifies financial difficulties.

Y-13.7   Constant annoyances in your early years hinder your career.

Y-13.8   Your ambition to move into the front rank causes you to be extravagant; financial difficulties result.

Y-13.9   You have continual financial difficulty during the length of the mark between the approximate years of 30 and 45.

Y-15 CAREER LINE: THE STAR

Y-15.1   Denotes your death.

Y-15.2   Fatality caused by the position of the parents.

Y-15.3   An ill fate follows you through life, unless the lines promise unusual success.

Y-15.4   A catastrophe due to the family.

Y-15.5 A catastrophe due to a friend.

Y-15.6 A mark of misfortune.

Y-16 CAREER LINE: THE CROSS

Y-16.1 You have repeated reversals which you withstand between the ages of 30 and 45. This is the critical time in most business careers and is the formative financial period in life. Most people before this age have been cared for and guided by parents or relatives. As the time approaches when you are no longer as dependent upon these aids, you begin to be guided by your own ideas. If these are good, you get along all right, but if you believe that the experiences of others do not apply to you, you have disappointments and must pay for your experiences.

Y-16.2 Shows a change of life.

Y-16.3 Denotes misfortune.

Y-16.4 Trouble with relatives or friends.

Y-16.5 Anxieties and disappointments in reference to travel.

Z

Z-1 FATE LINE

Z-1.1 This has been variously called the line of the sun and the line of brilliancy; to it has been ascribed the gift of great artistic talents, wealth and fame. No better name has ever been given this line than the Line of Capability. This name expresses in a nutshell the idea which should be applied to the line. It indicates a capability or possibility of accomplishing a great deal and the field in which the capability best operates.

The Fate line must be viewed in the light of character development.

Z-2 FATE LINE IS ABSENT

Z-2.1 It is absolutely incorrect to say that the absence of a Fate line indicates that you possess a lack of success in life, but its presence makes success easier.

Z-3 FATE LINE: ITS STARTING POINT

Z-3.1 Reflects early years in life. This indicates that you possess imagination and the power of language; you could achieve success as an author, etc.

Z-3.2 Reflects early years in life. Indicates that by the display of calmness, resignation, resistance, and the fact that you do not allow yourself to become discouraged, you achieve success and reputation in the world of Handology. The study of character.

Z-3.3 Reflects early years in life. Success comes from love or friendship.

Z-3.4 Reflects early years in life. Denotes great creative power.

Z-3.5 Reflects early years in life. Indicates increased success; if the rest of your Fate line is good, your success will lead to fortune.

Z-4 FATE LINE: ITS LENGTH

Z-4.1 Indicates the possession of great talent, so great that it continues to develop during your life and you achieve much.

Z-4.2 Determines the extent of its influence; the shorter the line, the less important its influence. You have talents, but they do not produce great results.

Z-4.3 Your brilliance operates during the formative period of your life and assists you in passing this critical period with greater ease.

Z-4.4 Indicates that you are endowed with good characteristics; in whichever world you move, you are brilliant. You possess artistic tendencies, success, good health and a happy disposition.

Z-4.5 Shows that you have an appreciation of beauty in art and nature and, with other signs, that you gain an advantage by marrying late in life.

Z-5 FATE LINE: ITS COURSE

Z-5.1 Indicates a vacillating career. You are clever and able to do much in your particular world but are erratic, unstable, unreliable and unconventional. Such people are versatile but go off on tangents and waste their brilliance and talents in "chasing butterflies" instead of pushing forward steadily in one direction. You may do something wonderful or may pass everything by.

Z-5.2 Reflects middle years in life. You finally channel your energies in a specific direction. You may become a great wanderer, be erratic or a crank, but you earn a reputation for something.

Z-5.3   Reflects middle years in life. Your life ends brilliantly. You achieve a wide reputation and, though an unsteady but talented person, have your work finally crowned with success.

Z-6   FATE LINE: ITS TERMINATION

Z-6.1   Reflects ending years in life. Indicates protection from misfortunes of all kinds, not only towards the end of life, but during the whole of it.

Z-6.2   Reflects ending years in life. This is a corrective mark which offsets any poor mark terminating under the 3rd finger.

Z-6.3   Reflects ending years in life. No matter how good the line may be, this mark clouds your latter days; it indicates loss of money and reputation.

Z-6.4   Reflects ending years in life. This may denote wealth from two sources.

Z-6.5   Reflects ending years in life. Denotes success, wealth and position.

Z-7   FATE LINE: ITS CHARACTER

Z-7.1   Indicates success and a high reputation. You possess creative power in whichever world you operate. You are not merely fond of color, painting and art but have the creative power to produce work of merit.

Z-7.2   The great creative power indicated by a deep line is missing. If you are an artist, for example, you are guided by the effects produced by other artists; if the mental, business or material worlds rule, you might achieve less celebrity and make less money. If the Head line is partially thick, you may lose the mental capacity to be successful; if the Head line is thin from beginning to end, you have to work harder to be successful.

Z-7.3   Indicates that little power of success is left; you like pretty things, are fond of artists, affect a slightly unconventional, nonconforming manner, but avoid attempting any productions yourself.

Z-7.4   Indicates an utter lack of artistic talent, although you may be impressed with your own knowledge on matters of art. You do not realize your own shallowness, and most of your effort is in talk.

Z-7.5   Indicates that you have a series of successes and failures, but there is no even, steady operation of a strong line. You make some efforts which bring money and reputation and then relapse into a state of

287

inaction, periodically replaced by other series of efforts followed by stagnation. Such people are brilliant "spurters" but cannot be relied upon for continuous action.

Z-7.6 A much more favorable indication of final success and reputation. The last period of your life contains one of your better efforts.

Z-7.7 The early part of your life is best, and your wealth-producing capacity diminishes as life progresses.

Z-9 FATE LINE: THE SPLIT

Z-9.1 Indicates constant impediments to your success, affecting your career.

Z-9.2 You overcome obstacles.

Z-9.3 Shows that the obstacles are annoying interferences, which keep you constantly worried and, by disturbing your mental peace, impede your progress. Also shows a menace to your reputation.

Z-9.4 Some obstruction near the end is insurmountable.

Z-9.5 Indicates that you have ill health and delicacy at this age, from which you may never recover and which could ruin your prospects of success at chosen endeavors.

Z-9.6 Indicates that your mental powers fail; this checks your career and puts an end to your success.

Z-9.7 An error in calculation causes an impediment to your career from which you do not recover. Often, this refers to investments made early in life which turn out badly.

Z-9.8 Indicates that you have a diversity of talent but achieve less with what you have than if your efforts were concentrated.

Z-9.9 Indicates that you have combined wisdom, brilliance and shrewdness. This combination could reap wealth and renown.

Z-9.10 Increases the good effect of the line and, when seen on a good line, gives a more certain indication of success. Your life seems buoyant enough to rise above obstacles that may get in the way; you float over difficulties instead of being dragged under by them.

Z-9.11 You need greater and more constant effort to achieve success. You are pulling a load uphill and there are times when it gets very heavy. You do not overcome obstacles easily; such a line bears no promise of a brilliant life.

Z-9.12 Coupled with great talent, you have strong ambition and the power of leadership. You are successful and are sure to win fame if you do not secure wealth.

Z-9.13 Your ambition is crowned with success.

Z-9.14 You are certain to achieve great renown.

Z-9.15 Wisdom, soberness, frugality, a scientific turn of mind and the balancing qualities of your character increase your success. You are not led by traditions, but think for yourself.

Z-9.16 Your qualities of wisdom, soberness and balance bring great success.

Z-9.17 Indicates that you are unsuccessful and lose reputation rather than gain.

Z-9.18 Indicates great success as a leader.

Z-9.19 Indicates great success using common sense.

Z-9.20 Indicates great success in business, science and industry.

Z-9.21 Indicates that you fail to achieve ultimate success by reason of too great a diversity of effort.

Z-9.22 Indicates that you fail to achieve ultimate success by reason of too great a diversity of effort.

Z-9.23 Indicates that you fail to achieve ultimate success by reason of too great a diversity of effort.

Z-9.24 Indicates that you have shrewdness, business ability, a scientific turn of mind and great powers of expression in addition to your brilliant character; you achieve distinction.

Z-9.25 Your success is intensified.

Z-9.26 Sterling qualities are added. You are self-reliant, able to defend yourself, not easily discouraged and, if necessary, force your way through the world.

Z-9.27 Renown is added to your success.

Z-9.28 Indicates the power of imagination, the ability to paint word pictures and the power of expression. As an author you could become successful. If the hand is musical, you love only the classical form.

Z-9.29 You are passionately fond of music of a melodious nature. If you are an instrumentalist, you excel in playing with expression and feeling.

Z-9.30 These marks must be interpreted as indicating impediments to your success from mental stress and/or influences from friends or relatives.

Z-9.31 Indicates good mental powers.

Z-9.32 Indicates that a powerful brain has given you judgment and self-control, which have contributed to your success.

Z-9.33 Indicates unusual mental powers.

Z-9.34 Indicates that you benefit greatly by your goodness of heart, sympathy, and an affectionate disposition towards friends who assist in promoting your interests.

Z-9.35 These marks have often been interpreted as indicating inheritances from relatives, but they do not necessarily indicate this particular form of help. You have received good counsel, sympathy and support, as well as financial aid.

Z-9.36 Your affections stand in the way of success.

Z-9.37 Indicates that money assists your career; sometimes it denotes marriage.

Z-9.38 Shows that you receive money from relatives or friends.

Z-9.39 Shows that you receive money from strangers.

Z-9.40 Too many vertical lines under the 3rd finger destroy your power of concentration; results are nil.

Z-9.41 Shows want of means, preventing development of your talents.

Z-9.42 Denotes robbery. You do not protect your material items; you leave doors open, and so on.

Z-9.43 Denotes robbery with the threat of violence.

Z-9.44 Indicates that an enemy causes injury to your reputation.

Z-10 FATE LINE: THE BREAK

Z-10.1 Indicates that your talents during the period covered by this mark are simply latent. Ill health may render inoperative even the most brilliant talents.

Z-10.2 Your talents during the period covered by this mark are simply latent.

Z-10.3 Delicate health prevents the use of your talents.

Z-10.4 Your mental powers are weak and you cannot give the attention necessary to make your affairs successful.

Z-10.5 Indicates setbacks to your ambition and upward course. These are impediments which destroy the usefulness of the line and render inoperative all of its beneficial influences. Such a line shows that you may have a strong liking for art, if that world rules, but you will never be a producer or a creator of it; you are, if wealthy, an art patron.

Z-10.6 Any repair sign tends to overcome the obstacles and bring about better conditions. You like pretty things, are fond of artists, at times affect a little Bohemianism, but avoid attempting any productions yourself.

Z-11 FATE LINE: THE TRIDENT

Z-11.1 Indicates celebrity and wealth from mental efforts.

Z-11.2 You scatter your efforts in so many directions that you accomplish little. Your talent is too diversified.

Z-12 FATE LINE: THE DOT

Z-12.1 Tells of a menace to your reputation.

Z-12.2 Indicates loss of your good name.

Z-12.3 Indicates the whisperings of enemies.

Z-12.4 After a life of prosperity, you lose your reputation.

Z-13 FATE LINE: THE ISLAND

Z-13.1 Indicates that your gambling disposition is increased by extreme self-confidence.

Z-13.2 Indicates that your gambling disposition is increased by extreme self-confidence.

Z-13.3 Indicates that your gambling disposition is increased by extreme self-confidence.

Z-15 FATE LINE: THE STAR

Z-15.1 An indication of brilliant success; this star is like an electric light ending a good line and intensifying the whole combination.

Z-15.2 Indicates that you are dazzling in your brilliance and that the greatest fame comes to you. Prosperity and renown continue to the end of your life.

Z-15.3 You are brilliant and successful throughout your entire life.

Z-15.4 Denotes great success.

Z-16 FATE LINE: THE CROSS

Z-16.1 Indicates a blemish on your reputation. It also indicates poor judgment; you make many mistakes in the course of your life, which consequently terminates unfavorably.

Z-16.2 Shows disappointment in obtaining a position.

Z-16.3 Shows many disappointments and obstacles.

Z-17 FATE AND SISTER LINES

Z-17.1 Gives added strength to an already fine indication. You could have the greatest success.

Z-17.2 Frequently the Career and Fate lines are interdependent, and in many cases one is strong at a time when the other is weak. In such cases they act upon each other as Sister lines and one repairs the damage to the other. It is so in this case.

ZA

ZA-1 HEALTH LINE

ZA-1.1 The Health line has been variously called the line of liver and the Hepatica line. It is exceedingly useful as a guide to business success, as no factor better enables one to cope with the affairs of the world than a clear brain, and nothing more surely keeps the brain from clogging than a good digestion and an active liver.

The Health line is not found on all hands. At least half of all hands are without it. I do not regard the absence of the Health line as necessarily a detriment, because many people without this line enjoy good health.

ZA-2   HEALTH LINE IS ABSENT

ZA-2.1   Shows that in health matters there are no disturbances to cause you trouble and, if you take care of your stomach and liver, etc., you give yourself the possibility of having no trouble from your organs. Your health in these directions is largely "self-made" and proportionate to the care you take of yourself.

ZA-4   HEALTH LINE: ITS LENGTH

ZA-4.1   The influence of this line is felt during your entire life.

ZA-5   HEALTH LINE: ITS COURSE

ZA-5.1   Indicates a chronic biliousness. You may have attacks of bilious fever and various liver problems. With biliousness there is very frequently a complication of rheumatism. Your business career is unsteady and subject to many changes or variations.

ZA-6   HEALTH LINE: ITS TERMINATION

ZA-6.1   Reflects ending years in life. There is an influence which prevents your best interests from being realized.

ZA-6.2   Reflects ending years in life. Your career is hampered.

ZA-6.3   Reflects ending years in life. Even worse difficulties are indicated, resulting from either poor health or dishonesty.

ZA-6.4   Reflects ending years in life. You could lose your reputation.

ZA-6.5   Reflects ending years in life. Indicates that you divide your energy among several talents and do not achieve as great a success as would be possible by concentrating your energy.

ZA-7   HEALTH LINE: ITS CHARACTER

ZA-7.1   Indicates a good digestion, a healthy action of the liver, good vitality, strong constitution, a clear brain and good memory. Whatever type you are and whatever your occupation, you have the assistance of these powerful allies.

ZA-7.2   The effect of this line upon the Life line is as favorable as that of a strong Warrior line: it builds up and gives strength to the areas where weakness exists. Many times such a Health line replaces the functions of the Life line; this often accounts for the health of a person with a poor Life line.

ZA-7.3   Indicates that you may still have a good digestive system and proper action of the liver, and that your health and character attributes act in conjunction to produce success in business.

ZA-7.4   You are not vitally strong and any severe stress to your stomach results in its derangement. As a consequence you are frequently despondent and predisposed to sudden and violent headaches, heartburn, stir stomach and indigestion.

When the vital functions are performing, you get along all right; however, with such a line, constant care is necessary as to diet and hygiene, for while such people cannot be said to be sickly, they are not particularly healthy. This weakened condition tells upon the energies, the ambitions and the ability to conduct business.

ZA-7.5   You have a diseased liver and stomach. You are predisposed to inflammation of the gall duct, gall stones, cirrhosis and numerous structural liver troubles which are always serious. People with this mark suffer from mental sluggishness and depression.

You are pessimistic, suspicious, intensely nervous and cross; life is a burden both to yourself and to your friends. You cannot have a clear head, keen foresight, command of self, energy and kindred qualities necessary to the successful pursuit of business.

ZA-7.6   There is a period when health is impaired; at such a time you must use great care, get lots of sleep and avoid dissipation. If this is done, the trouble may be avoided.

ZA-7.7   The good health of your first years is followed by a serious ailment of the liver and consequent stomach derangement which could impair health and success.

ZA-7.8   The good health of your first years is followed by a serious ailment of the liver and consequent stomach derangement which impairs your health and success. The Life line shows this problem to be quite serious.

ZA-7.9   Could indicate a fitful condition of the stomach and liver. There are periods when the liver does not properly perform its functions, the digestion is poor and life becomes a drag. These alternating intervals of good health and weakness mar life's steadiness and prevent you from getting good results.

ZA-7.10   This mark is often associated with sudden attacks of temporary insanity.

ZA-7.11   Indicates troubles to the digestive system.

ZA-9   HEALTH LINE: THE SPLIT

ZA-9.1   Indicates biliousness or severe headaches.

ZA-9.2   Indicates that a severe illness may have occurred.

ZA-9.3   Indicates a continuous sickness or headaches for the full length of the mark.

ZA-9.4   Indicates great suffering from nervousness, biliousness or severe headaches, all arising from imperfect action of the stomach and liver.

ZA-9.5   You have excellent health and great success in business.

ZA-9.6   You succeed but have to work harder to accomplish results.

ZA-9.7   Indicates success in business, aided by your ambition and your ability to lead and control people.

ZA-9.8   Influential acquaintances and friends greatly assist you.

ZA-9.9   You are aided by soberness, wisdom, frugality and carefulness. Because you look on the dark as well as the bright side of undertakings, you are successful in business. This is an ideal mark for a person who deals with money.

ZA-9.10   Indicates that you have great shrewdness and business ability, aided by a brilliant mind and agreeable manner; you are very successful. This is an ideal mark for a merchant.

ZA-9.11   You could succeed as a writer.

ZA-9.12   Indicates success due to mental powers of concentration; such a person is best adapted to a literary or scientific career.

ZA-9.13   Shows a change which is of advantage to you in business relations or a profession.

ZA-9.14   Shows that your health has been injured by unsuitable surroundings.

ZA-10 HEALTH LINE: THE BREAK

ZA-10.1   There are no more potent factors in the healthy and vigorous operation of the brain than a good digestion and proper bile secretion. The first effect of indigestion is intense depression. A person with indigestion becomes morbid and sees everything through a glass colored by a disordered stomach. When the attack has passed, the person's head clears and he or she sees things in their proper light.

ZA-10.2   A defective condition of the head may be accounted for by a poor digestive system and/or disturbed action of the stomach.

ZA-10.3   Disturbed action of the stomach sometimes produces functional derangement of the heart. Health lines also indicate such excellent digestion and liver action that the effects of a weak heart may never be markedly exhibited.

ZA-10.4   Indicates a person who virtually never knows a day's sickness. If this is present in someone who is animal in character, the intense good health and strength of vitality renders the person fierce in passions, inordinate in appetites; from this class (if male) often comes the rapist and drunkard. Such persons should never choose indoor occupations.

ZA-10.5   Indicates the worst form of stomach trouble and indigestion with their train of ills; gastric fever and inflammation of the bowels are among the possible acute disorders.

ZA-10.6   Severe stomach disorder could occur at the approximate age indicated.

ZA-10.7   Indicates that you need to do as much as possible before the age of 30, for at that time the powerful allies of the good Health line desert you. The years between 30 and 45 are among the most difficult in your life. You may recover in later years if care is used.

ZA-10.8   Indicates that you may not recover from ill health. This could happen between the ages of 30 and 45.

ZA-10.9   Indicates that your health is impaired at the time of this mark and, consequently, your business career may suffer.

ZA-10.10   Indicates extreme delicacy of the stomach; shows a person to be in a continual state of indigestion. Such a person has many headaches and must use constant care not to disturb the digestion.

ZA-10.11   A danger to your life has been averted. The cause may have come from several directions.

ZA-10.12   A danger to your life and health is being averted. The cause could have come from several directions.

ZA-11 HEALTH LINE: THE TRIDENT

ZA-11.1   Reflects ending years in life. Your efforts are so scattered that no great success can be achieved.

ZA-12 HEALTH LINE: THE DOT

ZA-12.1   Indicates acute attacks of biliousness or stomach trouble.

ZA-12.2   Could mean that the natural stomach delicacy associated with your leadership qualities has caused this trouble.

ZA-12.3   An acute attack of bilious fever.

ZA-12.4   Indicates an attack of gout or rheumatism that could become more serious.

ZA-12.5   A severe attack of heart trouble brought on by derangement of the digestive organ occurs at the age indicated.

ZA-12.6   An indication of chronic heart attacks.

ZA-12.7   A severe attack of biliousness or gastric fever at the age indicated.

ZA-12.8   A severe attack of inflammation of the intestines, appendicitis, peritonitis or some other acute intestinal disorder at the age indicated.

ZA-12.9   Gout or, more likely, rheumatic fever has occurred or will occur at the age indicated.

ZA-12.10   A severe attack of inflammation of the intestines, appendicitis, peritonitis or some other acute intestinal disorder has occurred or will occur at the age indicated.

ZA-13 HEALTH LINE: THE ISLAND

ZA-13.1   Indicates a delicacy of health. This may arise from the liver and stomach or from appendicitis or inflammation of the intestines or a difficulty of the head, heart or any other organ, which can be determined by further examination of the hand.

ZA-13.2   An indication of great delicacy of the throat and lungs.

ZA-13.3   Indicates that you need to use the greatest care to avoid any exposure which might induce the development of consumption, bronchitis, pneumonia or any disease of the throat, bronchia or lungs. Cancer of the throat has also been noted with this mark.

ZA-15 HEALTH LINE: THE STAR

ZA-15.1   You are successful in the world, as indicated by your character statements.

ZA-15.2   Strengthens a successful career.

ZA-15.3   An indication of serious female trouble.

ZA-15.4   Indicates added brilliance.

ZA-15.5   Could indicate serious head trouble, even insanity.

ZA-15.6   An indication of serious female trouble.

ZA-15.7   The female weakness is very serious. Such a person has great difficulty in child-bearing.

ZA-15.8   The female weakness is very serious. Such a person has great difficulty in child-bearing.

ZA-15.9   The female weakness is very serious. Such a person has great difficulty in child-bearing. Modern medicine can sometimes remedy this problem.

ZA-16 HEALTH LINE: THE CROSS

ZA-16.1   Reflects ending years in life. Your career is hampered.

ZA-16.2   Reflects ending years in life. Even worse difficulties are indicated, resulting from either poor health or dishonesty.

ZA-16.3   Reflects ending years in life. You could lose your reputation.

ZA-16.4   By illness, a worldly advantage was lost.

ZB

ZB-1 NEUROSIS LINE

ZB-1.1   The Neurosis line nearly always indicates an intense state of nervousness and, in a great majority of cases, great liability to hysteria.

ZB-7 NEUROSIS LINE: ITS CHARACTER

ZB-7.1 A nervous force electrifies your physical and mental organization to a great degree. Such a person suffers from any slight or inattention, can easily be depressed and, in the world of today when even people with the best intentions have no time to humor the eccentricities of others, soon comes to think that he or she has no place in the world and that no one cares.

This brooding, once begun, grows until every act of even good friends is distorted, every grief is magnified, pain is imagined where there is none; a fully developed case of hysteria.

ZB-7.2 Your tendency to lasciviousness is indulged.

ZB-7.3 This person could, because of imaginings, masturbate a lot. The habit is difficult to break, for lack of a real physical heart makes self-abuse preferable to actual intercourse. Such a person is shy and difficult and neither courts nor loves the society of people in general or the opposite sex in particular.

ZB-7.4 This is most often seen in hands of people who are not in the least nervous, and is not so frequently an indication of hysteria as it is of the increase in animal appetites.

ZB-7.5 Indicates that you may die suddenly as a result of dissipation and excess.

ZB-7.6 Indicates that your excesses ruin your career and end your good reputation.

ZB-7.7 Indicates that your excesses ruin your married life and cause great sorrow, finally ending with an impairment of your mental faculties, insanity, and the ruining of your career.

ZB-10 NEUROSIS LINE: THE BREAK

ZB-10.1 Indicates increased nervousness, the danger of hysteria, and a retiring disposition.

ZB-10.2 Makes the indication of the Neurosis line, whether it be of health or of temperament, doubly strong.

ZB-10.3 Danger from hysteria is great and all nervous symptoms are intensified.

ZB-10.4 You are a great sufferer; you suffer from nervous depression and ill health; constant discontent and unhappiness surround you.

ZB-10.5 Could show a grave danger of insanity.

ZB-10.6 Indicates that you may be in grave danger of insanity as a result of intense nervousness and excessive imagination; you are erratic, cranky, and difficult to get along with.

ZB-10.7 You may be in grave danger of being paralyzed.

ZC

ZC-1 WARRIOR LINE

ZC-1.1 The Warrior line's effect is to strengthen its Sister line (the Life line) and to indicate a stronger constitution than is shown by even a good Life line.

ZC-4 WARRIOR LINE: ITS LENGTH

ZC-4.1 The strengthening power of this line is present during your entire life. Indicates a smooth career, unclouded by ill health and with vital force enough to meet all challenges. You live well, peacefully and long, die beloved and respected.

ZC-4.2 The strengthening power of this line is present only until the age indicated on your Life line.

ZC-6 WARRIOR LINE: ITS TERMINATION

ZC-6.1 Reflects ending years in life. Indicates so much vitality that the ordinary length of life is not sufficient to expend it. Such people are great travelers and expend a good deal of energy in this way. The rest is used in revelry.

ZC-6.2 Reflects ending years in life. You may die suddenly after a life of great excess.

ZC-6.3 Reflects ending years in life. Shows that your pace is too rapid and your brain is being exhausted.

ZC-6.4 Reflects ending years in life. Indicates that you may become insane at the age indicated. Mental stress due to business strain causes self-harm.

ZC-6.5 Reflects ending years in life. Indicates that you may become insane at the age indicated. Death is self-inflicted.

ZC-6.6   Reflects ending years in life. Indicates that you may become insane at the age indicated, followed by death due to mental strain which causes self-harm.

ZC-7   WARRIOR LINE: ITS CHARACTER

ZC-7.1   You are inherently delicate, but an underlying vital strength prevents the delicacy from taking any serious form.

ZC-7.2   You have tremendous vitality, great endurance and much aggression. Such people are intense and they run the risk of overdoing things. The great vital force they possess is constantly impelling them to action, and they never do anything by halves. They have vitality to spare and are constantly seeking an outlet for their energy.

ZC-7.3   The delicacy or danger shown by the mark on the Life line does not prove fatal, owing to the underlying vitality indicated by the Warrior line.

ZC-7.4   This mark always improves life.

ZC-9   WARRIOR LINE: THE SPLIT

ZC-9.1   Indicates a constant tendency for you to rise in life.

ZC-9.2   You have increased mental strength, owing to the overflow into mental channels of some of the vitality indicated by the Warrior line.

ZC-9.3   Indicates that the upward path of your career is more certain, owing to the strong force behind you.

ZC-9.4   Split mark indicates great vitality. This vitality is too strong for the head, which is injured by constant straining. Such people are so strong that they do not know when they have overtaxed their strength. The head shows the first indications of wear.

ZC-9.5   Indicates excessiveness in the indulgence of sexual appetites. Such people are so healthy that their sexual powers are great. They do not stop to consider morality, but simply indulge their appetites.

ZC-9.6   Split mark indicates that the indulgence of your desires is a decided check to your career.

ZC-9.7   The reputation you have built could be lost.

ZC-9.8   Indicates that your unfaithfulness ruins the happiness of your married life.

ZC-9.9 Indicates that your unfaithfulness is intensified and ruins the happiness of your married life.

ZD

ZD-1 MYSTICAL LINE

ZD-1.1 The Mystical line indicates love for occult interests and an ability to obtain proficiency in them if other necessary Handology indications are present.

ZD-1.2 Indicates that you may develop a great aptitude for occult studies and a fondness for psychology. This is only an indication.

ZD-1.3 Indicates great impressionability and numerous emotions; such people are always interested in new things.

ZE

ZE-1 BALANCE LINE

ZE-1.1 The Balance line shuts out wisdom, seriousness and balancing qualities.

ZE-1.2 People with this line either develop into bad characters, often reaching the stage where they do not stop at crime, or they shift from one thing to another with no continuity in any direction, until their lives are total failures.

ZE-1.3 The presence of this line shows a disposition to jump from one occupation to another and not stick to any occupation long enough to make it successful. There is a lack of continuity of purpose in those having this mark, and poor success in their undertakings is the usual result. This mark does not make failure in life a certainty; it is seen in the hands of successful people.

ZE-1.4 With a bad hand in the Handology sense, this shows a possible suicide victim.

ZF

ZF-1 1ST RASCETTE

> *ZF-1.1* The 1st Rascette provides additional confirmation to other indications of a strong constitution.

ZF-5 1ST RASCETTE: ITS COURSE

> *ZF-5.1* Could indicate a delicacy of abdominal organs.
>
> *ZF-5.2* Indicates to women possible delicacy of the procreative organs and a danger in maternity. While these marks do not show sterility, they show a defective condition which could produce the same results.

ZF-7 1ST RASCETTE: ITS CHARACTER

> *ZF-7.1* Indicates an added strength to the constitution and an added strength to your life.
>
> *ZF-7.2* Indicates that your constitution is the driving force behind your life.
>
> *ZF-7.3* Indicates that your constitution is not strong.
>
> *ZF-7.4* Indicates a rising tendency in your life, ambitious efforts and a desire to improve.

ZG

ZG-1 TRAVEL LINES

> *ZG-1.1* The Travel lines indicate journeys. These lines increase restlessness and the desire to travel.
>
> *ZG-1.2* A long Travel line indicates more restlessness and longer journeys.
>
> *ZG-1.3* Travel lines can indicate a period when you retire from business or another occupation, change your thoughts from business to books, and mentally travel a great deal, though actually taking few journeys.

ZH

ZH-1 INTUITION LINE

ZH-1.1 The presence of this line, if well marked, adds greatly to your intuitive faculty, though this may only be another name for your character's shrewdness. For those who are likely to become unbalanced from believing themselves to possess the powers of a medium or clairvoyant, an Intuition line is a poor possession.

If you are devoted to luxury and sensuous pleasures, this line is a menace to your career. Such people seem to receive impressions for which they cannot account. They form opinions which are accurate, but if asked the reason for these opinions they are unable to give any.

Such people seem to have an added faculty of sensitivity, of keenness in estimating people and of shrewdness in arriving at correct opinions concerning their fellows. Some people with this mark are not conscious of these faculties and, upon being asked to give a reason for some statements, tell us that they "feel it in their bones." This faculty of receiving impressions from those one meets can be cultivated. If such people are not conscious of these powers and do not use them, they experience many things concerning other people, but dismiss the impressions as fancies.

ZH-1.2 Such people dismiss their intuitions as foolishness.

ZH-1.3 Indicates that you may be psychic. Such people have visions, dreams and strong impressions of impending danger, and they see signs and believe in omens; they are dreamy, nervous and highly strung, and they wear out easily. From this class genuine "psychics" are recruited.

ZH-1.4 Your mental forces are injured by allowing too much free reign for your imagination and intuition.

ZH-9 INTUITION LINE: THE SPLIT

ZH-9.1 You are ambitious to accomplish something with your intuitive faculties; such people are successful psychics. You probably use these faculties as a medium or clairvoyant.

ZH-9.2 Indicates that you achieve renown through the exercise of your intuitive faculties.

ZH-9.3   Indicates that the exercise of your intuitive faculties impairs your career.

ZH-9.4   Because you have good common sense as well as intuition, the exercise of your intuitive faculties assists your career.

ZH-10 INTUITION LINE: THE BREAK

ZH-10.1   Indicates the existence of only a limited amount of intuition.

ZH-13 INTUITION LINE: THE ISLAND

ZH-13.1   Indicates that the faculty of intuition brings poor success and a tendency to sleepwalk.

ZH-15 INTUITION LINE: THE STAR

ZH-15.1   You have great success from the exercise of these faculties.

ZH-15.2   Indicates that you make money from the exercise of your faculties, or may not do so if you wish it.

ZH-15.3   Indicates that you resort to tricks and impersonation to make money from your intuitive faculties.

ZH-16 INTUITION LINE: THE CROSS

ZH-16.1   Indicates strongly that such people resort to tricks and impersonation to make money from their intuitive faculties.

ZI

ZI-1 LASCIVIA LINE

ZI-1.1   People with this line are likely to expend their surplus energy in the sphere of activity indicated by their hands. A fine high hand (intellectual) shows greater achievements; in a low animal hand, poor achievements. Lascivious means lewd, lustful and immoral.

ZI-7   LASCIVIA LINE: ITS CHARACTER

ZI-7.1   This line undoubtedly has a strong tendency to lower you in some direction; you are more apt to think evil, even if you do not practice it, and temptation surely causes you to fall.

ZI-7.2   You devote yourself to pleasure and pursue it regardless of the cost in dollars and cents or in consequences.

ZI-7.3   Excesses affect your mental capacity for a short period.

ZI-7.4   Pleasure-seeking causes financial embarrassment.

ZI-7.5   Excess ruins your reputation.

ZI-7.6   You debauch yourself continually.

ZI-7.7   You might commit rape, murder, arson or any crime to accomplish your desires or to hide your acts.

ZI-9   LASCIVIA LINE: THE SPLIT

ZI-9.1   Indicates that lasciviousness ruins your marriage.

ZI-9.2   Lewd tendencies ruin your success.

ZI-9.3   Immoral tendencies ruin your success.

ZI-9.4   Lascivious practices injure health and cause illness.

ZI-9.5   Excessive lascivious practices could permanently injure health.

ZI-9.6   Indicates that excesses could injure your health and prospects.

ZI-9.7   You drink heavily and commit intolerable excesses.

ZI-9.8   Indicates that excesses could cause a severe illness.

ZI-9.9   Indicates that excesses could weaken and impair your head; you could develop many headaches.

ZI-9.10   You could have an attack of brain fever; you may become insane as a result of excesses.

ZI-17   LASCIVIA LINE: SISTER LINE

ZI-17.1   This line repairs the Health line wherever it shows a mark on the Health line.

ZI-17.2   Reduces the bad effects of biliousness.

ZI-17.3   Indicates that you do not have such serious stomach troubles as shown by the Health line.

ZI-17.4   Indicates better health during the time it runs along the Health line.

ZI-17.5   You have good health and success; this mark makes it doubly certain.

Part 4

Quick Reference

This section may be used to look up a particular feature of the hand and quickly find its corresponding Description code in Part 3. But remember, for a complete and accurate picture to emerge, the worksheet in Part 2 should be filled out so that all pieces of information can be assembled.

DESCRIPTION	DESCRIPTION CODE
1st finger leans to 2nd	P-2
2nd finger leans to 1st	P-4
2nd finger leans to 3rd	P-5
3rd finger leans to 2nd	P-7
3rd finger leans to 4th	P-8
4th finger leans to 3rd	P-10

A

Absent Affection line	X-2
Absent Career line	Y-2
Absent Fate line	Z-2
Absent Life line	V-2
Absent Health line	ZA-2
Absent Heart line	T-2
AFFECTION LINE	X
Affection line, absent	X-2

DESCRIPTION	DESCRIPTION CODE
Affection line, breaks	X-10
Affection line, character	X-7
Affection line, crosses	X-16
Affection line, dots	X-12
Affection line, islands	X-13
Affection line, length	X-4
Affection line, splits	X-9
Affection line, starting point	X-3
Affection line, tassels	X-11
Affection line, termination	X-6
Affection line, tridents	X-11
APEX	Q
Apex, under 1st finger, centered	Q-1
Apex, under 1st finger, leans out	Q-2
Apex, under 1st finger, leans to 2nd	Q-3
Apex, under 1st finger, near Head line	Q-7
Apex, under 1st finger, near Heart line	Q-6
Apex, under 1st finger, points up	Q-4
Apex, under 1st finger, points down	Q-5
Apex, under 2nd finger, centered	Q-8
Apex, under 2nd finger, leans to 1st	Q-9
Apex, under 2nd finger, leans to 3rd	Q-10
Apex, under 2nd finger, points up	Q-11
Apex, under 2nd finger, points down	Q-12
Apex, under 3rd finger, centered	Q-13
Apex, under 3rd finger, leans to 2nd	Q-14
Apex, under 3rd finger, leans to 4th	Q-15
Apex, under 3rd finger, points up	Q-16
Apex, under 3rd finger, points down	Q-17
Apex, under 4th finger, centered	Q-18
Apex, under 4th finger, leans to 3rd	Q-19
Apex, under 4th finger, leans out	Q-20
Apex, under 4th finger, points up	Q-21
Apex, under 4th finger, points down	Q-22
Auburn hair	F-7

DESCRIPTION	DESCRIPTION CODE

B

Balanced hand	G-4
BALANCE LINE	ZE
Base of hand is larger	G-3
Base of hand is slightly smaller	G-6
Beau's lines, nails	E-20
Black, discolored nails	E-26
Black hair	F-3
Blond hair	F-2
Blotches on a big "A" Mount	R-92
Blotches on a big "B" Mount	R-93
Blotches on a big "C" Mount	R-94
Blotches on a big "D" Mount	R-95
Blotches on a big "E" Mount	R-96
Blotches on a big "F" Mount	R-97
Blotches on a big "G" Mount	R-98
Blue hands	D-5
Blue nails	E-14
Blue, faintly tinged, nails	E-15
Blunt 1/4 inch, flat nails	E-12
Breaks, Affection line	X-10
Breaks, Career line	Y-10
Breaks, Fate line	Z-10
Breaks, Head line	U-10
Breaks, Health line	ZA-10
Breaks, Heart line	T-10
Breaks, Influence line	W-10
Breaks, Intuition line	ZH-10
Breaks, Life line	V-10
Breaks, Neurosis line	ZB-10
Broad nails	E-9
Broad thumb	N-13
Broad thumb phalanges, merely	N-46
Brown, discolored nails	E-26
Brown hair	F-7

DESCRIPTION	DESCRIPTION CODE
Bulbous nails	E-16

C

CAREER LINE	Y
Career line, absent	Y-2
Career line, breaks	Y-10
Career line, character	Y-7
Career line, course	Y-5
Career line, crosses	Y-16
Career line, islands	Y-13
Career line, splits	Y-9
Career line, stars	Y-15
Career line, starting point	Y-3
Career line, termination	Y-6
Character, Affection line	X-7
Character, Career line	Y-7
Character, Fate line	Z-7
Character, Head line	U-7
Character, Health line	ZA-7
Character, Heart line	T-7
Character, Influence line	W-7
Character, Lascivia line	ZI-7
Character, Life line	V-7
Character, Neurosis line	ZB-7
Character, Rascette, 1st	ZF-7
Character, Warrior line	ZC-7
CHARACTER OF THE LINES	S
Circle on a big "A" Mount	R-50
Circle on a big "B" Mount	R-51
Circle on a big "C" Mount	R-52
Circle on a big "D" Mount	R-53
Circle on a big "E" Mount	R-54
Circle on a big "F" Mount	R-55
Circle on a big "G" Mount	R-56
Circles, Head line	U-14

DESCRIPTION	DESCRIPTION CODE
Circles, Heart line	T-14
Clubbed nails	E-18
Clubbed thumb tip	N-34
Coarse nails, skin fine	E-2
Coarse texture, skin	A-2
COLOR	D
Color, blue hands	D-5
Color, Head line	U-8
Color, Heart line	T-8
Color, Life line	V-8
Color, pink hands	D-2
Color, purple hands	D-5
Color, red hands	D-3
Color, white hands	D-1
Color, yellow hands	D-4
Conic fingertips	I-5
Conic fingertips, slightly	I-4
Conic thumb tip	N-25
CONSISTENCY	B
Consistency, elastic	B-3
Consistency, flabby	B-1
Consistency, hard	B-4
Consistency, soft	B-2
Course, Career line	Y-5
Course, Fate line	Z-5
Course, Head line	U-5
Course, Health line	ZA-5
Course, Heart line	T-5
Course, Influence line	W-5
Course, Life line	V-5
Course, Rascette, 1st	ZF-5
Crossbars on a big "A" Mount	R-78
Crossbars on a big "B" Mount	R-79
Crossbars on a big "C" Mount	R-80
Crossbars on a big "D" Mount	R-81

DESCRIPTION	DESCRIPTION CODE
Crossbars on a big "E" Mount	R-82
Crossbars on a big "F" Mount	R-83
Crossbars on a big "G" Mount	R-84
Cross on a big "A" Mount	R-64
Cross on a big "B" Mount	R-65
Cross on a big "C" Mount	R-66
Cross on a big "D" Mount	R-67
Cross on a big "E" Mount	R-68
Cross on a big "F" Mount	R-69
Cross on a big "G" Mount	R-70
Crosses, Affection line	X-16
Crosses, Career line	Y-16
Crosses, Fate line	Z-16
Crosses, Head line	U-16
Crosses, Health line	ZA-16
Crosses, Heart line	T-16
Crosses, Intuition line	ZH-16
Crosses, Life line	V-16
Crosswise, nails ridged	E-5

D

Depressed "A" Mount	R-15
Depressed "B" Mount	R-16
Depressed "C" Mount	R-17
Depressed "D" Mount	R-18
Depressed "E" Mount	R-19
Depressed "F" Mount	R-20
Depressed "G" Mount	R-21
Depressed upper "E" Mount	R-19
Dot on a big "A" Mount	R-92
Dot on a big "B" Mount	R-93
Dot on a big "C" Mount	R-94
Dot on a big "D" Mount	R-95
Dot on a big "E" Mount	R-96
Dot on a big "F" Mount	R-97

DESCRIPTION	DESCRIPTION CODE
Dot on a big "G" Mount	R-98
Dots, Affection line	X-12
Dots, Fate line	Z-12
Dots, Head line	U-12
Dots, Health line	ZA-12
Dots, Heart line	T-12
Dots, Influence line	W-12
Dots, Life line	V-12

E

Elastic hands, consistency	B-3
Elementary thumb	N-11
Equally separated fingers	H-14
Extremely flexible hands	C-3
Extremely short, flat nails	E-11

F

FATE LINE	Z
Fate line, absent	Z-2
Fate line, breaks	Z-10
Fate line, character	Z-7
Fate line, course	Z-5
Fate line, crosses	Z-16
Fate line, dots	Z-12
Fate line, islands	Z-13
Fate line, length	Z-4
Fate line, Sister lines	Z-17
Fate line, splits	Z-9
Fate line, stars	Z-15
Fate line, starting point	Z-3
Fate line, tassels	Z-11
Fate line, termination	Z-6
Fate line, tridents	Z-11
Flabby hands, consistency	B-1
Flat, extremely short nails	E-11

DESCRIPTION	DESCRIPTION CODE
Flat, blunt nails	E-12
Flat thumb	N-12
Fine texture, skin	A-1
Fingers excessively long	G-1
FINGER STANCE	P
Finger stance, 1st finger straight	P-1
Finger stance, 1st leans to 2nd	P-2
Finger stance, 2nd finger straight	P-3
Finger stance, 2nd leans to 1st	P-4
Finger stance, 2nd leans to 3rd	P-5
Finger stance, 3rd finger straight	P-6
Finger stance, 3rd leans to 2nd	P-7
Finger stance, 3rd leans to 4th	P-8
Finger stance, 4th finger straight	P-9
Finger stance, 4th leans to 3rd	P-10
FINGERS	H
Fingers, cannot expand wide	H-15
Fingers, equally separated	H-14
Fingers, phalanges	H-16
Fingers, 1st phalange long	H-17
Fingers, 1st phalange short	H-19
Fingers, 1st phalange square	H-20
Fingers, 1st phalange thick	H-18
Fingers, 2nd phalange long	H-21
Fingers, 2nd phalange short	H-22
Fingers, 2nd phalange thick	H-21
Fingers, 3rd phalange long	H-23
Fingers, 3rd phalange narrow	H-24
Fingers, 3rd phalange short	H-25
Fingers, 3rd phalange thick	H-23
Fingers, long	L-1
Fingers, long and thick	L-6
Fingers, long and thin	L-3
Fingers, long 1st finger	H-1
Fingers, long 2nd finger	H-2

DESCRIPTION	DESCRIPTION CODE
Fingers, long 3rd finger	H-3
Fingers, long 4th finger	H-4
Fingers, normally set	H-9
Fingers, short	M-1
Fingers, short 1st finger	H-5
Fingers, short 2nd finger	H-6
Fingers, short 3rd finger	H-7
Fingers, short 4th finger	H-8
Fingers, slightly smaller	G-7
Fingers, smooth	K-1
Fingers, spaced wide, thumb and 1st	H-10
Fingers, spaced wide, 1st and 2nd	H-11
Fingers, spaced wide, 2nd and 3rd	H-12
Fingers, spaced wide, 3rd and 4th	H-13
FINGERTIPS	I
Fingertips and phalanges	I-7
Fingertips, conic	I-5
Fingertips, slightly conic	I-4
Fingertips, pointed	I-6
Fingertips, spatulate	I-1
Fingertips, square	I-2
Fingertips, very square	I-3
Flat and blunt nails	E-12
Flat and extremely short nails	E-11
Flat and flabby 2nd thumb phalange	N-41
Flat thumb	N-12
FLEXIBILITY	C
Flexibility, 1st phalanges	C-4
Flexibility, both hands	C-5
Flexibility, extreme	C-3
Flexibility, normal	C-2
Flexibility, stiff, hard to open	C-1
Fluted nails	E-3
Fluted badly, new nail	E-7
Frank and open nails	E-13

DESCRIPTION	DESCRIPTION CODE
G	
Gray hair	F-5
Grille on a big "A" Mount	R-71
Grille on a big "B" Mount	R-72
Grille on a big "C" Mount	R-73
Grille on a big "D" Mount	R-74
Grille on a big "E" Mount	R-75
Grille on a big "F" Mount	R-76
Grille on a big "G" Mount	R-77
H	
HAIR	F
Hair, auburn	F-7
Hair, black	F-3
Hair, blond	F-2
Hair, brown	F-7
Hair, gray	F-5
Hair, light	F-2
Hair, none	F-1
Hair, red	F-6
Hair, white	F-4
Hand is balanced	G-4
Hard hands, consistency	B-4
Hard to open hands, flexibility	C-1
HEAD LINE	U
Head line, breaks	U-10
Head line, character	U-7
Head line, circles	U-14
Head line, colors	U-8
Head line, course	U-5
Head line, crosses	U-16
Head line, dots	U-12
Head line, islands	U-13
Head line, length	U-4
Head line, Sister lines	U-17

DESCRIPTION	DESCRIPTION CODE
Head line, splits	U-9
Head line, stars	U-15
Head line, starting point	U-3
Head line, termination	U-6
Head line, tridents	U-11
HEALTH LINE	ZA
Health line, absent	ZA-2
Health line, breaks	ZA-10
Health line, character	ZA-7
Health line, course	ZA-5
Health line, crosses	ZA-16
Health line, dots	ZA-12
Health line, islands	ZA-13
Health line, length	ZA-4
Health line, splits	ZA-9
Health line, stars	ZA-15
Health line, termination	ZA-6
Health line, tridents	ZA-11
HEART LINE	T
Heart line, absent	T-2
Heart line, breaks	T-10
Heart line, character	T-7
Heart line, circles	T-14
Heart line, color	T-8
Heart line, course	T-5
Heart line, crosses	T-16
Heart line, dots	T-12
Heart line, islands	T-13
Heart line, length	T-4
Heart line, Sister lines	T-17
Heart line, splits	T-9
Heart line, stars	T-15
Heart line, starting point	T-3
Heart line, termination	T-6
Heart line, tridents	T-11

DESCRIPTION	DESCRIPTION CODE
Heavy thumb	N-11
Hemorrhaging or splintered nails	E-24
High-set 1st finger	H-1
High-set 2nd finger	H-2
High-set 3rd finger	H-3
High-set 4th finger	H-4
High-set thumb	N-4

I

INFLUENCE LINE	W
Influence line, breaks	W-10
Influence line, character	W-7
Influence line, course	W-5
Influence line, dots	W-12
Influence line, islands	W-13
Influence line, length	W-4
Influence line, splits	W-9
Influence line, stars	W-15
Influence line, starting point	W-3
Influence line, termination	W-6
INTUITION LINE	ZH
Intuition line, breaks	ZH-10
Intuition line, crosses	ZH-16
Intuition line, islands	ZH-13
Intuition line, splits	ZH-9
Intuition line, stars	ZH-15
Irregular pitting or pitting in rows, nails	E-25
Island on a big "A" Mount	R-85
Island on a big "B" Mount	R-86
Island on a big "C" Mount	R-87
Island on a big "D" Mount	R-88
Island on a big "E" Mount	R-89
Island on a big "F" Mount	R-90
Island on a big "G" Mount	R-91
Islands, Affection line	X-13

DESCRIPTION	DESCRIPTION CODE
Islands, Career line	Y-13
Islands, Fate line	Z-13
Islands, Head line	U-13
Islands, Health line	ZA-13
Islands, Heart line	T-13
Islands, Influence line	W-13
Islands, Intuition line	ZH-13
Islands, Life line	V-13

K

KNOTTY FINGERS	J
Knotty fingers, 1st joints large	J-2
Knotty fingers, 2nd joints large	J-3
Knotty fingers, general	J-1
Knuckles — see Knotty Fingers	

L

LASCIVIA LINE	ZI
Lascivia line, character	ZI-7
Lascivia line, Sister lines	ZI-17
Lascivia line, splits	ZI-9
Large 3rd phalange, thumb	N-23
Large "A" Mount	R-1
Large "B" Mount	R-2
Large "C" Mount	R-3
Large "D" Mount	R-4
Large "E" Mount	R-5
Large "F" Mount	R-6
Large "G" Mount	R-7
Large lower "E" Mount	R-5
Large upper "E" Mount	R-5
Large base of hand	G-3
Large middle portion of hand	G-2
Large nails	E-17

DESCRIPTION	DESCRIPTION CODE
Large thumb	N-1
Large thumb joint	N-35
Length, Affection line	X-4
Length, Fate line	Z-4
Length, Head line	U-4
Length, Health line	ZA-4
Length, Heart line	T-4
Length, Influence line	W-4
Length, Life line	V-4
Length, Warrior line	ZC-4
LIFE LINE	V
Life line, absent	V-2
Life line, breaks	V-10
Life line, character	V-7
Life line, color	V-8
Life line, course	V-5
Life line, crosses	V-16
Life line, dots	V-12
Life line, islands	V-13
Life line, length	V-4
Life line, Sister lines	V-17
Life line, splits	V-9
Life line, stars	V-15
Life line, starting point	V-3
Life line, termination	V-6
Light hair	F-2
Lindsay's nails	E-22
LONG FINGERS	L
Long 1st finger	H-1
Long 1st phalanges, fingers	H-17
Long 1st phalange, thumb	N-17
Long 2nd phalanges, fingers	H-21
Long 2nd phalange, thumb	N-20
Long 2nd phalange, thumb	N-37
Long 3rd phalanges, fingers	H-23

DESCRIPTION	DESCRIPTION CODE
Long 2nd finger	H-2
Long 3rd finger	H-3
Long 4th finger	H-4
Long fingers	L-1
Long fingers, excessively	G-1
Long hands	L-2
Long, narrow nail	E-8
Long, thick fingers	L-6
Long, thin fingers	L-3
Long thumb, set low	N-6
Low-set 1st finger	H-5
Low-set 2nd finger	H-6
Low-set 3rd finger	H-7
Low-set 4th finger	H-8
Low-set thumb	N-5
Low-set thumb, long	N-6
Low-set thumb, short	N-7

M

Medium flexibility, hands	C-2
Medium-set thumb	N-8
Medium texture, skin	A-3
Merely broad thumb phalange	N-46
Middle of hand is larger	G-2
Middle of hand is smaller	G-8
MOUNTS	R
Mount "A," blotches	R-92
Mount "A," circle	R-50
Mount "A," cross	R-64
Mount "A," crossbar	R-78
Mount "A," depressed	R-15
Mount "A," dots	R-92
Mount "A," grille	R-71
Mount "A," island	R-85
Mount "A," large	R-1

DESCRIPTION	DESCRIPTION CODE
Mount "A," smooth	R-8
Mount "A," spots	R-92
Mount "A," square	R-57
Mount "A," star, perfect	R-36
Mount "A," star, imperfect	R-99
Mount "A," triangle	R-43
Mount "A," trident	R-29
Mount "A," vertical lines, 1 to 3	R-22
Mount "A," vertical lines, more than 3	R-106
Mount "B," blotches	R-93
Mount "B," circle	R-51
Mount "B," cross	R-65
Mount "B," crossbar	R-79
Mount "B," depressed	R-16
Mount "B," dots	R-93
Mount "B," grille	R-72
Mount "B," island	R-86
Mount "B," large	R-2
Mount "B," smooth	R-9
Mount "B," spots	R-93
Mount "B," square	R-58
Mount "B," star, perfect	R-37
Mount "B," star, imperfect	R-100
Mount "B," triangle	R-44
Mount "B," trident	R-30
Mount "B," vertical lines, 1 to 3	R-23
Mount "B," vertical lines, more than 3	R-107
Mount "C," blotches	R-94
Mount "C," circle	R-52
Mount "C," cross	R-66
Mount "C," crossbar	R-80
Mount "C," depressed	R-17
Mount "C," dots	R-94
Mount "C," grille	R-73
Mount "C," island	R-87

DESCRIPTION

DESCRIPTION CODE

Description	Code
Mount "C," large	R-3
Mount "C," smooth	R-10
Mount "C," spots	R-94
Mount "C," square	R-59
Mount "C," star, perfect	R-38
Mount "C," star, imperfect	R-101
Mount "C," triangle	R-45
Mount "C," trident	R-31
Mount "C," vertical lines, 1 to 3	R-24
Mount "C," vertical lines, more than 3	R-108
Mount "D," blotches	R-95
Mount "D," circle	R-53
Mount "D," cross	R-67
Mount "D," crossbar	R-81
Mount "D," depressed	R-18
Mount "D," dots	R-95
Mount "D," grille	R-74
Mount "D," island	R-88
Mount "D," large	R-4
Mount "D," smooth	R-11
Mount "D," spots	R-95
Mount "D," square	R-60
Mount "D," star, perfect	R-39
Mount "D," star, imperfect	R-102
Mount "D," triangle	R-46
Mount "D," trident	R-32
Mount "D," vertical lines, 1 to 3	R-25
Mount "D," vertical lines, more than 3	R-109
Mount "E," blotches	R-96
Mount "E," circle	R-54
Mount "E," cross	R-68
Mount "E," crossbar	R-82
Mount "E," depressed	R-19
Mount "E," depressed, upper	R-19
Mount "E," dots	R-96

DESCRIPTION	DESCRIPTION CODE
Mount "E," grille	R-75
Mount "E," island	R-89
Mount "E," large	R-5
Mount "E," large, upper	R-5
Mount "E," puffy, lower	R-5
Mount "E," smooth	R-12
Mount "E," spots	R-96
Mount "E," square	R-61
Mount "E," star, perfect	R-40
Mount "E," star, imperfect	R-103
Mount "E," triangle	R-47
Mount "E," trident	R-33
Mount "E," vertical lines, 1 to 3	R-26
Mount "E," vertical lines, more than 3	R-110
Mount "F," blotches	R-97
Mount "F," circle	R-55
Mount "F," cross	R-69
Mount "F," crossbar	R-83
Mount "F," depressed	R-20
Mount "F," dots	R-97
Mount "F," grille	R-76
Mount "F," island	R-90
Mount "F," large	R-6
Mount "F," smooth	R-13
Mount "F," spots	R-97
Mount "F," square	R-62
Mount "F," star, perfect	R-41
Mount "F," star, imperfect	R-104
Mount "F," triangle	R-48
Mount "F," trident	R-34
Mount "F," vertical lines, 1 to 3	R-27
Mount "F," vertical lines, more than 3	R-111
Mount "G," blotches	R-98
Mount "G," circle	R-56
Mount "G," cross	R-70

DESCRIPTION	DESCRIPTION CODE
Mount "G," crossbar	R-84
Mount "G," depressed	R-21
Mount "G," dots	R-98
Mount "G," grille	R-77
Mount "G," island	R-91
Mount "G," large	R-7
Mount "G," smooth	R-14
Mount "G," spots	R-98
Mount "G," square	R-63
Mount "G," star, perfect	R-42
Mount "G," star, imperfect	R-105
Mount "G," triangle	R-49
Mount "G," trident	R-35
Mount "G," vertical lines, 1 to 3	R-28
Mount "G," vertical lines, more than 3	R-112
MYSTICAL LINE	ZD

N

NAILS	E
Nails, Beau's lines	E-20
Nails, black	E-26
Nails, blue	E-14
Nails, blue, faintly tinged	E-15
Nails, broad	E-9
Nails, brown	E-26
Nails, bulbous	E-16
Nails, clubbed	E-18
Nails, coarse	E-2
Nails, extremely short and flat	E-11
Nails, faint blue color	E-15
Nails, flat and extremely short	E-11
Nails, flat and blunt	E-12
Nails, fluted	E-3
Nails, fluted badly	E-7
Nails, general data	E-1

DESCRIPTION	DESCRIPTION CODE
Nails, grow upon themselves	E-4
Nails, hemorrhages or splinters	E-24
Nails, irregular pitting	E-25
Nails, large	E-17
Nails, Lindsay's	E-22
Nails, narrow and long	E-8
Nails, newly grown	E-6
Nails, open and frank	E-13
Nails, pitting, irregular or in rows	E-25
Nails, ridged crosswise	E-5
Nails, short	E-10
Nails, splinters or hemorrhages	E-24
Nails, spoon	E-19
Nails, Terry's	E-21
Nails, white spots	E-3
Nails, Yellow-nail syndrome	E-23
Narrow 3rd phalanges, fingers	H-24
Narrow and long nails	E-8
NEUROSIS LINE	ZB
Neurosis line, breaks	ZB-10
Neurosis line, character	ZB-7
New nail badly fluted	E-7
Newly grown nail	E-6
Normal 1st phalange, thumb	N-31
Normally flexible hands	C-2
Normally set fingers	H-8

O

One-thickness thumb	N-14
Open and frank nails	E-13
Ordinary "A" Mount	R-8
Ordinary "B" Mount	R-9
Ordinary "C" Mount	R-10
Ordinary "D" Mount	R-11
Ordinary "E" Mount	R-12
Ordinary "F" Mount	R-13

DESCRIPTION	DESCRIPTION CODE
Ordinary "G" Mount	R-14

P

Paddle-shaped thumb tip	N-33
Phalanges, 1st flexible, fingers	C-4
Phalanges, 1st long, fingers	H-17
Phalange, 1st long, thumb	N-17
Phalange, 1st normal, thumb	N-31
Phalanges, 1st short, fingers	H-19
Phalange, 1st short, thumb	N-18
Phalanges, 1st square, fingers	H-20
Phalanges, 1st thick and long, fingers	H-18
Phalange, 1st, thumb	N-16
Phalange, 2nd flat and flabby, thumb	N-41
Phalange, 2nd long, fingers	H-21
Phalange, 2nd long, thumb	N-20
Phalange, 2nd long, thumb	N-37
Phalange, 2nd, thumb	N-19
Phalange, 2nd, thumb	N-36
Phalanges, 2nd short, fingers	H-22
Phalange, 2nd short, thumb	N-38
Phalange, 2nd very short, thumb	N-40
Phalange, 2nd thick and short, thumb	N-39
Phalange, 2nd thick, fingers	H-21
Phalange, 2nd waist-like, thumb	N-44
Phalange, 3rd large, thumb	N-23
Phalanges, 3rd long, fingers	H-23
Phalanges, 3rd narrow, fingers	H-24
Phalanges, 3rd short, fingers	H-25
Phalanges, 3rd thick, fingers	H-23
Phalanges and fingertips	I-7
Phalange, merely broad, thumb	N-46
Phalanges of the fingers	H-16
Phalanges, shapes, thumb	N-45
Phalanges, thumb	N-15

DESCRIPTION	DESCRIPTION CODE
Pink hands	D-2
Pitting, irregular or in rows, nails	E-25
Pointed fingertips	I-6
Puffy lower "E" Mount	R-5
Purple hands	D-5

R

RASCETTE, 1ST	ZF
Rascette, 1st, character	ZF-7
Rascette, 1st, course	ZF-5
Red hair	F-6
Red hands	D-3
Ridged, crosswise, nails	E-5

S

Separated equally, fingers	H-14
Shapes of the thumb phalange	N-45
Short 1st finger	H-5
Short 1st phalanges, fingers	H-19
Short 1st phalange, thumb	N-18
Short 1st phalange, thumb	N-21
Short 2nd finger	H-6
Short 2nd phalanges, fingers	H-22
Short 2nd phalange, thumb	N-38
Short 3rd finger	H-7
Short 3rd phalanges, fingers	H-25
Short 4th finger	H-8
SHORT FINGERS	M
Short fingers	M-1
Short nails	E-10
Short thumb, set low	N-7
Sister line, Head line	U-17
Sister line, Fate line	Z-17
Sister line, Heart line	T-17
Sister line, Lascivia line	ZI-17

DESCRIPTION	DESCRIPTION CODE
Sister line, Life line	V-17
Skin, course texture	A-2
Skin, fine texture	A-1
Skin, fine texture, with coarse nails	E-2
Skin, medium texture	A-3
Small thumb	N-2
Smaller, slightly, base of hand	G-6
Smaller, slightly, fingers	G-7
Smaller, slightly, middle portion of hand	G-8
Smooth "A" Mount	R-8
Smooth "B" Mount	R-9
Smooth "C" Mount	R-10
Smooth "D" Mount	R-11
Smooth "E" Mount	R-12
Smooth "F" Mount	R-13
Smooth "G" Mount	R-14
SMOOTH FINGERS	K
Smooth fingers	K-1
Smooth fingertip pads	A-4
Soft hands, consistency	B-2
Spaced wide, thumb and 1st finger	H-10
Spaced wide, 1st and 2nd finger	H-11
Spaced wide, 2nd and 3rd finger	H-12
Spaced wide, 3rd and 4th finger	H-13
Spatulate fingertips	I-1
Spatulate thumb tip	N-29
Splintered or hemorrhaging nails	E-24
Splits, Affection line	X-9
Splits, Career line	Y-9
Splits, Fate line	Z-9
Splits, Head line	U-9
Splits, Health line	ZA-9
Splits, Heart line	T-9
Splits, Influence line	W-9

DESCRIPTION	DESCRIPTION CODE
Splits, Intuition line	ZH-9
Splits, Lascivia line	ZI-9
Splits, Life line	V-9
Splits, Warrior line	ZC-9
Spoon nails	E-19
Spots on a big "A" Mount	R-92
Spots on a big "B" Mount	R-93
Spots on a big "C" Mount	R-94
Spots on a big "D" Mount	R-95
Spots on a big "E" Mount	R-96
Spots on a big "F" Mount	R-97
Spots on a big "G" Mount	R-98
Square 1st phalanges, fingers	H-20
Square on a big "A" Mount	R-57
Square on a big "B" Mount	R-58
Square on a big "C" Mount	R-59
Square on a big "D" Mount	R-60
Square on a big "E" Mount	R-61
Square on a big "F" Mount	R-62
Square on a big "G" Mount	R-63
Square fingertips	I-2
Square fingertips, very	I-3
Square thumb tip	N-27
Star on a big "A" Mount	R-36
Star on a big "B" Mount	R-37
Star on a big "C" Mount	R-38
Star on a big "D" Mount	R-39
Star on a big "E" Mount	R-40
Star on a big "F" Mount	R-41
Star on a big "G" Mount	R-42
Star, imperfect, on a big "A" Mount	R-99
Star, imperfect, on a big "B" Mount	R-100
Star, imperfect, on a big "C" Mount	R-101
Star, imperfect, on a big "D" Mount	R-102
Star, imperfect, on a big "E" Mount	R-103

DESCRIPTION	DESCRIPTION CODE
Star, imperfect, on a big "F" Mount	R-104
Star, imperfect, on a big "G" Mount	R-105
Stars, Career line	Y-15
Stars, Fate line	Z-15
Stars, Head line	U-15
Stars, Health line	ZA-15
Stars, Heart line	T-15
Stars, Influence line	W-15
Stars, Intuition line	ZH-15
Stars, Life line	V-15
Starting point, Affection line	X-3
Starting point, Career line	Y-3
Starting point, Fate line	Z-3
Starting point, Head line	U-3
Starting point, Heart line	T-3
Starting point, Influence line	W-3
Starting point, Life line	V-3
Stiff hands, flexibility	C-1
Stiff thumb	N-48
Straight 1st finger	P-1
Straight 2nd finger	P-3
Straight 3rd finger	P-6
Straight 4th finger	P-9
Straight thumb	N-9
Supple thumb	N-47

T

Tassels, Affection line	X-11
Tassels, Fate line	Z-11
Termination, Affection line	X-6
Termination, Career line	Y-6
Termination, Fate line	Z-6
Termination, Head line	U-6
Termination, Health line	ZA-6
Termination, Heart line	T-6

DESCRIPTION	DESCRIPTION CODE
Termination, Influence line	W-6
Termination, Life line	V-6
Termination, Warrior line	ZC-6
Terry's nails	E-21
TEXTURE	A
Texture, skin is coarse	A-2
Texture, skin is fine	A-1
Texture, skin is medium	A-3
Texture, smooth fingertip pads	A-4
Thick 1st phalanges, fingers	H-18
Thick 2nd phalanges, fingers	H-21
Thick 2nd phalange, thumb	N-39
Thick 3rd phalanges, fingers	H-23
THUMB	N
Thumb as a whole	N-3
Thumb, elementary	N-11
Thumb, heavy	N-11
Thumb is broad	N-13
Thumb is flat	N-12
Thumb is large	N-1
Thumb is one thickness	N-14
Thumb is small	N-2
Thumb is set high	N-4
Thumb is set low	N-5
Thumb is straight	N-9
Thumb joint is large	N-35
Thumb, medium set	N-8
Thumb phalanges	N-15
Thumb phalanges, 1st	N-16
Thumb phalanges, 1st long	N-17
Thumb phalanges, 1st normal	N-31
Thumb phalanges, 1st short	N-18
Thumb phalanges, 1st short, 2nd long	N-21
Thumb phalanges, 1st weak or strong	N-32
Thumb phalanges, 2nd flat and flabby	N-41

DESCRIPTION	DESCRIPTION CODE
Thumb phalanges, 2nd long	N-20
Thumb phalanges, 2nd long	N-37
Thumb phalanges, 2nd long, 1st short	N-21
Thumb phalanges, 2nd	N-19
Thumb phalanges, 2nd	N-36
Thumb phalanges, 2nd short	N-38
Thumb phalanges, 2nd short and thick	N-39
Thumb phalanges, 2nd very short	N-40
Thumb phalanges, 2nd waist-like	N-44
Thumb phalanges, 3rd large	N-23
Thumb phalanges, both same length	N-22
Thumb phalanges, merely broad	N-46
Thumb phalanges, shapes	N-45
Thumb set low, long	N-6
Thumb set low, short	N-7
Thumb shape as a whole	N-10
Thumb supple	N-47
Thumb stiff	N-48
Thumb tip	N-24
Thumb tip is conic	N-25
Thumb tip is clubbed	N-34
Thumb tip is paddle-shaped	N-33
Thumb tip is spatulate	N-29
Thumb tip is square	N-27
Tip of the thumb	N-24
TRAVEL LINES	ZG
Triangle on a big "A" Mount	R-43
Triangle on a big "B" Mount	R-44
Triangle on a big "C" Mount	R-45
Triangle on a big "D" Mount	R-46
Triangle on a big "E" Mount	R-47
Triangle on a big "F" Mount	R-48
Triangle on a big "G" Mount	R-49
Trident on a big "A" Mount	R-29
Trident on a big "B" Mount	R-30

DESCRIPTION	DESCRIPTION CODE
Trident on a big "C" Mount	R-31
Trident on a big "D" Mount	R-32
Trident on a big "E" Mount	R-33
Trident on a big "F" Mount	R-34
Trident on a big "G" Mount	R-35
Tridents, Affection line	X-11
Tridents, Fate line	Z-11
Tridents, Head line	U-11
Tridents, Health line	ZA-11
Tridents, Heart line	T-11

V

Vertical lines, 1 to 3, "A" Mount	R-22
Vertical lines, 1 to 3, "B" Mount	R-23
Vertical lines, 1 to 3, "C" Mount	R-24
Vertical lines, 1 to 3, "D" Mount	R-25
Vertical lines, 1 to 3, "E" Mount	R-26
Vertical lines, 1 to 3, "F" Mount	R-27
Vertical lines, 1 to 3, "G" Mount	R-28
Vertical lines, more than 3, "A" Mount	R-106
Vertical lines, more than 3, "B" Mount	R-107
Vertical lines, more than 3, "C" Mount	R-108
Vertical lines, more than 3, "D" Mount	R-109
Vertical lines, more than 3, "E" Mount	R-110
Vertical lines, more than 3, "F" Mount	R-111
Vertical lines, more than 3, "G" Mount	R-112
Very short, 2nd thumb phalange	N-40

W

WARRIOR LINE	ZC
Warrior line, character	ZC-7
Warrior line, length	ZC-4
Warrior line, splits	ZC-9
Warrior line, termination	ZC-6
White hair	F-4

DESCRIPTION	DESCRIPTION CODE
White hands	D-1
White spots, nails	E-3
WHOLE HAND	G
Whole hand, balanced	G-4
Whole hand, base is larger	G-3
Whole hand, base is slightly smaller	G-6
Whole hand, fingers excessively long	G-1
Whole hand, fingers slightly smaller	G-7
Whole hand, middle portion larger	G-2
Whole hand, middle portion smaller	G-8
Whole hand, one part slightly smaller	G-5
Whole thumb	N-3
Wide spaces, thumb and 1st finger	H-10
Wide spaces, 1st and 2nd fingers	H-11
Wide spaces, 2nd and 3rd fingers	H-12
Wide spaces, 3rd and 4th fingers	H-13

Y

Yellow hands	D-4
Yellow-nail syndrome	E-23

Handology Notes

_____

_____

_____

_____

_____

_____

_____

_____

_____

_____

_____

_____

_____

_____

_____

_____

_____

_____

_____

_____

_____

_____

_____